RESCUING HUMAN RIGHTS

The development of human rights norms is one of the most significant achievements in international relations and law since 1945, but the continuing influence of human rights is increasingly being questioned by authoritarian governments, nationalists, and pundits. Unfortunately, the credibility of human rights is undermined by the proliferation of new rights, the linkage of rights to other issues such as international crimes or the activities of business, and the attempt to address every social problem from a human rights perspective. *Rescuing Human Rights* calls for understanding human rights as international human rights law and maintaining the distinctions between binding legal obligations on governments and broader issues of ethics, politics, and social change. Resolving complex social problems requires more than simplistic appeals to rights, and adopting a "radically moderate" approach that recognizes both the potential and the limits of international human rights law offers the best hope of preserving the principle that we all have rights, simply because we are human.

HURST HANNUM is professor of international law at The Fletcher School of Law and Diplomacy, Tufts University, Massachusetts. He has authored numerous books and articles on human rights and has served as counsel and advocate before European, inter-American, and UN human rights institutions.

Rescuing Human Rights

A RADICALLY MODERATE APPROACH

HURST HANNUM

The Fletcher School of Law and Diplomacy,
Tufts University, Massachusetts

CAMBRIDGE
UNIVERSITY PRESS

CAMBRIDGE
UNIVERSITY PRESS

University Printing House, Cambridge CB2 8BS, United Kingdom

One Liberty Plaza, 20th Floor, New York, NY 10006, USA

477 Williamstown Road, Port Melbourne, VIC 3207, Australia

314–321, 3rd Floor, Plot 3, Splendor Forum, Jasola District Centre, New Delhi – 110025, India

79 Anson Road, #06–04/06, Singapore 079906

Cambridge University Press is part of the University of Cambridge.

It furthers the University's mission by disseminating knowledge in the pursuit of education, learning, and research at the highest international levels of excellence.

www.cambridge.org
Information on this title: www.cambridge.org/9781108417488
DOI: 10.1017/9781108277730

© Hurst Hannum 2019

First published 2019

Printed and bound in Great Britain by Clays Ltd, Elcograf S.p.A.

A catalog record for this publication is available from the British Library.

Library of Congress Cataloging-in-Publication Data
NAMES: Hannum, Hurst, author.
TITLE: Rescuing human rights : a radically moderate approach / Hurst Hannum,
Tufts University, Massachusetts.
DESCRIPTION: Cambridge, United Kingdom ; New York, NY, USA :
Cambridge University Press, 2019. | Includes bibliographical references and index.
IDENTIFIERS: LCCN 2018042533 | ISBN 9781108417488 (hardback : alk. paper) |
ISBN 9781108405362 (paperback : alk. paper)
SUBJECTS: LCSH: Human rights. | Human rights–Government policy. |
Human rights–International cooperation.
CLASSIFICATION: LCC JC571 .H347657 2019 | DDC 323–dc23
LC record available at https://lccn.loc.gov/2018042533

ISBN 978-1-108-41748-8 Hardback
ISBN 978-1-108-40536-2 Paperback

In memory and appreciation of Kevin Boyle
(1943–2010)

Dear friend, colleague, and human rights visionary

"When I use a word," Humpty Dumpty said, in rather a scornful tone, "it means just what I choose it to mean – neither more nor less."

"The question is," said Alice, "whether you can make words mean so many different things."

"The question is," said Humpty Dumpty, "which is to be master – that's all."

Lewis Carroll, *Though the Looking-Glass, and What Alice Found There* (1871), chap. 6

Contents

Contents

Acknowledgments

The opinions expressed in this book have been shaped by a great number of conversations – some of them with individuals who would probably disagree with many of the views expressed herein. Among the constructive critics have been students and colleagues in a number of academic and other institutions at which I presented many of the ideas found in these pages over the past several years, and I wish to thank The Fletcher School of Law and Diplomacy; University of Hong Kong; Central European University; Harvard Law School; King's College, London; Princeton University's Woodrow Wilson School of Public and International Affairs; the University of Minnesota; the Hertie School of Governance, Berlin; Georgetown University Law School; the University of Glasgow Human Rights Project/Program; and the Legal Vice Presidency of the World Bank for allowing me to present my thoughts to a variety of audiences. I benefited greatly from each of these opportunities.

A great number of colleagues and friends have contributed in various ways to my thinking (sometimes encouraging, sometimes discouraging), including Malin Oud, John Shattuck, Kevin Boyle, Elsa Stamatopoulou, Nigel Rodley, Michael O'Boyle, David Weissbrodt, Patrick Thornberry, Richard Goldstone, Cecile Aptel, Allen Buchanan, Bert Lockwood, Anna-Maria Biro, Samuel Moyn, Achim Ladwig, Zohrab Mnatsakanyan, Maria Varaki, Benyam Dawit Mezmur, Ho-Ming So Denduan-grudee, Chip Pitts, Stephen Marks, Tom Hadden, Norah Niland, Antonio Donini, Janelle Diller, Shane Darcy, Dapo Akande, and Fletcher colleagues Eileen Babbitt, Michael Glennon, Joel Trachtman, and Alan Henrikson. For their comments on sections of the manuscript and/or the article that preceded it, I would particularly like to thank John Cerone, Christina Cerna, Meg DeGuzman, Patricia Fagen, Sofia Gruskin, Kathleen Hamill, David Harris, Banafsheh Keynoush, Mark Lattimer, David Kinley, Steven Koh, Siobhan McInerney-Lankford, Robert McCorquodale, Sean Murphy, Sejal Parmar, Tara Sepehrifar, Nadja Skaljic, Ivana Vuco, and

Alexandra Xanthaki. None of these individuals, of course, is responsible for any of the views expressed here.

Thank you to the two anonymous reviewers of the book proposal to Cambridge University Press, for both their supportive words and their good advice. Thank you, too, to John Berger of CUP for his encouragement, help, and good humor over the years, and to Emma Collison for her help during the editorial process. Elodie Graham, Jeanne Koré Salvato, my wife, Ann, and CUP's excellent design team helped to select the title, cover, and design for the book.

I also thank my research assistants at Fletcher during the earlier phases of the book, Alliya Anjum, Casey Hogle, Aruni Jayakody, Nida Paracha, and Kathrin Strobel, without whom I never would have surfaced from beneath the stacks of materials in my office.

This manuscript was written in part in autumn 2017, while I was a visiting fellow at Mansfield College and a research visitor at the Bonavero Institute for Human Rights, Faculty of Law, University of Oxford, and I wish to thank the director, Kate O'Regan, as well as the always helpful staff, Annelen Micus and Zoe Davis-Heaney, for their warm welcome and assistance. I also thank my fellow fellows at the time, Johanna Gusman, Malcolm Wallis, and bob watt, for their enjoyable and intellectually stimulating company.

I could not have completed this book without the support and encouragement of my wife, Ann Barger Hannum, and I thank her as well for her extremely helpful comments and suggestions on parts of the manuscript. Now that this particular task is completed, I promise to become more social in the months to come, and I hope that our next voyage will be somewhat less hectic than this most recent one has been.

List of Abbreviations

ACHPR	African Charter on Human and Peoples' Rights
AfCommHPR	African Commission on Human and Peoples' Rights
AfCtHPR	African Court on Human and Peoples' Rights
AmConvHR	American Convention on Human Rights
CEDAW	Convention on the Elimination of All Forms of Discrimination against Women
CEDAW Committee	Committee on the Elimination of All Forms of Discrimination against Women
CERD	Convention on the Elimination of All Forms of Racial Discrimination
CERD Committee	Committee on the Elimination of All Forms of Racial Discrimination
CP	civil and political
CP Covenant	International Covenant on Civil and Political Rights
CRC	Convention on the Rights of the Child
ESC	economic, social, and cultural
ESC Covenant	International Covenant on Economic, Social, and Cultural Rights
Eur. Ct. Hum. Rts.	European Court of Human Rights
Eur. Ct. Justice	European Court of Justice
ECHR	European Convention on Human Rights and Fundamental Freedoms
GA	UN General Assembly
HR Committee	UN Human Rights Committee
HR Council	UN Human Rights Council
IACommHR	Inter-American Commission on Human Rights
IACtHR	Inter-American Court of Human Rights

ILO	International Labor Organization
NGO	nongovernmental organization
OHCHR	Office of the UN High Commissioner for Human Rights
UDHR	Universal Declaration of Human Rights
UN	United Nations
UK	United Kingdom
US	United States
WTO	World Trade Organization

Preface

Human rights are in danger of becoming the victims of their own success. The purpose of this book is to support human rights and human rights advocacy and to argue for their continuing relevance in the twenty-first century and beyond. For this relevance to be sustained and even increased, however, the human rights movement must evaluate its strategies, successes, and failures in an open and honest fashion. Similarly, politicians, diplomats, donors, and the public need to understand more clearly what human rights intend to achieve and how their advocates propose to do this. Many critics simply don't understand the purpose of human rights and mistakenly attack them for not being imagined in a different way, rather than analyzing them on their own terms.

Understanding human rights includes recognizing that their goals and capabilities are limited. Human rights were never intended to provide a solution to all of the world's problems, and those who offer human rights as a panacea for such problems do a disservice both to human rights and to the causes they seek to promote. Many of the criticisms in this book are directed at the unrealistic expansion or overreach of human rights, which undermines their legitimacy and acceptance.

The primary contribution of the book is to reconsider the basic purposes of human rights from a normative perspective, taking into account the treaties and other legal texts that set forth the rights in detail, in the context of today's domestic and international political realities. This is not an easy task, since the phrase *human rights* has come to mean almost anything that anyone thinks that it should mean. No ideology or political movement will survive long if it means all things to all people – that is the problem with contemporary appeals to vague concepts such as populism, nationalism, self-determination, and national security. Activists may be disappointed to discover that human rights do not provide simplistic solutions to sincerely felt, legitimate grievances, but their response should not be to twist human rights to suit their own agendas.

While there are many critical comments in the book about the ways in which advocates and supportive governments have understood and used human rights as part of their campaigns, this should not imply any lack of appreciation or respect for human rights defenders, advocates, and NGOs, many of whom carry out their work not only with tremendous dedication but frequently at tremendous risk to themselves, their colleagues, and their families. There would be no human rights regime without this work, and human rights defenders deserve much more credit for bringing about positive change than they generally receive. Their impact may be difficult to measure, but the work of human rights advocates, international and domestic, is absolutely crucial to continued progress in making human rights a reality.

The thesis of this book is grounded in law and legal concepts, but the arguments are pragmatic, not technical. There are frequent references to treaties, declarations, and the judgments and decisions of international human rights bodies, but the goal is to understand the proper role of human rights in the world, not to win a case or parse legal theories about the role of international law.

There is little discussion of the sources of human rights norms; we can read the texts agreed to by diplomats and governments, and we can leave it to the drafters to explain where their formulations originated rather than speculate about their antecedents. This does not mean that the existing texts are perfect or even good, but formal international agreements do give specific (if not always clear) content to human rights. As the co-author of an international human rights law textbook, I have spent a great deal of time understanding and writing about the institutions that have been created to encourage and oversee compliance with human rights norms. This book devotes very little space to these mechanisms, which have been the subject of innumerable analyses, both inside and outside the United Nations.[1] I also make no attempt to trace the history of human rights, whether from time immemorial or since 1945.

I am a lawyer, not a social scientist, and I leave it to the quantifiers to measure the impact that various human rights instruments and mechanisms have had on the behavior of states. As methodology improves and findings of correlation permit us to judge causation with greater confidence, such work may become even more important. For the moment, however, I simply offer my agreement with the following conclusion that human rights norms and advocacy have had a generally positive impact, at least under certain conditions:

> International human rights law has not failed or succeeded, and we should stop thinking in such dichotomies. Based on a variety of studies using a good deal of newly uncovered evidence, we are comfortable arguing that human rights protections have improved over the last three decades, and that the development of international human rights law is associated in multiple ways with that change.[2]

A BRIEF BIOGRAPHICAL NOTE

The opinions in this book are derived from more than four decades of experience in international human rights, as a practitioner, academic, and consultant. I began my career with the Northern Ireland Civil Rights Association in the 1970s, where I was co-counsel in cases brought to the European Commission on Human Rights concerning ill treatment by British security forces during the "Troubles" in Northern Ireland. In the early 2000s, I was lead counsel in a case argued before the Grand Chamber of the European Court of Human Rights that challenged (unsuccessfully, I should add) the use of force by NATO countries in the 1999 bombing of Serbia and Kosovo. I also have contributed to complaints brought in the inter-American and UN systems and testified on human rights and refugee issues on several occasions before US Congressional subcommittees in the 1980s and 1990s.

I have been active in several human rights NGOs, serving as a member of the International Council of Minority Rights Group International (London); on the board of directors of Amnesty International–USA; as president of Survival International–USA; and as an adviser to the International Human Rights Law Group (now Global Rights, based in Abuja, Nigeria), International Service for Human Rights (Geneva), and Chittagong Hill Tracts Commission (Dhaka). As executive director of the Washington-based Procedural Aspects of International Law Institute prior to moving to Fletcher, I participated in numerous meetings of the UN Commission on Human Rights and its Sub-Commission on the Promotion and Protection of Human Rights throughout the 1980s and 1990s; I have also attended meetings of the UN Human Rights Council, Universal Periodic Review process, treaty body sessions, Permanent Forum on Indigenous Issues, and UN working groups or forums on minorities and business and human rights. Other NGO work, focusing primarily on human rights and conflict resolution, has concerned Aceh, Afghanistan, Bosnia and Hercegovina, the Caucuses, China, Kashmir, and Sri Lanka.

While I have never worked full time for any government or international organization, I have been a short-term paid consultant for the US State Department (on the meaning of autonomy in international law), the UN Department of Political Affairs (on Portuguese-Indonesian talks on East Timor and as an adviser to former US Secretary of State James Baker on Western Sahara), and the UN Office of the High Commissioner on Human Rights (as author/editor of a handbook on minority rights). In 1990, I was a public member of the US delegation to the Copenhagen Conference on the Human Dimension of the Conference on Security and Cooperation in Europe.

I have been professor of international law at The Fletcher School of Law and Diplomacy, Tufts University, since 1990 and have also held full-time visiting positions at the University of Hong Kong (2006–2008) and Central European University (Budapest, 2010–2011). I have published widely and am on the editorial advisory boards of *Human Rights Quarterly* and *Human Rights Law Review*.

Other than the United States, I have lived for periods ranging from roughly three months to two and a half years in Guam, US Virgin Islands, France, Northern Ireland, England, Hong Kong, and Hungary. I have traveled for talks, meetings, and other human rights-related activities to Morocco, Rwanda, Egypt, Israel and the Occupied Territories, Italy, Spain, Scotland, Greece, Serbia, Bosnia and Herzegovina, Czechoslovakia, Austria, Germany, Netherlands, Åland Islands, Finland, Norway, Sweden, Greenland, Poland, Switzerland, Georgia, Russia, China, India, Sri Lanka, Philippines, South Korea, Macao, Malaysia, Indonesia, Australia, Singapore, Canada, Haiti, Argentina, and Nicaragua.

I offer this bio not to impress but to ensure transparency; we all have our biases, and I am sure that I have mine. At the very least, my experiences have exposed me to a wide range of issues, personalities, and politics, all of which have informed the opinions set forth in the following pages. Some of these people are further recognized in the Acknowledgments.

1

Introduction: Assumptions and Principles

The imagining, proclamation, and eventual codification of international human rights law rank among the most significant accomplishments in international relations of the post-1945 era. While the concept of rights on the domestic level had been evolving for centuries, the notion that all people in the world possess certain rights – which their own government is obliged to protect – was nothing short of revolutionary.

The intrusion of human rights into the formerly sacrosanct realm of national sovereignty upended 350 years of viewing sovereignty primarily as a shield against outside influence. While sovereignty was never absolute, its limits were few. One of the only limits relating to rights was the customary international law norm that required states to protect aliens within their jurisdiction, although this protection stemmed from respect for the sovereignty of the alien's state rather than from any broader concern for the rights of individuals within a state's territory. Other limits reflected the responsibility of countries for acts within their territories that might harm another state or the perceived necessities of conducting international relations, such as the immunity of diplomats and freedom of the high seas.

Individual rights, on the other hand, are not in their essence international. Their violation affects other states only indirectly, and the idea that the way in which a state treats its own citizens within its own jurisdiction is a legitimate matter for international concern was truly novel. Illustrative of this hesitance is the long struggle to outlaw slavery. Abolitionist campaigns within countries began to bear fruit in the late 18th and early 19th centuries, and the United States and United Kingdom in 1807 prohibited their ships from participating in international slave trading. However, the first international treaty that banned slavery itself was adopted only in 1926.[3]

The origins and growth of international human rights norms and what became the international human rights movement have been analyzed by a number of scholars, but it is not particularly relevant to a contemporary understanding of the content of human rights to decide whether the meaningful internationalization of rights began in the 1930s, 1940s, or 1970s.[4] Formally, however, identifying as one of the purposes of the United Nations "promoting and encouraging respect for human rights and fundamental freedoms for all without distinction as to race, sex, language, or religion"[5] was surely a landmark. The language of the charter left implementation of this goal primarily in the hands of states themselves, but it made clear that human rights were no longer solely a domestic concern of individual countries.

While some countries still claim occasionally that international human rights norms violate traditional norms of state sovereignty,[6] sovereignty today no longer permits states to act with impunity with respect to the treatment of individuals within their jurisdiction. This fact is reflected not only in hortatory declarations and diplomatic speeches but in practice. The United Nations and many other multilateral international organizations include the promotion of human rights within their mandates, and regional human rights courts exist in Europe, Africa, and the Western Hemisphere. Every country in the world has ratified at least one of the nine global treaties adopted under the auspices of the United Nations: as of January 2018, more than 165 states had ratified the two core conventions on civil and political rights and economic, social, and cultural rights, respectively; 179 states had ratified the Convention on the Elimination of All Forms of Racial Discrimination; 189 had ratified the Convention on the Elimination of All Forms of Discrimination against Women; and 196 states[7] had ratified the Convention on the Rights of the Child.

On the regional level, 23 states have ratified the American Convention on Human Rights, of which 20 have recognized the jurisdiction of the Inter-American Court of Human Rights; all 47 members of the Council of Europe have ratified the European Convention on Human Rights, which includes acceptance of the compulsory jurisdiction of the European Court of Human Rights; and 53 of the 55 members of the African Union have ratified the African Charter of Human and Peoples' Rights, of which 24 have accepted the optional jurisdiction of the African Court on Human and Peoples' Rights. Thus, over 90 countries from all regions of the world (except Asia and the Pacific, where there is no regional or subregional human rights mechanism that includes a court) have accepted the jurisdiction of international courts with the authority to issue legally binding judgments on human rights within individual states.

In 2006, the UN Human Rights Council adopted a new procedure, the Universal Periodic Review (UPR), under which the human rights situation in every member state of the United Nations is reviewed on a regular basis, irrespective of which – if any – treaties the state has ratified. The UPR procedure was adopted by consensus, and every UN member has submitted reports on their domestic human rights practices and participated in the quadrennial four-year review process.

In light of these facts and the actions of states themselves, no matter what quibbles or questions remain about the legal and political impact of human rights treaties, the relevance of "soft law" principles and declarations, or the lack of sufficiently robust implementation or compliance mechanisms, the argument that human rights are purely a domestic matter is no longer sustainable.

THE PROBLEM

10 December 2018 marked the 70th anniversary of the adoption of the Universal Declaration of Human Rights (UDHR). This should have been an occasion for celebration; instead, human rights are on the verge of becoming a victim of their own success. China, Russia, and other authoritarian states that have consistently opposed attempts to induce compliance with human rights norms have become increasingly influential in international affairs. The relatively solid support for human rights within the so-called West is shaky, as the financial crisis that began in 2008 and the migrant crisis that hit Europe in 2015 weakened support for international commitments of all kinds. The rise of nationalism and populism in Hungary, Poland, the United States, the United Kingdom, Italy, Greece, Venezuela, Turkey, India, and many other countries is, in part, a reaction against the unfulfilled promises of liberal democracy and an international economic and trade regime that seems uncontrollable. The tide of repression in the name of the fight against terrorism continues to grow; fear and uncertainty have replaced the hope and confidence that were shortsightedly proclaimed as the Berlin Wall fell and the Soviet Union disintegrated in the late 1980s and early 1990s.

Academics and pundits now reflect on the "limits,"[8] "twilight,"[9] or "endtimes"[10] of human rights; the demise of "the last utopia"[11]; or their very survival.[12] The more generous write about human rights being at a "crossroads"[13] or "in crisis,"[14] and write that now is the time for asking "hard questions,"[15] examining "critical perspectives,"[16] or imagining varying kinds of human rights "futures,"[17] many of them pessimistic.

What went wrong? Is the very concept of universal rights becoming irrelevant, even as the world becomes increasingly interconnected? Were human rights always too idealistic to survive the economic and political shocks of the past decade, or have they been "subsumed by the politics of American power and market-based democratic liberalism?"[18] Is it true that "[t]he ubiquity of human rights talk, campaigns, and demands is best explained not by impact but marketing?"[19] Should we abandon legalistic references to rights in favor of concentrating on such pressing matters as climate change, sustainable development, corruption, and the increasing polarization of the body politic? Is it enough just to recognize the hubris of liberal internationalists who hailed the "end of history"[20] and the inevitable triumph of liberalism and democracy, and then, after a mea culpa, continue on the same path? Or is it time to undertake a realistic analysis of why human rights now seem to be struggling, despite the fact that they continue to appeal to people (if not always their governments) all over the world who are victims of dictatorship, discrimination, violence, and disappointment at economic and social systems that have failed to improve their standards of living?

It is the thesis of this book that human rights are not only relevant but essential as we move fully into the twenty-first century. I hope to counter those who deny the existence or importance of human rights; educate those who view human rights too narrowly, by excluding economic, social, and cultural rights and/or reasonable interpretative expansions of norms that were formulated decades ago; and discourage those who unthinkingly or irresponsibly expand the idea of human rights in ways that undermine their originally more modest purpose. Human rights, properly understood, are indeed universally applicable, and their abandonment would be an unconscionable rejection of the simple proposition that all human beings share fundamental rights to be respected and ensured by their governments.

It is not enough to simply follow the accepted wisdom of the past several decades. The revitalization of human rights requires not a change in goals but a change in tactics, strategies, and understandings of what human rights can and cannot deliver. Governments that ignore or violate rights remain the primary culprits, but human rights advocates, governmental and nongovernmental, must become more realistic idealists who understand the role and the limitations of human rights in a world never contemplated by those who first articulated international norms in the decades after the Second World War. Foundations and other donors need to do more than simply respond to current crises or popular causes.

Often strident calls from European and other, primarily Western, human rights activists for adherence to the contemporary liberal European construct of society are increasingly feeding a backlash in the rest of the world. This tendency is exacerbated by activists who see an expansive concept of rights as the primary means to effect domestic social and political change; ironically, the same tactic is used rhetorically by anti-rights governments in order to burden human rights with larger geopolitical problems, as a means of undermining and delegitimizing them.

There must be a conscious attempt to return to the principles of consensus and universality that were at the heart of human rights at least through the 1970s. Human rights must be distinguished from other worthy initiatives, such as the prosecution of international criminals, saving the environment, reducing poverty, making business more responsible, and preventing or ending violent conflict. We also must recognize that universality does not mean uniformity and that local variations in interpretation and practice should not automatically be rejected. Overreaching and overselling human rights will only strengthen anti–human rights governments and others who challenge the universal application of human rights by privileging cultural relativism over globally shared values.

THE CONTEXT

A few recent examples may be useful. Mainstream academics have called for the extension of human rights obligations not only to international organizations but to corporations, other non-state actors, and even individuals.[21] An Argentine law professor argues that the "constitutionalisation of the international human rights regime" in Latin America now imposes obligations on states to, for example, "adopt ... adequate and transformational compensation measures to address widespread situations of systematic patterns that produce or reproduce inequality amongst citizens[,] ... produce public information ... [and] prevent undue media concentration ..."[22] Amnesty International, one of the oldest and most well-respected international human rights nongovernmental organizations (NGOs), has promoted drafting a treaty to control the arms trade[23] and called for the full decriminalization of all aspects of consensual sex work.[24] In comments about Belarus, the committee that oversees the Convention on the Elimination of All Forms of Discrimination against Women (CEDAW) expressed its concern at "the continuing prevalence of sex-role stereotypes and by the reintroduction of such symbols as a Mothers' Day and a Mothers' Award, which it sees as encouraging women's traditional roles."[25] The UN Human Rights Council has appointed individual experts to consider the relationship between human rights and, e.g., transnational corporations, dumping of toxic waste, the use of mercenaries, the effects of economic reform policies and foreign debt, the promotion of a democratic and equitable international order, and "international solidarity."[26]

Some of these initiatives or claims are morally defensible, indeed admirable, and calling for greater social equity or attempting to regulate the global trade in arms is laudable and necessary. However, it stretches the imagination to believe that these issues were even present in the minds of those who adopted the Universal Declaration of Human Rights in 1948. That instrument, although not in and of itself legally binding, remains the most widely accepted articulation of human rights, but the popularity of the term *human rights* as a mantra for change has led to a significant expansion of the rights proclaimed in 1948. The unintended consequence of this expansion and accompanying calls to coerce countries to comply with human rights norms may be to set back an entire movement that is based on the proposition that all human beings enjoy certain universal rights that their governments must protect.

Of course, interpretations of international norms change over time, and we should welcome the fact that we have a much fuller understanding of human rights than we did in 1948. Just as "equal protection" in the United States was understood to permit racial segregation until the Supreme Court issued its famous 1954 judgment in *Brown v. Board of Education*,[27] people and international human rights bodies today are less likely to tolerate inequities and ill-treatment that were common a half century ago. Calls for restraint in formulating new rights should not serve as cover to justify attempts to turn the clock back to an earlier time, when women, children, minorities, and other disempowered groups "knew their place."

The UDHR refers to itself in the preamble simply as "a common standard of achievement for all peoples and all nations." Subsequent global treaties have built on the rights proclaimed in the declaration and created specialized committees of experts to oversee their implementation, but countries have not been willing to grant these bodies the authority to issue legally binding judgments. The committees' observations and recommendations merit serious consideration, but countries were not (and most still are not) willing to countenance an international human rights body with the authority to issue binding judgments on issues fraught with domestic sensitivity. While states cannot deny that human rights treaties *do* create binding legal obligations, in most instances the ultimate power to determine just what these obligations entail remains with the countries themselves.

NATIONALISM AND POPULISM

Most of the issues identified above predate the political shift to the right that has occurred in Europe, the United States, and many other countries in recent years. To cite only a few examples, a military coup overthrew the democratically elected government of Thailand in 2014. Elsewhere in Southeast Asia, "hoped-for [democratic] openings never came in Laos and Vietnam, where the Communist Party has always been nakedly repressive. Singapore remains an illiberal, albeit effective, technocracy. The leaders of Malaysia and Cambodia ... have proved depressingly adept at locking up critics and persecuting opponents ... Opposition figures in Malaysia find themselves in court on charges as varied as corruption and sodomy ... [In Indonesia and the Philippines,] liberals have more cause for fear than hope."[28] Cambodia banned opposition parties from fielding candidates in the 2018 elections and closed the office of the US National Democratic Institute, accusing it of political interference.[29]

In 2018, China amended its constitution to permit current President Xi Jinping to remain in power without limit, and suppression of dissent and dissenters has increased considerably under Xi's rule. The European Council on Foreign Relations described as "impossible topics" to discuss with China both human rights, "for which Europe's definition is rejected by China," and international law, "when it does not serve China's interests."[30]

In Europe, "[p]rogress towards full democracy and commitment to the rule of law in the western Balkans is either stagnating or going backwards," according to a committee of the UK House of Lords.[31] Hungary and Poland continue to move toward authoritarianism, by electing parties that are centralizing control over all branches of government in the executive. UK Prime Minister Theresa May declared that "she is prepared to rip up human rights laws to impose new restrictions on terror suspects."[32] Turkish voters approved a series of constitutional amendments in 2017 that gave President Recep Erdogan "sweeping new powers."[33] Soon thereafter, Turkey was described as "sliding into dictatorship,"[34] and Erdogan was reelected as president in June 2018.

In Africa, the leaders of Equatorial Guinea, Republic of Congo, Uganda, Cameroon, Sudan, Chad, and Eritrea have all been in power for 20 successive years or more, generally pursuant to sham elections in which no viable opposition was permitted.[35] Only in 2017 were two of its most infamous dictators – Robert Mugabe in Zimbabwe (37 years in power) and José Eduardo dos Santos in Angola (38 years) – removed from office. Neither Joseph Kabila in Democratic Republic of the Congo nor Paul Kagame in Rwanda show any signs of leaving soon, and a 2017 New York Times editorial was entitled "Democracy Is Rwanda's Losing Candidate."[36] Outside of Africa, the list of those in power for more than 20 years includes Cambodian Prime Minister Hun Sen, Iran's Supreme Leader Ayatollah Ali Khamenei, Kazakhstan's President Nursultan Nazarbayev, and Tajikistan's President Emomali Rakhmon.[37]

In 2015, the UN High Commissioner for Human Rights, Zeid Ra'ad Al Hussein, addressed the Human Rights Council in unusually direct terms. While his comments address a wide range of human rights violations, not only those related to populism or democracy, they underscore the challenges that human rights continue to face.

I will focus in this statement on the broad conduct of Member States regarding their obligations to uphold human rights ...

[W]ith alarming regularity, human rights are disregarded, and violated, sometimes to a shocking degree.

States claim exceptional circumstances. They pick and choose between rights. One Government will thoroughly support women's human rights and those of the LGBT communities, but will balk at any suggestion that those rights be extended to migrants of irregular status. Another State may observe scrupulously the right to education, but will brutally stamp out opposing political views. A third State comprehensively violates the political, civil, economic, social and cultural rights of its people, while vigorously defending the ideals of human rights before its peers ...

In recent months I have been disturbed deeply by the contempt and disregard displayed by several States towards the women and men appointed by you as this Council's independent experts – and also by the reprisals and smear campaigns that are all too frequently exercised against representatives of civil society, including those who engage with the Council and its bodies. I appeal to all of you, once again, to focus on the substance of the complaint, rather than lash out at the critic – whether that person is mandated by States, is a member of my Office, or is a human rights defender ...

[T]he reality, in far too many countries, of massacres and sexual violence; crushing poverty; the exclusive bestowal of health-care and other vital resources to the wealthy and well-connected; the torture of powerless detainees; the denial of human dignity – these things are known. And Excellencies, they are what truly make up a State's reputation; together with the real steps – if any – taken by the State to prevent abuses and address social inequalities, and whether it honours the dignity of its people.

The only real measure of a Government's worth is not its place in the solemn ballet of grand diplomacy. It is the extent to which it is sensitive to the needs – and protects the rights – of its nationals and other people who fall under its jurisdiction, or over whom it has physical control.

Some policy-makers persuade themselves that their circumstances are exceptional, creating a wholly new reality unforeseen by the law. This logic is abundant around the world today: *I arrest arbitrarily and torture because a new type of war justifies it. I spy on my citizens because the fight against terrorism requires it. I don't want new immigrants, or I discriminate against minorities, because our communal identity is being threatened now as never before. I kill without any form of due process, because if I do not, others will kill me.* And so it goes, on and on, as we spiral into aggregating crises.

I must remind you of the enduring and universal validity of the international human rights treaties that your States wrote and ratified. In reality, neither terrorism, nor globalisation, nor migration are qualitatively new threats that can justify overturning the legal foundations of life on Earth. They are not new.[38]

HUMAN RIGHTS AS LAW

The phrase *human rights* is extraordinarily broad and can encompass many understandings of what rights are. As implied by the first sentence of this book, however, the contemporary content of human rights is defined most clearly and most powerfully as law. The relationship of law to other regulatory or aspirational frameworks – politics, ideology, religion, philosophy, social justice, or equality, to name only a few – is a recurring theme of the present work. The underlying assumption is that the status of human rights *as law* needs to be protected and that the distinction between legal obligations and other obligations of a moral or political nature needs to be maintained. Human rights may mean all things to all people, but international human rights law cannot.

This understanding of human rights as connoting international human rights law may be criticized as narrow, and it certainly does not encompass every right that someone or some group seeks to assert. As discussed in Chapter 7, this narrow scope should not be confused with an attempt to achieve uniformity in interpretation and application. Law does, however, provide a structural context in which human rights can be best understood in today's world. Law also provides (1) the best evidence of the content of human rights and (2) the best evidence of the essential universality of the human rights commitments that states have actually undertaken. As aptly put by Duke University professor Allen Buchanan, "Human rights law, not any philosophical or 'folk' theory of moral human rights, is the authoritative lingua franca of modern human rights practice."[39]

This approach does not seek to minimize the role of human rights understood more broadly as an inspirational moral framework that has motivated activists and ordinary people around the world. It also recognizes the political value that many governments have found in human rights, whether it is to promote them or to hold them up as foils for nationalist rhetoric. However, understanding the role of human rights as law is essential if one hopes to clarify the other roles that human rights may play, as ideology, utopia, or political weapon.

This dichotomy is expressed by the former executive director of Minority Rights Group International, Mark Lattimer. He accepts that, "[a]s human rights demands become more detailed and comprehensive, more constitutive, the weight of human diversity they attempt to bear becomes too much – and the edifice collapses."[40] However, Lattimer notes that a more expansive claim for human rights based on politics, morals, or justice "is made so persistently by human rights lawyers around the world, as well as finding a grounding in the history and philosophy of human rights, that it surely deserves to be treated seriously, even if this means rethinking legal categories or touching on the relationship of justice to human dignity, or what it means to be human."[41] While I disagree that expansive claims are what is needed now, these are, indeed, options that need to be treated seriously.

Law can change, and international human rights law is no exception. Neither the Universal Declaration nor any other human rights instrument was handed down on golden tablets or otherwise revealed through divine intervention. Human rights were consciously created by diplomats, lawyers, and lobbyists to respond to the lessons of the two major wars of the twentieth century. Human rights are linked to modernity, to constrain the capacity of the twentieth century state to coerce its citizens and to recognize the obligations of government to promote equitable development and protect those in need, rather than simply consolidating its own power.

The continuing evolution of international human rights law is demonstrated by the adoption of numerous treaties at the global and regional levels that expand, nuance, or occasionally limit the broad norms articulated in the UN Charter or by the UDHR. New norms await further elaboration and agreement, and interpretations of existing norms may shift – just as domestic statutes and constitutions acquire new meaning in order to respond to new situations and new problems. We should welcome this process, although proclaiming too many new norms without ensuring that meaningful consensus exists within all regions of the world can be problematic, as discussed further in Chapters 5 and 10.

THE GENERAL APPROACH

The arguments set forth in this book are pragmatic rather than philosophical, realist rather than visionary. They assume that the constraints of the current international system of states will continue to exist for the foreseeable future and that neither a world government nor a new "super" or "hyper" state will have the capacity or legitimacy to mold the world into any particularly orderly shape. These assumptions do not flow from a conclusion that today's governmental institutions, national or international, are perfect or even particularly functional. However, with all due respect to the necessary work of philosophers and theorists, there is no alternative set of international institutions on the horizon (or even in distant mirages) that is likely to develop in the foreseeable future. Greater effectiveness, transparency, and accountability from all levels of government must be sought, but no system of global governance will ever be able to assume responsibility for protecting the rights of billions of people around the world.

Perhaps the best hope for significant change in international structures was the European Union, and the EU remains a laudable example of what sufficient political will can accomplish on a regional level. However, even prior to the 2016 referendum in the United Kingdom that narrowly resulted in a vote to withdraw from the EU, the limits of "Europe" in replacing national feelings with transnational competence or allegiance were already evident. While the articulation of and respect for human rights within Europe have been constant concerns of the EU and the more inclusive Council of Europe, Chapter 7 discusses the many ways in which even regional consensus and consistency have reached their limits. Debates over whether the EU suffers from a *democracy deficit,* due to the fact that European citizens are thought to have insufficient direct influence on EU decision making, only reinforces the fact that states, not the European Union, remain the fundamental building blocks of international politics and economics.

My arguments also are premised on the proposition that international human rights law has had a positive influence on the situation of individuals across the globe and that maintenance and better implementation of that law should be encouraged.[42] It does *not* presume that either human rights or law generally is the primary agent of change within or across societies, but it does argue that human rights norms can facilitate the development and influence of other socio-economic-political-moral change agents in ways that are likely to respond to the needs of most people in the world.

As just suggested, I do not believe that human rights are the answer to all of the world's problems, an issue discussed particularly in Chapters 3, 4, and 5. Properly understood, human rights articulate a minimum standard for the relationship between individuals and their governments, but they should not be utilized to impose any particular conception of the ideal society in every corner of the world. At the same time, human rights constrain some of the acts that might have been legally and politically viable options for states before 1948. Just as colonialism and slavery are no longer legally or morally acceptable in the world, neither are genocide, torture, unfair trials, despotism, discrimination, unjustified limitations on basic freedoms, or government failure to put the rights of its population above the interests of its entrenched elites. Without international law, we risk a return to the nineteenth century, in which war was a legal and oft-used instrument of policy, and international cooperation was achieved through royal marriages and secret negotiations. While progress toward a better world has been ragged, this is not the time to go back to national isolationism or to pretend that a benevolent world government is a viable option.

2

Crime and (Occasional) Punishment

A recurrent theme in this book is the unfortunate tendency of advocates, critics, and academics to conflate human rights with other undertakings that have an impact on the human condition. That tendency is exemplified to the greatest degree by the juxtaposition of human rights with international criminal justice, in particular with the creation of the International Criminal Court (ICC) in 2002. Indeed, many of the most vocal critics of human rights pay as much attention to the disappointments of the ICC as they do to the perceived failure of human rights, as they define them, to achieve their goals. For example, Hopgood refers to international criminal justice as "the vanguard of human rights" since the 1990s and to the ICC as "a European vanity project."[43] Dispelling this confusion is the first step to understanding the legitimate goals, scope, and limits of international human rights norms.

CONFUSING VIOLATIONS WITH CRIMES

Confusion between the responsibility of a state to protect human rights and the culpability of an individual who commits a crime is paradigmatic of attempts to infuse human rights into unrelated concepts, usually to the detriment of both. For example, it is common to find references to human rights crimes in the context of violent conflicts, without any explanation of what the characterization of a crime as a human rights crime adds to our understanding of either criminal justice or international law. A similar approach may be found in discussions of transitional justice or post–regime-change situations, when the issue of punishing past human rights violations arises.[44]

International law has imposed obligations on individuals for centuries, predating concern with international human rights and the obligations of governments to those within their jurisdiction. It is difficult to see, for example, what punishing the pirate, hijacker, drug trafficker, terrorist, money launderer, or polluter has to do with human rights. Of course, all involve harm to people or property, combined with widespread international agreement that punishing such acts need not be restricted by the normal limitations of state sovereignty. (Most states exercise jurisdiction over crimes only if the crime occurs within that state's territory or if either the victim or perpetrator is a citizen of the country.) On the other hand, most harms are neither international crimes nor human rights violations, even if they may give rise to personal civil or criminal liability at the domestic level. Although we may bemoan the lack of enforcement, the international community also has defined and attempted to punish war crimes at least since the nineteenth century, including what might now be termed by some as human rights crimes, such as rape and torture, in addition to crimes of mistreating prisoners of war or attacking civilian targets.

The rejoinder of many human rights activists is that only certain kinds of crimes are human rights crimes, i.e., those that involve either widespread killing or particularly heinous acts; today, these are often referred simply as "atrocity crimes." The most common examples given are genocide, war crimes, crimes against humanity, and torture. However, the body of law concerning the first three of these crimes arose independently of and prior to the articulation of the human rights obligations of governments. Indeed, it is now axiomatic that international crimes need not have any connection at all to acts of a government, although many do. Thus, whether or not particular acts may rise to the level of crimes against humanity depends on the acts themselves, not whether they are committed by government officials (such as the military dictatorships in Argentina, Chile, and elsewhere in South America in the 1970s and 1980s), by individuals or groups encouraged or supported by governments (such as militias or other armed groups during the Yugoslav wars in the 1990s or in Syria and Yemen today), or by groups independent of government control or even enemies of the governing authority (such as Boko Haram in Nigeria, the Lord's Resistance Army in Uganda, Al Shabab in Somalia, or FARC in Colombia).

Since the 1990s, international crime and punishment have spawned hundreds of international jobs and cost billions of dollars, including the aborted trial of Slobodan Milosevic and the successful prosecution of many who committed crimes in former Yugoslavia and Rwanda. Oxford University Press has two scholarly journals on the topic, the *Journal of International Criminal Justice* and the *International Journal of Transitional Justice*. A permanent International Criminal Court (ICC), based in The Hague, was created in 2002 pursuant to the 1998 Rome Statute of the ICC,[45] and 123 countries had submitted to its jurisdiction as of early 2018. Its jurisdiction extends not to human rights violations or to mass atrocities but to the three traditional categories of international crimes already mentioned, namely genocide, war crimes, and crimes against humanity. In July 2018, the court began to exercise jurisdiction over a fourth crime, aggression, a definition of which was agreed on in 2010 pursuant to article 5.2 of the Statute; thirty-five countries had accepted this expanded jurisdiction as of early 2018. In the Rome Statute itself, human rights are mentioned only three times, in the contexts of ensuring that the court interprets applicable law in a nondiscriminatory manner and consistently with "internationally recognized human rights" (article 21(3)); prohibiting, in most instances, evidence obtained by means that violate human rights norms (article 69(7)); and, oddly, as being an area of competence relevant to the selection of judges (article 36(3)(b)(ii)).

As of February 2018, the ICC had been seized with 24 cases involving 37 individuals.[46] Four accused have had charges against them dismissed or vacated; four have died; and twelve remain at large. Of those tried, five have been found guilty (some of these cases are still on appeal), and one has been acquitted. Once commenced, trials generally take two to four years to be completed. The court was investigating eleven situations, and another ten situations were at the stage of preliminary examination. A separate Trust Fund for Victims has been created to provide reparations and assistance; Sweden is the top donor, followed by the United Kingdom, Germany, the Netherlands, Finland, Norway, France, Ireland, Australia, and Japan.[47]

Human rights activists have adopted the cause of combating international crimes as a way of deterring human rights abuses, although it is difficult to find evidence of the deterrent value of such norms. To offer only two obvious examples, the existence of the UN Security Council–created International Criminal Tribunal for the former Yugoslavia (ICTY) did nothing to stop the execution of several thousand men and boys in Srebrenica in 1995 or mass expulsions and widespread killings of ethnic Albanians in Kosovo by Serb forces in 1999. Anecdotal evidence has suggested that some government officials and members of armed groups have expressed concern about possible prosecution by the ICC, but it is difficult to identify any conflict in the world today where international crimes are not occurring on a widespread basis. This does not mean that the effort to bring international criminals to justice is not worth making, but criminal justice does not automatically lead to respecting human rights generally.

One example of the increasing importance of international criminal law with respect to both governmental attention and resources may be found in the number of international criminal tribunals created in the past couple of decades. The ICC, already mentioned, expended nearly $1 billion before it reached its first verdict in 2012;[48] the 2017 budget was 145 million euros.[49] Budgets for the ICTY and International Criminal Tribunal for Rwanda (ICTR), both of which were in existence for over two decades to consider crimes committed in the early 1990s, reached $250–300 million annually at their heights.[50] A somewhat dated 2010 analysis (written before creation by the UN of the Special Tribunal for Lebanon in 2007) estimated that $6.3 billion would have been spent on international criminal tribunals during the period 1993–2015; it noted that expenditures were declining and would likely be less than $200 million annually in 2015.[51]

For comparison, the annual amount of the UN's regular budget allocated to the Office of the High Commissioner for Human Rights (today approximately 3.5% of the total UN budget) has risen gradually from approximately $50 million in 2000 to $190 million for the two years 2016–2017. In addition, OHCHR receives more than that amount in voluntary contributions from states,[52] for a total annual budget of roughly $230 million. Of course, there is no guarantee (and perhaps little likelihood) that funds not spent on international criminal tribunals would be spent on international human rights institutions. Given that the responsibilities of OHCHR extend to over seven billion people, however, the overwhelming majority of whom are not victims of international crimes, the disparity in funding is striking.[53]

While UN and NGO reports themselves are often reasonably careful to distinguish international crimes from human rights violations, journalists, government officials, and academics are far less discerning. For example, UN Wire, a respected online compilation of daily news concerning the United Nations, headlined "Security Council told attack on Ukraine port city violates human rights";[54] the actual article to which the headline referred was more precise: "Attacks on civilians in Mariupol, Ukraine were war crime – UN."[55] A similar sloppiness occurred after publication by the UN of its report on North Korea,[56] which the BBC headlined as "World must act on North Korea rights abuse, says UN report."[57] A caption on a photograph of North Korean leader Kim Jung-Un stated that he "could be held personally responsible for human rights abuses."[58] An ICC judge has been described as a person who "helps decide the planet's thorniest human rights cases."[59] A three-part course series on human rights jointly offered by the American Society of International Law, American University Academy on Human Rights and Humanitarian Law, and the Continuing Legal Education Institute addressed "Prosecution of Gender-based Crimes by International Criminal Tribunals" at its final session.[60] Among seven topics suggested for discussion at the 2016 annual meeting of the American Society of International Law was "human rights, international criminal law," as though the connection between the two should be obvious to everyone.[61] Even careful and knowledgeable scholars use the shorthand of human rights charges and trials to refer to criminal trials under international or domestic law.[62]

Particularly within the past decade, OHCHR involvement in situations of armed conflict and alleged international crimes has increased, and it may not be coincidental that the three UN High Commissioners for Human Rights prior to the 2018 appointment of former Chilean president Michelle Bachelet had significant experience with international criminal tribunals prior to their appointment; none had served on an international human rights body.[63] When Navi Pillay left office in 2014, for example, she castigated the Security Council for not having shown greater responsiveness that "would have saved hundreds of thousands of lives" and for the international community's "failure to prevent conflict."[64] In one of his earliest speeches to the Human Rights Council, High Commissioner Zeid Ra'ad Al Hussein stated, "From a human rights perspective, it is clear that the immediate and urgent priority of the international community should be to halt the increasingly conjoined conflicts in Iraq and Syria."[65] When explaining the reasons for the delay of a report on the situation in Sri Lanka, he stressed that those responsible for committing abuses would not escape justice.[66]

"United Nations mandated commissions of inquiry, fact-finding missions and investigations are increasingly being used to respond to situations of serious violations of international humanitarian law and international human rights law, whether protracted or resulting from sudden events, and to promote accountability for such violations and counter impunity."[67] Since 2006, there have been twenty-seven such missions (excluding an unimplemented mandate concerning the Israeli-occupied Palestinian territories): six concerning aspects of the Israeli-Palestinian conflict, including the 2009 and 2014 conflicts in Gaza; three on Burundi; two each on Libya, Central African Republic, South Sudan, and Syria; and one each concerning Lebanon, Sudan (Darfur), Ivory Coast, North Korea, Sri Lanka, Eritrea, Iraq (ISIL), Myanmar, Democratic Republic of Congo, and Yemen.[68]

The mandates of these investigations generally refer more often to crimes against humanity and criminal prosecution than they do to human rights violations, although the former would seem to fall more squarely within the competence of the ICC than the OHCHR. For example, there have been three separate mandates for the Syrian Commission of Inquiry created in 2011. The initial mandate was "to dispatch urgently an independent international commission of inquiry ... to investigate all alleged violations of international human rights law since March 2011 in the Syrian Arab Republic, to establish the facts and circumstances that may amount to such violations and of the crimes perpetrated and, where possible, to identify those responsible with a view to ensuring that perpetrators of violations, including those that may constitute crimes against humanity, are held accountable."[69] The second resolution requests the commission to "conduct a ... special inquiry ... into the events [of an alleged massacre] in El-Houleh and, if possible, to publicly identify those who appear responsible for these atrocities, and to preserve the evidence of crimes for possible future criminal prosecutions."[70] The third resolution asks the commission to follow up on its report, "with a view to hold to account those responsible for violations and abuses, including those that may amount to crimes against humanity and war crimes."[71] While each of the resolutions also refers to human rights violations, the emphasis on international crimes and criminal liability is clear.

The 2014 Gaza resolution similarly requests the commission of inquiry "to investigate all violations of international humanitarian law and international human rights law in the Occupied Palestinian Territory ... to establish the facts and circumstances of such violations and of the crimes perpetrated and to identify those responsible ... all with a view to avoiding and ending impunity and ensuring that those responsible are held accountable ..."[72] The mandate for the Sri Lanka investigation was similar.[73] The High Commissioner for Human Rights, in announcing the members of the Group of Eminent Experts on the situation of human rights in Yemen, stated, "The group's creation is an important step toward accountability and ending impunity for the serious violations of human rights committed by all sides in Yemen amid a worsening humanitarian crisis in the country, and ensuring justice and remedy for the victims."[74]

The Human Rights Council, at the request of the Iraqi government, created a $1.2 million fact-finding commission to investigate alleged crimes committed by the Islamic State in Iraq, hardly a situation that had been ignored by governments or the press; the press release announcing release of the subsequent report does not even mention the phrase "human rights."[75] In 2015, OHCHR responded to a Council request adopted at a special session to document gross human rights abuses and violations of international humanitarian law by the non-state group Boko Haram in Nigeria, Cameroon, Niger, and Chad.[76]

Governments also confuse human rights violations and crimes. For example, the US Department of Homeland Security created a "Human Rights Violators & War Crimes Unit" as part of its US immigration and customs authorities, in order to prevent the entry into the United States of "foreign war crimes suspects, persecutors and human rights abusers"; one of its missions is to "identify and prosecute individuals who have been involved in and/or responsible for the commission of human rights abuses across the globe."[77]

As noted above, the juxtaposition of these two distinct issues is common in many different circumstances, but this does not imply that it is warranted or helpful.

AMNESTY AND ACCOUNTABILITY

The human rights connection to criminality began in Latin America, where the primary concern of human rights advocates since the 1980s has been to overcome the impunity or "self-amnesty" of government (often military) officials who escaped punishment for the crimes they committed during their reign. This view crystallized around the case of General Pinochet and his henchman in Chile, who granted themselves amnesties before leaving office after a murderous seventeen years in power; a similar situation obtained in Argentina and elsewhere in Latin America in the 1970s and 1980s. While massive human rights violations (and many crimes) certainly occurred under Pinochet and the Argentine generals, most of them (such as clamping down on free expression, imposing martial law, detention without trial, persecuting political opponents, and the forceful overthrow of the political system itself) were not crimes under international law.

As democratic governments in Latin America became more stable, they were able to reverse earlier amnesty laws and charge former government officials with a host of crimes under domestic law, including kidnapping, rape, torture, and murder. Local human rights activists and the relatives of victims were in the forefront of these campaigns, and they often called on foreign colleagues for support. Combating impunity became a new human rights mantra, and little attention was paid to the fact that the acts being punished were generally crimes under domestic law and not necessarily internationally defined human rights violations. The human rights "hook" was that human rights norms require the prevention of future abuses and that victims have the right to an appropriate remedy for violations that occurred in the past.[78] Taken together, these two principles supported the battle against impunity and general amnesties.[79]

While jurisdiction over some relatively narrow charges against Pinochet was upheld in the United Kingdom under the specific terms of the 1984 Convention against Torture,[80] almost none of the other government officials involved in the crimes just mentioned were tried outside their own country.[81] Happily, many were eventually stripped of their immunity and tried within their respective countries – Pinochet himself was returned by the United Kingdom to Chile on humanitarian grounds and never tried in Britain on torture charges; he died before he could be tried in Chile on domestic charges. Since the international anti-impunity lobby happens to be composed, in large part, of people who also consider themselves to be human rights advocates, it was easy for them and others to conflate satisfaction over the punishment of crimes with satisfaction over the formal confirmation through criminal trials that regimes committed human rights violations, as well.

One of the leading activists and lawyers in combating impunity has been Juan Mendez, a former Argentine political prisoner who, among many other distinctions, served as general counsel to Human Rights Watch, member of the Inter-American Commission on Human Rights, special advisor on genocide to the UN Secretary-General, president of the International Center for Transitional Justice, and UN special rapporteur on torture.

> When it comes to mass atrocities, the appropriate response has to be the investigation, prosecution and punishment of those responsible ...
>
> In addition to the contributions of the inter-American court and commission, other international human rights institutions have added to the body of emerging law about what states owe to the victims of mass atrocities ... The state is obliged to:
>
> 1. Investigate, prosecute and punish mass atrocities (justice),
> 2. Find out and disclose all the circumstances of their commission (truth),
> 3. Offer appropriate compensation to the victims (reparations),
> 4. Conduct an overhaul of state institutions that have been the vehicle of those violations in the recent past (institutional reform) ...
>
> While reconciliation should be the ultimate objective of a policy of transitional justice, true reconciliation can come about only as a result of justice, meaning criminal prosecution of at least those bearing the highest responsibility for the crimes.[82]

Another perspective, however, is highly critical of the impact of the anti-impunity advocates.

> In the twenty-first century, fighting impunity has become both the rallying cry and a metric of progress for human rights. Criminal prosecutions are central to this fight ...

In various ways, ... a dominant emphasis on anti-impunity has qualitatively transformed human rights and transitional justice discourses, and in turn practices, particularly by narrowing their gaze to certain types of impunity. Contrary to what is suggested by the trend in scholarship, activism, and politics, we contend that the turn is not the logical, necessary, nor preferred outcome of a linear process of maturation in either field. Rather ... this laser focus on anti-impunity has created blindspots in practice and scholarship that result in a constricted response to human rights violations, a narrowed conception of justice, and an impoverished approach to peace ...

[P]roponents of international criminal law persistently fail to justify its utility, necessity, or efficacy ...[83]

In 2011, the Transitional Justice Institute at the University of Ulster convened a working group of experts to consider amnesties and related issues. Two years later, the group adopted the Belfast Guidelines on Amnesties and Accountability, which note that "[w]ithin international human rights law, there are differences in the approach of the regional human rights courts on whether there is an obligation to prosecute gross violations of human rights or whether it is sufficient that states investigate such violations and provide remedies for those affected. Amnesties enacted in different regions of the world may be subject to different standards."[84] The principles do refer to human rights, but they clarify that "'[g]ross violations of human rights' is used here to denote acts that constitute serious crimes under national or international law and, if committed by a government, would violate the state's human rights obligations."[85]

Of course, issues of amnesties, transitional justice, and punishment for crimes are properly viewed as falling within the scope of international human rights norms, and governments cannot violate international human rights law in order to pursue their own version of "justice." The questions are (1) to what extent granting or denying amnesty or punishing criminals is limited by human rights norms and (2) whether human rights norms *require* that prosecutions be undertaken under particular circumstances.

The first question has been addressed in a number of judgments by the European Court of Human Rights, often in the context of restrictions imposed on an individual's political participation based on his or her past acts or political beliefs. The court has generally deferred to the government's determination of such issues in transitional situations, for example, by upholding a prohibition on former active members of communist parties standing for office in Latvia following Latvia's resumption of independence in 2006.[86] On the other hand, the court found that granting special status and political access to ethnic Serbs, Croats, and Bosniaks in Bosnia and Herzegovina violated the European Convention's prohibition against racial discrimination.[87] While these cases concern restrictions on political activity rather than criminal prosecutions, each assumes that the particular historical circumstances of a state is a legitimate issue to be taken into account.[88]

A different perspective is found in Latin America, where the Latin American human rights system has consistently determined that blanket amnesties are impermissible and equates the obligation to provide a "remedy" for a human rights violation with providing a victim with "truth" and requiring criminal prosecution of any individual who committed at least some international crimes.

[The Inter-American Court of Human Rights] considers that all amnesty provisions, provisions on prescription and the establishment of measures designed to eliminate responsibility are inadmissible, because they are intended to prevent the investigation and punishment of those responsible for serious human rights violations such as torture, extrajudicial, summary or arbitrary execution and forced disappearance, all of them prohibited because they violate non-derogable rights recognized by international human rights law.[89]

Compliance with the Inter-American Court's judgments has been problematic.[90] For example, the court determined in 2010 that "[t]he provisions of the [1979] Brazilian Amnesty Law that prevent the investigation and punishment of serious human rights violations are not compatible with the American Convention . . . [and] lack legal effect." Among the court's wide-ranging orders were that Brazil conduct criminal investigations that would have been otherwise precluded by the amnesty law; provide medical and psychological treatment for the victims; publish the court's judgment; "carry out a public act of acknowledgment of its international responsibility in regard to the facts of the present case"; and develop human rights training programs for the armed forces.[91] As of early 2018, Brazil appears not to have complied with the judgment and has not revoked its amnesty.

The OAS General Assembly adopted a resolution recognizing "the importance of respecting and ensuring the right to the truth so as to contribute to ending impunity and to promoting and protecting human rights."[92] At the global level, a set of principles "for the protection and promotion of human rights through action to combat impunity" was submitted by the UN Commission on Human Rights in 2005,[93] and its successor, the UN Human Rights Council, created a new special procedure on "the promotion of truth, justice, reparation and guarantees of non-recurrence" in 2011.

It is difficult to find consistent state practice outside Latin America. Eastern Europe after the fall of Soviet-backed regimes, post-apartheid South Africa, Northern Ireland, Cambodia, Sudan, Kenya after electoral violence in 2009, Sierra Leone, Liberia, Philippines, Colombia – all have adopted different approaches to transitional or post-conflict justice. For example, apartheid is a crime against humanity, defined as such in a treaty ratified by 109 states,[94] and it surely falls within the scope of the mass atrocities referred to above by Mendez. However, when South Africans after the end of apartheid decided that a "truth and reconciliation" commission was more appropriate in most instances than individual criminal prosecution, foreign states, NGOs, and international organizations unanimously accepted this determination – despite the fact that article IV(b) of the Apartheid Convention specifically demands that states "adopt legislative, judicial and administrative measures to prosecute, bring to trial and punish in accordance with their jurisdiction persons responsible for, or accused of" apartheid as defined in the treaty.

Rather than being based on illusory interpretations of international law, decisions regarding amnesties – such as creating the South African truth commission – are better left to domestic authorities (assuming that the alleged criminals do not adopt self-amnesties simply to protect themselves), who are better positioned to determine whether punishment, forgiveness, or something in between is more likely to lead to a more stable, rights-respecting polity in the future. Where, as in Brazil, the population has freely and knowingly endorsed an amnesty through a referendum, it is even more difficult to conclude that this necessarily violates human rights. What is ultimately required is the much more difficult and time-consuming task of helping to change the behavior of governments and their officials and ensuring that violations are not repeated. Demands to put all those guilty of even the most serious human rights crimes in prison may or may not contribute to this goal.

Focusing on international criminal prosecutions may even undermine human rights concerns by essentially sweeping them under the rug. This arguably happened in Cambodia, where a decades-long process eventually led to a mechanism to try leaders of the Khmer Rouge for the deaths of 1.7 million people during their brief reign in 1975–1979. "Although this was one of the largest and most egregious crimes of the twentieth century, a generation went by before the Extraordinary Chambers in the Courts of Cambodia (ECCC) was established in February 2006, following many years of failed attempts to achieve justice, geopolitical manoeuvring and tortuous and difficult international negotiations."[95] The geopolitical maneuvering included a euphemistic reference to the "non-return to the policies and practices of the recent past" contained in the 1991 peace agreement between the Hun Sen government (created by the Vietnamese-backed invasion in 1979 that overthrew the Khmer Rouge) and the Khmer Rouge, as well as the continued recognition by the United Nations of a coalition government headed by the Khmer Rouge as the legitimate government of Cambodia until 1999. Following elections in 1993 and creation of a fig-leaf government of national unity, the UN General Assembly decided in 1998 to consider a request for assistance in bringing the Khmer Rouge leaders to justice by then Co-Prime Ministers Hun Sen and Norodom Ranariddh.[96]

More than a decade later, the United Nations and the Cambodian government – still headed by Hun Sen – agreed to create a hybrid or mixed Cambodian-international tribunal within the Cambodian judicial system, the Extraordinary Chambers, 90% of the funding for which came from the United Nations and international donors. The chambers were, to say the least, controversial and wracked with problems. Following the convictions of three senior Khmer Rouge leaders in two of the four planned cases set for trial, the Hun Sen government opposed any further trials, and some of the international judges resigned, citing political pressure from the government.[97] In 2018, two of these three accused were found guilty of genocide, in addition to their 2014 convictions for crimes against humanity.

Whether the trials were a success or failure depends very much on one's perspective. Columbia University professor Peter Maguire "derided as 'therapeutic legalism' the notion that war crimes trials can offer such benefits as healing, national reconciliation and closure for the victims."[98]

However, Philippe Sands, professor of law at University College London, questions whether "it's a fair sign of success or failure just to look at dollar signs and convictions ... The bigger question is, To what extent has this tribunal contributed to beginning the process of embedding the idea of justice, the absence of impunity, into public consciousness, to help Cambodia transition to a better place?"[99]

From the perspective of human rights, however, the protracted negotiations over establishment of the chambers and the trials themselves appear to have necessitated turning a blind eye to the rampant human rights violations committed under the rule of Hun Sen, who has been in power for over 30 years. While violations have been regularly documented by human rights NGOs and others, the United Nations was surprisingly quiet during the negotiation period in the 1990s and since the establishment of the Extraordinary Chambers. While the UN has had a human rights presence in Cambodia[100] and there has been a special representative/rapporteur on human rights in Cambodia[101] since 1993, the only resolutions adopted on the situation by the Human Rights Council or its predecessor, the Commission on Human Rights, have been under the diplomatically more polite agenda item of "advisory services and technical assistance." While many of these resolutions do express concern or even serious concern over various human rights violations, the tone is hardly what one would expect from a de facto one-party state whose leader recently announced that he was prepared to serve for "at least another 10 years."[102]

The 2018 report of the UN Special Rapporteur on the Situation of Human Rights in Cambodia charitably concludes:

> The progress made by Cambodia over the past 25 years is immense. The country has been transformed economically, although extreme poverty remains and the benefits of development have not been enjoyed equally by all Cambodians ... There remain a number of outstanding recommendations to which the Government is invited to respond. It is hoped that the action plan and strategy for realizing the Sustainable Development Goals will go some way to addressing those concerns and will enable the Government to work with other stakeholders in furthering the promotion and protection of human rights in Cambodia. The Special Rapporteur reiterates her willingness to work with the Government to better protect, respect and promote human rights for the benefit of all Cambodians.[103]

Non-UN sources are less charitable. The entry on Cambodia in Human Rights Watch's *World Report 2018* begins, "The civil and political rights environment in

Cambodia markedly deteriorated in 2017 ..."[104] Amnesty International notes in its 2017/2018 overview of Cambodia, "The crackdown on human rights defenders, media, civil society and the political opposition intensified ahead of elections scheduled for July 2018," including by crackdowns on opposition party leaders, civil society, and the media.[105] The Executive Summary of the Cambodian entry in the US Country Reports on Human Rights Practices for 2016 refers to "a politicized and ineffective judiciary; increased restrictions on freedoms of speech, assembly, and association; and the use of violence and imprisonment – both actual and threatened – to intimidate the political opposition and civil society as well as to suppress dissenting voices. Other human rights problems included continued prisoner abuse, restrictions on press freedom and online expression, failure to grant equal access and fair treatment to asylum seekers, pervasive corruption, and trafficking in persons."[106] In March 2018, 45 of the 47 state members of the UN Human Rights Council called on Cambodia to release all political prisoners and ensure a fair vote in the upcoming elections.[107]

It may be impossible to establish whether combating past impunity in Cambodia was implicitly prioritized by the UN and other actors over safeguarding human rights in the present. That possibility, however, is a powerful argument in most situations for separating the issues of criminal responsibility and human rights protection.

PEACE AND JUSTICE

The New York–based International Center for Transitional Justice was founded in 2001. One of the goals of its "new direction in human rights advocacy" was described as "helping societies to heal by accounting for and addressing past crimes after a period of repressive rule or armed conflict."[108] The mission is now couched somewhat differently, emphasizing human rights rather than crimes: "ICTJ works across society and borders to challenge the causes and address the consequences of massive human rights violations. We affirm victims' dignity, fight impunity, and promote responsive institutions. Societies break the cycle of massive human rights violations and lay the foundations for peace, justice, and inclusion."[109]

Without entering fully into the "peace versus justice" debate, the point is simply to reiterate that human rights violations, even serious or gross or massive violations, are often not crimes and are attributable to governments, not to individuals. No one believes that international law mandates criminal punishment for every government official who authorizes or tolerates religious or gender discrimination, denies free expression, or suppresses trade union activity, for example, although such acts certainly constitute serious violations of human rights and may also constitute crimes under domestic law. Nor is criminal punishment the only means of dealing with the consequences of war or dictatorship.

The punitive approach of criminal law is also quite different from the transformative goals of international human rights law, and post-apartheid South Africa again offers a compelling example:

> As interpreted by the human rights movement, the lesson of Nuremberg is twofold: one, that responsibility for mass violence must be ascribed to individual agents; and, two, that criminal justice is the only politically viable and morally acceptable response to mass violence ...
>
> This kind of logic ill fits the context of a civil war. Victims and perpetrators in civil wars often trade places in ongoing cycles of violence. No one is wholly innocent and none wholly guilty ...
>
> To break out of the cycle of violence we need to displace the victim narrative with that of the survivor. A survivor narrative is less perpetrator-driven, more issue driven. Atrocities become part of a historical narrative, no longer seen as so many standalone acts but as parts of an ongoing cycle of violence. To acknowledge that victim and perpetrator have traded places is to accept that neither can be marked as a permanent identity. The consequence is to de-demonize—and thus to humanize—the perpetrator ...
>
> Neither victors' justice nor victims' justice, CODESA [the Convention for a Democratic South Africa, which were the negotiations that ended apartheid] shed the zero-sum logic of criminal justice for the inclusive nature of political justice, inclusion through the reform of the political community in which yesterday's victims, perpetrators, bystanders, and beneficiaries may participate as today's survivors. Political reform targets entire groups, not isolated individuals. Its object is not punishment, but a change of rules; not state creation, but state reform. By turning its back on revenge, it offers the possibility of creating new communities of survivors. By focusing on the link between creating an inclusive political order and an inclusive rule of law, it calls for a deep reflection on the relation between politics and law. The point of it all was not to avenge the dead, but to give the living a second chance.[110]

CONCLUDING REMARKS

What difference does all of this make? Both human rights and criminal prosecution serve goals that benefit individuals and society, and there is no inherent conflict between them. However, whether in domestic or international forums, prosecution is necessarily selective and incomplete. The jurisdiction of the International Criminal Court is limited to "the most serious crimes of concern to the international community as a whole."[111] Domestic crimes, such as murder, torture, or kidnapping, may be subject to statutes of limitations, and it will rarely be possible to hold everyone who committed such acts accountable. Where an entire government system has been taken over by murderers and those who collaborate with them, symbolic prosecution of the worst offenders may be the best hope.

Human rights, on the other hand, do not apply only to some people, and their guarantee cannot be deliberately selective. Human rights govern a vast range of relationships between individuals and their governments, and their violation affects billions of people. Governments cannot simply ignore these violations, but their remediation goes far beyond merely stopping criminal acts. Both the goals and the modalities of protecting human rights are distinct from those relevant to pursuing the criminal accountability of individual offenders, and confusing these goals and the means of achieving them will simply make the tasks – punishing criminals and ensuring human rights – more difficult.

Despite the implicit criticism above of their preoccupation with punishment, neither the Human Rights Council nor the High Commissioner for Human Rights has entirely neglected human rights per se. For example, among the investigations mentioned above, those concerning North Korea[112] and Eritrea[113] do not involve situations of widespread armed conflict. OHCHR continues to fulfill its functions, including servicing the human rights treaty bodies and the special procedures created by the Council, most of whose tasks concern human rights rather than alleged crimes. Most of the press statements of the High Commissioner continue to highlight more traditional human rights issues and violations. Nonetheless, the constant references to war and crimes – which clearly have great humanitarian and political importance – often seem to drown the more mundane and far more numerous violations of human rights that occur daily. In addition, neither the Human Rights Council nor the OHCHR is particularly well suited or qualified to determine whether or not criminal violations of international law have occurred.

There is unfortunately very little that the HR Council, OHCHR, or even the ICC can do to influence ongoing situations of widespread violence and armed conflict, which are certainly being highlighted by other UN actors, states, and the media. Appeals to human rights in such conflicts are unlikely to yield much fruit, and they risk diminishing the value or effectiveness of human rights in the minds of many. Greater respect for human rights in Syria prior to 2011, for example, might have helped prevent or mitigate the outbreak of violence, and human rights guarantees surely must be an integral part of any peace agreement. However, it is ludicrous to appeal for the parties to respect human rights in the midst of a murderous conflict in which all actors are committing war crimes and crimes against humanity.[114] Human rights norms and mechanisms alone cannot stop war, and asking them to do so will undoubtedly be used as yet another example of how meaningless human rights are in today's world.

A proposal made in 2015 by two former ambassadors to the United Nations to "strengthen the conflict prevention and peacebuilding roles of the International Court of Justice and U.N. Human Rights Council" would exacerbate this trend even more.[115] In the report from which their op-ed is drawn, the phrase *human rights* appears only three times in the three-page table of contents, once in "human rights and transitional justice" and twice as "international courts and human rights bodies".[116] In order to "[s]treamline the global human rights architecture," the report encourages "a human rights dialogue between the Security Council,

Human Rights Council, and International Criminal Court … [in order to respond to] large-scale human rights abuses," i.e., international crimes.[17] The OHCHR already briefs the president of the Security Council on a regular basis, and the ICC's work is hardly secret. Thus, the only impact of the proposal would likely be to blur even further the judicial tasks of the ICC, the theoretically objective human rights analyses of OHCHR, and the avowedly political perspective of the Security Council.

States should continue to try to capture, try, and punish international criminals, and in some circumstances international criminal tribunals may be the most appropriate options for prosecution. Confusing these goals with human rights, however, distorts priorities and diminishes the attention that should be paid to the more boring yet more pervasive human rights violations faced by most of the world's population most of the time.

3

The Importance of Government, for Better or Worse

Changing a government's behavior is no small task, and donors, whether of expertise or financial resources, are often too impatient or conservative to take the leap of faith that is required if one expects to see visible progress on human rights issues in the short term. Similarly, human rights activists often find it easier to go after softer, more readily identifiable targets rather than amorphous "government" in all of its complexity.

When governments remain recalcitrant, donors and activists see mutually beneficial alternatives in turning their attention and resources to civil society, business, political parties, educators, and other actors, as a way of indirectly pressuring the only entities who truly have human rights obligations under international law, governments. This chapter examines the impact and implications of these directional shifts on the two sets of actors that have received the most attention in the past couple of decades, business and civil society.

BUSINESS AND HUMAN RIGHTS (B&HR)

Transnational or multinational corporations (TNCs) have long been accused of either conspiring with governments to violate human rights for economic gain or simply ignoring governments and infringing rights directly. Oddly, they are rarely given credit for contributing to the fulfillment of economic rights when development goes well, despite evidence that both extreme poverty and the degree of overall economic inequality in the world have improved markedly since the 1960s. For example, even while noting that he was "keenly aware that inequalities persist and that progress has been uneven," UN Secretary-General Ban Ki-Moon observed in the UN's report on the Millennium Development Goals, "The MDGs helped to lift more than one billion people out of extreme poverty, to make inroads against hunger, to enable more girls to attend school than ever before and to protect our planet . . . By putting people and their immediate needs at the forefront, the MDGs reshaped decision-making in developed and developing countries alike."[118] A significant portion of the credit should go to the efforts of business, entrepreneurs, workers, and others who have made economic and material progress possible in recent decades.

The more dominant conversation, however, reflects the following perspective.

> The root cause of the business and human rights predicament today lies in the governance gaps created by globalization – between the scope and impact of economic forces and actors, and the capacity of societies to manage their adverse consequences. These governance gaps provide the permissive environment for wrongful acts by companies of all kinds without adequate sanctioning or reparation. How to narrow and ultimately bridge the gaps in relation to human rights is our fundamental challenge."[119]

A TNC may collaborate with a repressive government in many ways, and there is no doubt that many TNCs are willing to do so.[120] When the collaboration amounts to complicity or aiding and abetting an international crime, then the individuals involved (generally not the company) may be subject to international criminal sanctions.

The United Nations has attempted on a number of occasions to address corporate responsibility for human rights, and these attempts culminated in adoption of the Guiding Principles on Business and Human Rights by the Human Rights Council in 2011 (hereafter Guiding Principles). Prior to that initiative, the General Assembly spent many years in the 1970s and 1980s discussing a Code of Conduct for Transnational Corporations, an initiative that eventually foundered on north–south divisions, continuing disagreements over the New International Economic Order that was proclaimed by the UN General Assembly in 1974,[121] and a growing desire on the part of developing countries to encourage rather than discourage foreign investment.[122]

In 1999, the United Nations adopted a set of principles known as the Global Compact, announced by Secretary-General Kofi Annan to encourage business leaders to ensure that globalization was pursued responsibly. As of early 2018, approximately 10,000 companies and medium- and small-sized enterprises had declared their acceptance of the ten principles that constitute the compact, which has as its motto "business as a force for good."[123] Of the ten principles, the first two address human rights specifically:

> Principle 1: Businesses should support and respect the protection of internationally proclaimed human rights; and
> Principle 2: make sure that they are not complicit in human rights abuses.

The remaining principles address labor rights, the environment, and combating corruption. The Global Compact has more in common with the concept of corporate social responsibility than international human rights law, and its commitments are purely voluntary, but they reflect the increasing attention paid to corporate activity and accountability by both civil society and government.

The most rights-oriented attempt to articulate the relationship between business and human rights were the Norms on the Responsibilities of Transnational Corporations and Other Business Enterprises with Regard to Human Rights, adopted by the UN Sub-Commission on the Promotion and Protection of Human Rights in 2003.[124] According to their primary author, US law professor and member of the Sub-Commission David Weissbrodt, the norms "applied human rights law under ratified conventions to the activities of … [businesses]. Moreover, the language of the document emphasized binding responsibilities through the use of the term 'shall' rather than 'should,' and the draft norms included measures for implementation."[125]

While many NGOs welcomed the norms, they received a chilly reception from the business community and the Sub-Commission's parent body, the UN Commission on Human Rights. The latter pointed out that, "as a draft proposal, [the Sub-Commission report] has no legal standing" and directed the Sub-Commission not to attempt to monitor the norms in any way.[126] Nonetheless, it was not politically feasible for the commission simply to drop the issue, and it requested the High Commissioner for Human Rights to prepare a report on the topic. Following the report's submission, the commission requested the Secretary-General to appoint a special representative on human rights and business, whose work over the next several years eventually resulted in adoption by the UN Human Rights Council (which succeeded the commission in 2006) of the Guiding Principles.[127]

The principles were drafted by the Secretary-General's special representative, Harvard professor John Ruggie, after extensive research and a series of consultations with governments, businesses, NGOs, and other stakeholders. The principles are intended to implement the "protect, respect and remedy" framework for B&HR approved by the Council in 2010.[128] The special representative's introduction to the principles states that their "normative contribution lies not in the creation of new international law obligations but in elaborating the implications of existing standards and practices … [and] integrating them within a single, logically coherent and comprehensive template."[129]

The three pillars of the principles are "the *State* duty to protect against human rights abuses by third parties, including business …; the *corporate* responsibility to respect human rights, which means to act with due diligence to avoid infringing on the rights of others; and greater access by victims to effective remedy, judicial and non-judicial."[130] "The term 'responsibility' to respect [re businesses], rather than 'duty', is meant to indicate that respecting rights is *not* an obligation that current international human rights law generally imposes directly on companies … [although it reflects] a standard of expected conduct acknowledged in virtually every voluntary and soft-law instrument related to corporate responsibility."[131] This non-applicability of international legal norms to business was confirmed by the ESC Committee in 2017, when it adopted a general comment related to business in which it was highly critical of many business practices but that also stated, "The present general comment addresses the States parties to the Covenant, and in that context it only deals with the conduct of private actors – including business entities – indirectly."[32]

The Guiding Principles look much like what one would expect from a decent set of guidelines articulating corporate social responsibility. As their author himself notes, they do not purport to extend to business a legal obligation to ensure human rights; for this reason, many NGOs were disappointed. At the same time, however, the principles have reinforced social and political pressures on business to pay attention – "due diligence" – to human rights norms, and the principles themselves have been widely supported by the business community.

There is no question that the Guiding Principles have become the most significant articulation of the connection between business activities and human rights. Unfortunately, they suffer from a number of weaknesses that undermine not only appropriate standards for the conduct of business but one of the fundamental principles of international human rights law.

For example, professor Ruggie criticized the 2003 Sub-Commission Norms for "their imprecision in allocating human rights responsibilities to states and corporations ... By their very nature ... corporations do not have a general role in relation to human rights like states, but a specialized one ... But ... [the Norms] articulate no actual principle for differentiating human rights responsibilities based on the respective social roles performed by states and corporations."[33] The Guiding Principles fall into the same trap, in that they state that the responsibility of business to "respect" human rights extends to *all* human rights, defined as the UDHR, the two UN covenants, and the International Labor Organization's Declaration on Fundamental Principles and Rights at Work.[34] This overarching scope is amplified by the principle that "[t]he responsibility of business enterprises to respect human rights applies to all enterprises regardless of their size, sector, operational context, ownership and structure. Nevertheless, the scale and complexity of the means through which enterprises meet that responsibility may vary according to these factors and with the severity of the enterprise's adverse human rights impacts."[35]

What does it mean that a business must respect the rights to education, health, fair trial, freedom of assembly, and marriage, to name only a few of the rights found in the covenants? Would this require a business that otherwise conforms to health and safety standards and the prohibitions against nondiscrimination and child labor to cease operations in a country that imprisons political prisoners or ignores education for girls? It would appear not, unless one interprets "infringing on the rights of others" as doing business and therefore paying taxes to a rights-violating government (whether in the developed or developing world). Would a business have to abstain from operating in a country that forbids women from working outside the home, or would it be sufficient for the business to offer to employ women and men equally, with the knowledge that, in fact, it could employ only men?

The scope of rights for which a business is responsible is also relevant to what the business should include in its "human rights due diligence process," which is described in Principles 17–21. This process should cover "adverse human rights impacts that the business enterprise may cause or contribute to through its own activities, or which may be directly linked to its operations, products or services by its business relationships . . ."[136] However, "[a]s a non-legal matter, business enterprises may be perceived as being 'complicit' in the acts of another party where, for example, they are seen to benefit from an abuse committed by that party."[137] Thus, if a business relies on government security forces that are known for violating human rights to protect it, it would seem to be complicit, while merely doing business in a country in which there is generalized government repression might not be a sufficiently close connection to constitute complicity or to require being included in a company's due diligence process.

Two institutions were created by the Human Rights Council to promote the Guiding Principles. The first is a working group of five independent experts whose primary tasks are to promote the effective and comprehensive dissemination and implementation of the Guiding Principles; identify and promote good practices related to the principles, including making recommendations; and support capacity building.[138] The group also has the ability to receive communications alleging human rights related to its mandate, whether against states or individual companies. Approximately one-third of the 92 communications received by the working group through May 2017 concerned businesses, and often both a business and the country concerned were accused of violations.[139] The communications and any replies received are published three times a year, jointly with those addressed to other thematic procedures.[140]

The HR Council also created an annual three-day Forum on Business and Human Rights, which is to "discuss trends and challenges in the implementation of the Guiding Principles and promote dialogue and cooperation on issues linked to business and human rights, including challenges faced in particular sectors, operational environments or in relation to specific rights or groups, as well as identifying good practices." After a slow start, the forum has developed into a major meeting-place for NGOs, governments, and others involved in advising businesses on how they might comply with the Guiding Principles, drawing approximately 2,000 participants to its sessions in Geneva, Switzerland. The forum is open to all relevant stakeholders, including states, the wider UN system, intergovernmental and regional organizations, businesses, labor unions, national human rights institutions, nongovernmental organizations, and academics, among others.

The forum epitomizes both the potential and the pitfalls of linking human rights with the activities of business. Its agenda is certainly broad. In 2017 alone, under the central theme of realizing access to effective remedy, there were panels or discussions on, among other topics, the role of "shapers" of corporate practice; promoting inclusion and countering antimigrant narratives; living wages; corporate misconduct in sharing and processing personal data; remedy for workers and communities affected by toxic waste; how multinational enterprises can use their leverage to help enable remediation by their business partners; bringing an LGBTI "lens" to the Guiding Principles; worker recruitment fees; increasing the effectiveness of domestic public law regimes; cross-border corporate human rights crimes; financialization, housing, and human rights; the international investment regime; victims of industrial supply chain accidents; victims of modern slavery in supply chains; and respect for human rights in the 2020 Tokyo Olympics.[41] Many of these topics highlight serious problems, but their scope is astonishing for a three-day meeting.

The tone of many of the presentations – particularly those by governments and businesses – is often self-congratulatory rather than analytical or critical. At the 2016 session, for example, the Attorney-General of Kenya was greeted very warmly, despite the widespread and well-known human rights problems in the country, because Kenya was the first African country to introduce a B&HR "action plan." A representative of SwissRe, a large reinsurance company, stated that the company would decide not to reinsure a project "based on human rights reasons," but that it would often do so simply by not replying to a request rather than informing the requesting company directly of its decision. SwissRe could not "press for" human rights, according to the representative, suggesting rather strongly that SwissRe cares more about protecting its own purity and image rather than actually improving human rights in any particular country. No doubt the same observation would apply to many other businesses present at the forum.

James Harrison is a reader and associate professor in the School of Law at the University of Warwick, where he is co-director of the Centre for Human Rights in Practice. He attended the 2016 session of the Forum, and after lauding the work of the activists and journalists who uncover evidence of human rights violations (often at considerable risk to their own safety), as well as local and national governments that are taking specific steps to leverage public procurement to promote respect for labor rights, he offered the following observations:

> There are many companies at the forum who talk about their extensive efforts to make sure their supply chains respect human rights, from Apple to Coca Cola, from Nestlé to BP. But listening to their speeches it is impossible to know whom to trust. I have no way of judging whose efforts are extensive, genuine, and transformative. Whose are limited, questionable, aimed only at preserving and enhancing the company's brand ...
>
> At every session of the Forum, the UNGPs [Guiding Principles] are continuously namechecked, but their actual impacts are never discussed ...
>
> At another session, it is governmental representatives who talk about their engagement with the UNGPs. Representatives from Colombia, Kenya, South Korea, Mexico, Mozambique, Italy, France, Norway, Japan, Finland, Poland, the United Kingdom, the United States, Greece, Switzerland, Slovenia and Chile one by one describe their efforts to create a National Action Plan on business and

human rights. The audience gets restless, considerable numbers leave. But I stay. I feel hypnotised by the seemingly endless repetition of bureaucratic processes. It is only towards the end that Fernanda Hopenhaym, speaking on behalf of civil society, breaks the monotony: "It's not about how many action plans we have globally, it's also about their quality."[142]

In 2014, a third, presumably temporary, body appeared, when the Human Rights Council created an open-ended intergovernmental working group "to elaborate an international legally binding instrument to regulate, in international human rights law, the activities of transnational corporations and other business entities."[143] After three sessions (2015–2017), the group remained mired in disagreement, not least over whether its mandate extends to national businesses as well as those whose activities are transnational.[144] If the former are not included, many of the most egregious "human rights violations" will go unaddressed. For example, were transnational corporate headquarters responsible for the deadly collapse of the Rana Plaza building in Bangladesh in 2013, in which over 1,000 people were killed, or does the primary fault lie with unscrupulous local construction companies and corrupt local actors in both the private and public sectors?[145] How do outsiders pressure Chinese companies not to put harmful plastic in rice and milk?[146]

Among the elements of a new treaty discussed at the working group's 2017 session were ensuring "civil, administrative and criminal liability of TNCs and OBEs [other business enterprises] regarding human rights violations or abuses," including criminal liability for those who manage and control such entities; dismissing the need for a legal definition of TNCs and OBEs; protecting all internationally recognized human rights, including those in instruments related to "labour rights, environment, corruption;" adopting "a broad concept of jurisdiction" that would allow alleged victims to seek redress in either host or home states; and calling on TNCs and OBEs to "use their influence in order to help promote and ensure respect for human rights." The elements are replete with calls on states to "adopt legislative and other measures" to accomplish the goals of the proposed treaty, all of which are already within the authority of states to enact.[147] At the end, the session weakly "took note" of the elements and called upon the chair "to undertake informal consultations with States and other relevant stakeholders."[148]

It is the norm in every country in the world that, when a person or business harms someone else, that person or business must compensate the injured person; this the law of torts.[149] There are different degrees of liability and standards of care, but the basic principle that an individual or business cannot deliberately, recklessly, or negligently injure anyone without consequence is ubiquitous. Ensuring that appropriate compensation is paid to the person harmed is one of the most common kinds of legal cases brought in domestic courts, albeit with often highly contentious disagreements over both the degree of harm (if any) suffered; whether or not the civil defendant actually caused the harm; and, if so, whether the defendant should be held legally liable for the harm. There need be no human rights element present; all that matters is that someone was unjustly harmed, even (depending on the circumstances) by accident.

The word *tort* does not appear in the Guiding Principles, but part III of the principles is devoted to the responsibilities of business to remedy "adverse impacts" that they have caused or to which they have contributed, as well as to ensure that the victims have access to an effective remedy. In the non-state context, this means that business should create effective non-judicial grievance mechanisms.[150] In many respects, this is one of the most innovative aspects of the principles, and encouraging business to create factory-level or company-level grievance mechanisms would be a welcome addition to more time-consuming (and perhaps unavailable) judicial remedies.

Of course, if a company does not provide it voluntarily, remediation necessarily implies a functioning, effective, independent, and honest judicial system, an option sadly lacking in many countries. Corruption is often a significant impediment to a fair hearing, and this is when plaintiffs begin to look for both fairer tribunals and defendants with ample resources that will be able to pay adequate compensation, if harm and causation can be proved. Enter the issue of who should pay, the local subsidiary or supplier that actually caused the harm, or the rich, powerful parent company usually based in Europe or the United States. Because the concept of the "independent" subsidiary is fundamental to today's corporate or company law, "piercing the corporate veil"[151] is a significant barrier to victims who are harmed in a developing country with dysfunctional courts.

If this is beginning to sound like an introduction to business law, it should. Despite the juxtaposition of "business and human rights," the businesses involved are subject to and benefit from normal corporate/company law rules. Thus, any alleged "human rights abuses"[152] must also be torts or harms in order to be action-able in domestic courts. This would not necessarily be true in the nonjudicial grievance procedures recommended in the principles, where employee complaints of any kind might be addressed. It appears to be an open question how human rights abuses differ from ordinary torts, except that the former are narrower in scope.

In the United States, a direct means of attempting to hold corporations account-able for international harms that they cause was "discovered" in 1979. It is grounded in a unique statute, the 1789 Alien Tort Claims Act (ATCA), which had been adopted nearly two centuries earlier and almost never used until that time. ATCA reads, in full, "The district courts shall have original jurisdiction of any civil action by an alien for a tort only, committed in violation of the law of nations or a treaty of the United States." The law was originally intended to ensure that federal rather than state courts would address international wrongs, such as piracy or attacking a foreign ambassador, but a landmark case in 1979 held that ATCA also allowed jurisdiction to be exercised over a Paraguayan national and a Paraguayan victim (both resident in the United States at the time) for torture that had occurred in Paraguay.[153]

This set the stage for dozens of ATCA cases filed against both individuals and corporations for torts committed outside the United States (any tort committed within the United States would be actionable under domestic tort law), so long as they allegedly violated international law. In 2004, the US Supreme Court reaffirmed that an ATCA suit is permissible so long as the alleged violation of the law of nations (today known as customary international law) is widely accepted "and defined with a specificity comparable to the features of the 18-century paradigms we have recognized" (piracy, violations of safe conduct, and infringement of the rights of ambassadors).[154] However, a subsequent Supreme Court decision in 2013, *Kiobel v. Royal Dutch Shell*,[155] narrowed the scope of ATCA significantly, holding that the statute does not have extraterritorial application. It noted, in passing, that there was "no indication that the ATS [ATCA] was passed to make the United States a uniquely hospitable forum for the enforcement of international norms."[156] Suits against US-based corporations are likely to remain permissible, and Justice Breyer's concurring opinion proposed that jurisdiction also may be present if a defendant's conduct "substantially and adversely affects an important American national interest, and that includes a distinct interest in preventing the United States from becoming a safe harbor (free of civil as well as criminal liability) for a torturer or other common enemy of mankind."[157]

Some of the claims made by plaintiffs in ATCA cases have been fanciful, and the great majority of cases have either been dismissed or have resulted in default judgments with no hope of collecting damages. A few have been settled out of court for substantial sums (UNOCAL reportedly paid $25 million in one such suit concerning its activities in Burma, and Shell settled a case concerning its activities in the Niger Delta for $15.5 million in 2009), and the statute has enabled some human rights violations to be brought within the scope of litigation. Because international human rights violations do require some government involvement, the torts at issue are distinguishable from purely private wrongs, such as breaches of contract, auto accidents, murder, or kidnapping. While relatively few ATCA suits have resulted in compensation for victims, corporations must at least bear the possibility of liability under an ATCA suit in mind if they engage in activities that might rise to the level of violations of international law. The statute does not apply to all human rights norms but may be invoked only for violations of customary international law, such as torture, disappearances, forced labor, and international crimes (genocide, war crimes, and crimes against humanity), or of treaties to which the United States is a party.

While the responsibility of a foreign government is implicit in ATCA suits, even a successful case does not directly require the offending government to do anything, and damages have generally been sought from the impugned company or individual, not the state. In addition, targeting corporations may make it easier for the government itself to shift blame for the harm.

The Problems

Monitoring, regulating, and exposing the abuses of business are not only legitimate but necessary, whether it is termed corporate social responsibility (CSR) or responsible business conduct (RBC), which some in the OECD argue is a stronger concept.[158] Entwining corporate accountability with human rights, however, does serious damage to both causes.

First, identifying "respect" for human rights as the standard for corporate activity, as set forth in the Guiding Principles, is far too conservative to encompass the kind of conduct that we should expect from business. Social responsibility or responsible conduct entails much more than the "do no harm" approach that the principles advocate, even if we include the very useful language advocating access to judicial and nonjudicial remedies. For example, business could treat workers better than the law requires out of a sense of fairness, not just financial calculation; offer support to stakeholders when workers and others are hurt by events or circumstances for which a business is not legally liable; refrain from advertising and marketing that inappropriately targets vulnerable groups, such as children or the elderly; act in ways that will support a government's responsibilities to ensure human rights; and be generous toward charitable causes and institutions.[159] Businesses should be expected to lead, not follow, in their willingness to embrace diversity and set good examples, not just to do no harm.

Some of these responsibilities can be mandated by domestic law, and greater financial and decision-making transparency can be readily regulated in much greater detail than will ever be found in international norms. For example, the United Kingdom has amended company law to require companies to "have regard" to interests of stakeholders other than investors in determining corporate policies and priorities, including "the impact of the company's operations on the community and the environment" and "the desirability of the company maintaining a reputation for high standards of business conduct."[160] At the regional level, the European Union in 2014 began to require that companies that employ more than 500 people include in their annual reports nonfinancial statements containing "information to the extent necessary for an understanding of the undertaking's development, performance, position and impact of its activity, relating to, as a minimum, environmental, social and employee matters, respect for human rights, anti-corruption and bribery matters ..."[161] France followed suit in 2017 with a *loi de vigilence*, which imposes civil (tort) liability on companies of a certain size if they do not conduct adequate due diligence "while performing any acts that could foreseeably harm human rights or the environment."[162]

Second, when the real focus of business and human rights is on large transnational corporations, which are usually based in the global north, we reinforce the notion that human rights are more applicable to rich countries than to developing countries and that the latter can't really be trusted to respect or ensure human rights on their own. Much of the B&HR regime is top-down, and pressure is being placed primarily on large companies to impose compliance (or in the forum's terms, use their "leverage") on their subsidiaries or at least distance themselves from smaller businesses in their supply chain that ignore workers' rights or despoil the environment.

Third, linking business and human rights confuses two very different kinds of obligations. As Ruggie and many others note (but many advocates choose to forget), guidelines and principles do not create legal obligations for business enterprises, and compliance with such recommendations is purely voluntary. These include the Guiding Principles themselves, UN Global Compact, OECD Guidelines for Multi-national Enterprises, Business Social Compliance Code of Conduct, Consumer Charter for Global Business, Voluntary Principles on Security and Human Rights, Equator Principles, International Finance Corporation's Performance Standards, Principles for Responsible Investment, ISO 26000 Social Responsibility, and hundreds of other country-, industry-, or company-specific standards. Nearly 20 years ago, OECD identified 246 codes of conduct that had been subscribed to by entities within OECD countries, unsurprisingly noting that "[t]he codes examined differ considerably in terms of their content and degree of detail."[163] Even the guidelines have guidelines, e.g., the Australian government's Guidelines For Developing Effective Voluntary Industry Codes Of Conduct.[164] Such codes "may be useful first steps, but they are not alone sufficient. Worse, they may even be dangerous if human rights advocates and financiers alike rely on them too heavily, as the veneer of compliance checks could mask the need for more substantial and necessary systemic change."[165]

Human rights, on the other hand, constitute binding legal obligations on states and their governments; they cannot be accepted or ignored at whim or as a matter of public relations. The difficulties in implementing or ensuring compliance with human rights law are well-known, but they should not detract from the fact that it *is* law, accepted by the state itself, not merely the recommendations of experts or civil society groups. There is nothing wrong with more consultative or mediation-based approaches to disputes, which mirror efforts to achieve a "friendly settlement" that are regularly employed by regional human rights bodies. However, this under-scores the different approach of the B&HR regime, compared to the harder law of human rights. Particularly if the focus is on business to respect "all" human rights (as in the Guiding Principles), and businesses that fail to do so suffer no consequences, governments and the public at large may be tempted to see human rights generally as equally illusory.

An example from the 2017 session of the Forum illustrates the rather cavalier fashion in which human rights are inappropriately attached to often important problems, in the hope that it will give these problems greater gravitas and attention. The Director of Global Initiatives of Human Rights Watch opened her presentation at a panel on the 2020 Tokyo Olympics by presenting a tragic story of a worker involved in preparations for the Olympics who committed suicide, apparently from the stress of being overworked. This was offered as an example of the kind of human rights abuses that often occur at mega-sporting events, such as the Olympics and the World Cup.[166] When asked during the Q&A period whether the suicide was a human rights violation and, if so, who was responsible for the violation, the presenter did not respond directly, but privately she declared without hesitation that both the Japanese government and the company for whom the suicide victim worked had violated the human right to life. While it is certainly possible that a chain of causation leading to the government might be demonstrated, the facile assumption that, because there was a suicide (in a country in which work-related suicides are unfortunately not uncommon), a human right must have been violated reflects the way in which appeals to human rights often describe harms that should be prevented or remedied, but which are distinct from the obligations of governments under international law.

In fairness, it should be recognized that the International Olympic Committee itself has adopted new language that will be inserted in its host city contracts, beginning in 2024, which will require cities to prohibit any form of discrimination; "to protect and respect human rights and ensure any violation of human rights is remedied in a manner consistent with international agreements, laws, and regulations applicable in the Host Country and in a manner consistent with all internationally recognised human rights standards and principles, including the United Nations Guiding Principles on Business and Human Rights, applicable in the Host Country;" to refrain from fraud or corruption; to embrace sustainable development and the UN Sustainable Development Goals; and to conduct their activities to "comply with any international agreements, laws and regulations applicable in the Host Country, with regard to planning, construction, protection of the environment, health and safety, labour and working conditions and cultural heritage."[167] Laudable goals, to be sure, and a needed correction to the host of problems plaguing the IOC in recent years. At least this wish list is formally addressed to government entities – the host city and government – that do, indeed, have obligations to respect and ensure human rights.

Fourth, identifying the broad responsibilities of business with human rights obligations expands the concept of the latter to such an extent that human rights will inevitably be seen as failing to protect interests that it was never intended to protect. As noted above, the agendas of the 2016 and 2017 sessions of the UN Forum on B&HR, in which the author participated, are extraordinarily broad. Problems of human trafficking, abysmal working conditions, and attacks on indigenous and other human rights defenders were widely discussed, and the forum is, in part, a vehicle in which new situations can be brought to the attention of those present, including businesses and governments. However, it appeared that more of the materials distributed by companies and NGOs dealt with sustainability and the environment than with even labor rights, although the latter were certainly discussed.

Fifth, the prospect of using corporations to control governments rather than the reverse raises serious concerns, and attempts to impose human rights obligations directly on companies (whether foreign or domestic) may empower just those entities – corporations – that are the least accountable and transparent of all. Even Ruggie stated in his first report to the Human Rights Council that making corporations "in effect, co-equal duty bearers for the broad spectrum of human rights ... may undermine efforts to build indigenous social capacity and to make Governments more responsible to their own citizenry." [168] One might justifiably ask, for example, if relying on companies like Google, Apple, and Facebook to monitor internet content is either a feasible or good idea.[169]

A problematic recent article by the director-general of the London-based International Institute for Security Studies supports the views that corporations need to adopt a more expansive and self-referent view of the world.

> The reality in the twenty-first century is that companies cannot escape politics, nor can they consistently pretend to be politically neutral. The answer is to embrace the need to engage politically and diplomatically. Today's corporate foreign policy has two components: geopolitical due diligence and corporate diplomacy ...
>
> The role of corporate diplomacy is twofold: to enhance a company's general ability to operate internationally and to ensure its success in each particular country with which it is engaged ...
>
> The first principle of corporate diplomacy is that companies must develop their own approach to foreign governments, rather than manipulate or be manipulated by the policies of their home country ...
>
> Companies must engage all actors rather than attempt to mitigate geopolitical risk just through good government contacts (on the one hand) and good social practices (on the other). It is the dynamic relationship between the government, the business elite or oligarch class, and civil society that needs to be appreciated.[170]

The imposition of obligations on business to combat a wide range of human rights violations implicitly recognizes their authority and legitimacy to do what is necessary to achieve this goal. This brings us back to a basic conundrum: if business need only "respect" human rights, then the larger human rights situation in a country in which they operate should be irrelevant, and distancing a business from human rights abuses is sufficient. However, if the goal is to *protect* the human rights of people in that country, much more vigorous advocacy should be expected; if this is the case, the specter of corporate interference in governance should strike us more with alarm than with hope.

Finally, leaving aside the nuances of *obligation* versus *responsibility* and who should be expected to hoist the banner of human rights, is it realistic to target "70,000 transnational firms, together with roughly 700,000 subsidiaries and millions of suppliers spanning every corner of the globe,"[171] not to mention domestic businesses? Thus far, B&HR activists have looked primarily to large transnational firms, whose influence – while considerable – remains sporadic and indirect.

There is simply no alternative to seeking remedy where it must be found, no matter how difficult, and that means pressing governments whose legal as well as moral duty is to control activities within their jurisdiction that harm others, whether the perpetrators are spouses, drug traffickers, terrorists, corrupt officials, or businesses.

The B&HR ship has already sailed, and too many people – consultants, civil society organizations, compliance officers, factory monitors, academics, government bureaucrats, and others – are making too much money for this particular micro-industry to disappear. In addition, much of this effort has been valuable in increasing the attention paid to corporate abuses and encouraging business to make at least rhetorical (and sometimes real) commitments to behave better.

Given the limits on international enforcement mechanisms and the ultimate responsibility of states to control activities within their jurisdiction, however, it would seem better in the long run to prioritize the admittedly more difficult task of ensuring that governments live up to their obligations to regulate and hold accountable businesses that harm others. Calling businesses to task and demanding that they commit themselves to operating in a responsible, accountable, sustainable, environmentally friendly, and economically useful and equitable way should continue, but we cannot confuse ethical and moral principles with legal obligations. Little will be gained by imposing obligations to protect human rights on entities that have neither the capability nor the authority to do so.

A NOTE ON OTHER NON-STATE ACTORS

Many other non-state actors – criminals, terrorists, armed opposition groups beyond the control of governments, intergovernmental organizations, religious groups, and others – harm individuals. The issue is not whether ways should be found to hold such entities responsible for the harm that they cause, whether through criminal sanctions, civil sanctions, or both, but whether it is useful to characterize such acts as human rights violations. One of the strongest arguments for extending human rights obligations to non-state actors has been made by law professor Andrew Clapham, who would extend human rights obligations to the United Nations and other international organizations, corporations, non-state actors in times of armed conflict,[172] and even individuals.[173] While Clapham makes a strong case for why such entities should care about human rights broadly construed, the obligations he proposes most often fall within the scope of moral and political obligations, rather than legal ones.[174]

Nonetheless, a number of soft law guidelines, codes, and similar instruments have been adopted by United Nations and regional intergovernmental bodies, academics, NGOs, and industry associations.[175] Outside the field of business, these include subjects as diverse as the treatment of prisoners; use of force by law enforcement; treatment of juvenile defenders; the role of lawyers and prosecutors; independence of the judiciary; indigenous peoples; minorities; private security service providers;

amnesties and impunity; the right to truth; human rights defenders; extreme poverty; foreign debt; humanitarian emergency assistance; security of tenure for the urban poor; extraterritorial obligations of states; violations of economic, social, and cultural rights; religious intolerance; mental health; and the rights of noncitizens. The impact and persuasiveness of these and many other instruments vary widely, but they may be used by activists, NGOs, and human rights tribunals and committees as supplementary means of interpreting existing legal obligations and identifying ethical and political commitments. As is true for corporate codes of conduct, however, they do not in and of themselves create legal obligations, even if directed at governments.

OVERSELLING CIVIL SOCIETY

The counterpart to ignoring governments in favor of human rights targets such as corporations is the tendency to bypass governments by channeling human rights assistance primarily through NGOs or *civil society*, a broad term that seems to include every element of the nongovernmental sector except political parties and for-profit companies. Many such groups are composed of dedicated individuals willing to risk their freedom and even lives to protect human rights within a hostile society and government. A few are large, influential NGOs with international influence. Other groups are small, ad-hoc organizations whose primary purpose may be to receive foreign funds and support a few staff members.

A vibrant civil society is both a cause and a result of living in a system in which human rights, openness, and tolerance are the norm. Not all civil society is "good" – the concept includes right-wing nationalist groups, intolerant religions, libertarian organizations that reject socioeconomic rights, and many other groups that promote ideas with which many liberal human rights advocates would disagree. However, that is not the point. Human rights NGOs and other civil society groups are often in the forefront of pressing governments for positive change, whether that change is mandated by international human rights norms (such as nondiscrimination, equal access to education, fair trials and elections, etc.) or whether the goal is to address broader social issues (such as maldistribution of resources, immigration policy, corruption, government budget priorities, and technology).

Narrowing our focus to NGOs that are concerned with human rights, whether defined internationally or domestically, it is inevitable that fact-finding and raising awareness of problems within a country will take on an antigovernment (though not necessarily partisan or ideological) cast. No government, even one that fosters an open political environment, likes to have its failings identified publicly, and authoritarian or simply intolerant regimes are likely to dismiss serious allegations by NGOs as being politically motivated. If human rights become part of a domestic political debate, human rights NGOs will naturally support a political opposition that they view as more sympathetic to rights protection than a government that they view as a human rights violator. This is a dilemma that seems unresolvable, since robust protection of human rights obviously implies stopping violations, and such a course of action cannot avoid being political in its implementation, if not in its ideology.

As human rights become a more potent component of political change, the protection of human rights defenders[176] around the world is a growing focus of both international bodies and NGOs. Recognizing that human rights activism is frequently met with harassment, arrest, or worse, a number of new initiatives have appeared in recent years.[177] In 1999, the UN General Assembly adopted a Declaration on the Right and Responsibility of Individuals, Groups and Organs of Society to Promote and Protect Universally Recognized Human Rights and Fundamental Freedoms,[178] and there has been a UN special rapporteur on the situation of human rights defenders since 2000. The European Union also has adopted its own Guidelines on Human Rights Defenders.[179]

Unfortunately, attacks on those defending human rights becomes even more problematic if the vast majority of financial (and often political) support for NGOs comes from outside the country. When external funding dries up, it is often impossible to replace, and foreign-funded NGOs may lack a sufficient domestic political (and financial) base. In addition, reliance on foreign funding leaves NGOs open to criticism from their own governments, which can claim (occasionally with some justification) that they do not represent a real domestic constituency. This has led to increasing restrictions by states such as Russia, China, Egypt, Burundi, and India on foreign funding of NGOs.[180]

In the Middle East, it has been suggested that the problem that governments have with foreign-funded NGOs is not primarily based on fears of a democratic revolt but rather on the view that these civil society organizations are "agents of a neocolonial project."

> The hypocrisy of this position for governments that either receive copious amounts of foreign assistance or that rely on the West for their security is self-evident, but that does not necessarily diminish its effectiveness. The fact is that the history of the region and the nationalist narratives that developed and evolved over the twentieth century render civil society groups a natural target for Middle Eastern authoritarians, who are inclined to cast Western-funded human rights campaigners and good-governance activists as the most recent manifestation of the civilizing mission that originally brought European colonialists to North Africa and the Levant.[181]

Whatever their justification, such restrictions are almost always adopted as a means of stifling free debate and unwanted criticism in order to hide corruption, fraud, nepotism, human rights violations, or all four. At the same time, however, would Europe and the United States welcome the impact of a foreign billionaire's contributions to civil societies in their countries, with the avowed purpose of advocating Chinese, Russian, or Saudi values and Chinese, Russian, or Saudi interpretations of human rights?[182] While foreign contributions to civil society in the United States would be easily outmatched by domestic and US government sources, the reality and perception might be very different in a less wealthy society.

International human rights NGOs collaborate closely with domestic NGOs whenever possible, but they have sometimes been criticized for their advocacy methods. As Kenneth Roth, the long-time executive director of Human Rights Watch described it, "the core of . . . [HRW's] methodology is our ability to investigate, expose and shame. We are at our most effective when we can hold governmental (or, in some cases, nongovernmental) conduct up to a disapproving public."[183] However, as Tom Farer, an eminent human rights academic and former member of the Inter-American Commission on Human Rights, has observed, "[w]hile [human rights NGOs may hope] . . . to trigger pressure from morally sensitive and influential sectors within the target state, in most instances the real targets of shaming campaigns are citizens of liberal democratic countries."[184] Unfortunately, this is rarely enough. "No doubt many NGOs have helped people in need throughout the Middle East, but those dedicated to governance and human rights, for example, have hardly had an impact."[185]

Increasingly, both NGOs and the OHCHR are expanding their "field" presences, to facilitate local contacts with both NGOs and government officials.[186] However, Farer's observation remains relevant even twenty years later, and activities from consumer boycotts to issue-oriented human rights campaigns often receive much more attention in the developed world – where free expression may be protected more fully – than they do in target countries in the developing world.

A free and vibrant civil society is both a sign of a healthy democracy and necessary to the full enjoyment of many rights. While governments are ultimately responsible for human rights, many rights may be fulfilled through civil society groups. For example, the government cannot shirk its responsibility for ensuring that education and social services are available, but these activities may be undertaken by the private and nonprofit sectors, not only by government. No matter how rights-respecting a government may be, human rights defenders and broader civil society organizations are indispensable watchdogs.

At the same time, NGOs are not governments, and a lively civil society cannot conduct fair trials, impose taxes to be spent on guaranteeing economic rights, hold elections, or perform the myriad other tasks entrusted to government as part of its international obligations to ensure human rights. Reliance on civil society to solve what are essentially government problems is doomed to fail, since NGOs (themselves rarely accountable to more than a small board of directors and a few donors) simply cannot and should not become government. In the long run, the goal must be to make governments more accountable and to change their policies, not to ignore them. This does not mean that civil society is unimportant, but the balance between what can be legitimately expected from civil society and government respectively needs to be carefully monitored.

A final caveat about relying too much on civil society is that it is much easier to change a regime pursuant to pressures from civil society than to improve it. The 2011 uprisings in North Africa and the Middle East concluded with mixed results, at best, although civil society deserves much of the credit for the departure of long-serving dictators in Tunisia and Egypt. The former may be on its way to a new democratic understanding, although there also may be a cost in terms of decreasing acceptance of secular norms and a more conservative – but more democratic – society. The al-Sissi government in Egypt may be worse than the Mubarak dictatorship it ultimately replaced, and its post-elections coup was hardly reassuring; particularly worrisome was the acceptance by many "democracy" advocates of the second military coup, which overthrew a democratically elected government – however flawed – whose view probably did represent that of a majority of Egyptians.[187] The continuing turmoil in Libya and Syria speaks for itself, and what little still exists of civil society in either country is unlikely to be the key to a resolution in the near term. In none of these cases, despite their best efforts, were civil society organizations able to do much to protect human rights, and it is unclear whether either democracy or economic development will be significantly advanced by replacing old dictators with new authoritarians.[188]

CONCLUDING REMARKS

Bringing pressure on all political and economic actors who may be able to contribute to making the world a better place is a worthy endeavor. Ensuring that individuals, organizations, and businesses that harm others are held responsible for that harm is laudable. Much of such work is related to the civil, cultural, economic, political, and social rights guaranteed by international human rights law, but it also reaches – and should reach – much further, addressing issues of morality, social justice, equity, environmental sustainability, and enabling individuals and groups to live a "good life," however that term is defined.

Government's job is to oversee a legal and political system that is fair, nondiscriminatory, accountable, and tolerant of minority views, so that demands can be responsibly advocated and debated by all organs and individuals within society. Both advocacy and the targets of advocacy enjoy rights that enable them to express their views; the *outcome* of advocacy is not guaranteed, except insofar as the human rights of all must be ensured.

Struggles between government and civil society are inevitable – this is called democracy, which assumes that disagreement among different segments of society is better than enforcing an artificial consensus that primarily consolidates the power of those who already exercise it. Providing support, assistance, expertise, and resources to government is an essential part of ensuring human rights, and we should not expect the private sector – whether business, religious, or civil society actors – to accomplish or be held accountable for what is properly within the domain of government.

4

Human Rights and ... Whatever

In the 1970s, the rights revolution brought human rights into parliaments, courts, and the new, growing world of nongovernmental organizations (NGOs). The language of rights quickly became the lingua franca of the entire world ... Not surprisingly, rights and claims became widespread in politics, society, and personal relations ...

There is no surprise that when we have a particularly useful tool we want to believe that it will solve all our problems. So as science searches for that one universal all-encompassing principle of the universe, we attempt to find the key that opens every door to what we perceive as happiness or well-being.

Human rights are often considered such a key. But their success has led to an inflation of rights ... Many have placed excessive expectations on human rights, only to fault the concept as soon as it turned out that exclusion, wars, violence, and other vices persist.[189]

It is difficult to find a UN document or NGO advocacy brief that does not demand a "rights-based" approach to something. Among the better known of these "human rights and" issues are business, trade and globalization, the environment, corruption, and technology. Similar to the attempt to join human rights and business at the hip, discussed in Chapter 3, the hope seems to be that chanting the mantra of human rights will make the resolution of any complex problem easier. Alas, this is not the case, and the issues just mentioned have not mysteriously been resolved after emerging from the fog of rights-based approaches.

TRADE AND GLOBALIZATION

In the early years of the new millennium, a somewhat loose organization known as the Mobilization for Global Justice organized numerous protests against the policies of the International Monetary Fund (IMF) and World Trade Organization (WTO). It accused these institutions of "systematically oppressing and impoverishing Africa, Latin America, the Caribbean, Asia, and the Pacific for decades." It stated, "We are standing in solidarity with the people of the Global South, declaring that the rights of people in the North are wholly bound up with the rights of people in Nigeria, Brazil, the Philippines, Fiji, Haiti, Ecuador, India, and the rest of the world. We are identifying corporate globalization as one of the main factors in the widening divisions between rich and poor and continued attacks on the rights of the impoverished in the U.S. and other Northern societies."[190]

A few years later, the National Bureau of Asian Research stated that "[g]lobalization and free trade are prime drivers of economic growth, prosperity, and job creation in better-paying sectors of the economy. The increasing globalization of the world economy during the second half of the twentieth century led to the most rapid worldwide reduction in poverty and rise in living standards in the history of mankind."[191] This does not sound like just an economic debate, at least from the perspective of the protesters. The claim is that people's *rights* are being violated, and that the violations must be stopped. Are there international human rights that are violated by free trade agreements and other aspects of economic globalization? Is this a useful approach to understanding the issues involved?

Over 160 governments have formally committed themselves to upholding the rights found in the Covenant on Economic, Social, and Cultural Rights. This treaty guarantees, inter alia, the rights to work, social security, education, the "highest attainable standard of physical and mental health," and "an adequate standard of living ... including adequate food, clothing and housing." While some of these rights are set forth in rather general terms, they are no more vague than terms such as *due process* or *fair trial*, which courts have interpreted for centuries. Indeed, the South African Constitutional Court, for example, has adopted a number of well-reasoned, path-breaking judgments with respect to the rights to health, water, and housing in the course of interpreting provisions in the South African constitution.[192]

We can only scratch the surface of the complex arguments for and against the so-called Washington consensus, which favors expanding trade and economic globalization generally. Increased foreign direct investment by developed states and companies based within them is seen as either essential to development or exploitation masquerading as business. The protection of these investments through bilateral investment treaties (BITs), which mandate binding arbitration procedures for economic disputes between foreign companies and the governments of the countries in which they are investing, either provide a fair and neutral forum for the settlement of such disputes and protect companies from expropriation or unfairly limit a country's sovereign right to alter investment rules to better protect the country and its inhabitants.

> There is no consensus on how trade liberalization affects human rights, nor even a well-developed methodology for determining the human rights impacts of trade agreements. Many people in the mainstream trade policy community see no linkage whatsoever with human rights and consider such concerns outside their realm. Likewise, many human rights groups lack familiarity with trade issues.

They are puzzled by the language and suspicious of the entire process: from the negotiations of tariffs to the settlement of disputes. The two communities are so far apart that they do not even use the same vocabulary, let alone share a common philosophy.[193]

[Similarly,] [t]here is no consensus about the impact of globalization on human rights. Virtually every social science has its own definition of globalization and therefore a preferred way of measuring its impact. Thus, any debate regarding any link between globalization and human rights abuses suffers from conceptual, methodological, and measurement problems and results in variable and fragile conclusions. Moreover, it is not clear how the contemporary globalization differs from previous ones.[194]

Differences of opinion on the linkages between macroeconomic policy or trade decisions and their impact on individuals in specific countries continue. Neither human rights law nor economic reality can prevent unemployment, changing job patterns, or the cyclical nature of markets. The norms of the ESC Covenant only require states to work progressively toward goals that all countries are likely to support (at least in theory), such as fuller employment, fair wages, and the ability to make a decent living. When states ignore these obligations, they should be called to account, but it is disingenuous, at best, to suggest that the mere recitation of broad human rights norms is sufficient to determine global trade policy.

While WTO member countries should operate within the constraints imposed by the covenant and ILO norms on labor rights, calls for the WTO to incorporate human rights norms more formally into its decision-making processes are more likely to result in bad human rights interpretation than in good trade policies. Further, it does not seem helpful to shift attention from the obligations of *states* to guarantee rights in favor of placing those obligations on an amorphous international institution.

The simplistic equation of globalization with rights violations does little to address the much more difficult issues of how to ensure equitable economic progress for all countries of the world, in order to ensure that the beneficiaries are real people, not just stock market indexes, billionaires, and corrupt government officials. These are serious issues, and they deserve to be discussed in a manner that does not ignore the possibility that negative short-term impact may eventually yield long-term benefits.

As the Industrial Revolution began, workers naturally worried about being displaced by increasingly efficient machines . . .

People of the time recognized all the astonishing new benefits the Industrial Revolution conferred, but they also worried, as Carlyle put it in 1829, that technology was causing a "mighty change" in their "modes of thought and feeling. Men are grown mechanical in head and in heart, as well as in hand." Over time, worry about that kind of change led people to transform the original Luddites into the heroic defenders of a pretechnological way of life. "The indignation of nineteenth-century producers," the historian Edward Tenner has written, "has yielded to the irritation of late-twentieth-century consumers."[195]

Many of the consequences of under-regulated trade and predatory globalization are far more serious than "irritation." Unfortunately, the sloganeering of some globalization opponents accomplishes little more than making the protesters feel righteous. As is true with respect to business, slogans distract from the task of ensuring that governments live up to their actual human rights obligations and make it easier for governments and the private sector to reject the relevance of human rights in any form. Governments and civil society need to ensure the rights that the former have freely agreed to; economists, the WTO, and the private sector can seek to advance their legitimate goals of increasing trade and profit, while leveling the market's playing field so that the international economic system is more fair and open. Both sides of the debate must learn more about the other before proclaiming that they, and they alone, have all of the rights on their side.

ENVIRONMENT

Another issue frequently linked to human rights is protection of the environment, ranging from holding companies responsible for oil spills and other environmental degradation to asserting an obligation on – someone? everyone? – to address climate change. Since most UN human rights treaties were drafted before environmental protection became a matter of international concern, there are few specific references to environmental matters, and environmental concerns are most often addressed as part of the rights to life or health. As perceptively stated in the initial report of the UN independent expert "on the issue of human rights obligations relating to the enjoyment of a safe, clean, healthy and sustainable environment," his first priority was "to provide greater conceptual clarity" to the relationship between human rights and the environment.[196]

Some regional human rights instruments do refer to environmental issues, although in relatively general terms. The African Charter on Human and Peoples' Rights recognizes the right of "[a]ll peoples" [not individual persons] to a "general satisfactory environment favorable to their development."[197] The African Women's Convention recognizes in somewhat greater detail the right of women "to live in a healthy and sustainable environment."[198] As a component of the right to an adequate standard of living, the 2012 ASEAN Human Rights Declaration proclaims the right to a "safe, clean and sustainable environment"; it also mentions the environment in the context of the right to development.[199]

The additional protocol to the American Convention on Human Rights on socio-economic and cultural rights provides

1. Everyone shall have the right to live in a healthy environment and to have access to basic public services.
2. The States Parties shall promote the protection, preservation, and improvement of the environment.[200]

In late 2017, the Inter-American Court of Human Rights issued an advisory opinion on human rights and the environment. In keeping with its tendency to interpret rights broadly, the court recognized an autonomous right to a healthy environment under the American Convention, despite the fact that the word *environment* does not appear in the convention itself and that only 16 countries have ratified the protocol quoted immediately above.[201]

Human rights violations may either cause or result from environmental degradation, but the right to a clean/healthy/sustainable environment per se is difficult to define. As one leading expert on both environmental issues and human rights has stated, "The substance of environmental rights involves evaluating ecological systems, determining the impacts that can be tolerated and what is needed to maintain and protect the natural base on which life depends. Environmental quality standards, precaution, and principles of sustainability can establish the limits of environmental decision-making and continue to give specific content to environmental rights in law."[202] This is a realistic analysis of the problem, as opposed to the simplistic observation from a joint OHCHR/UN Environment Program meeting that "[m]ore than 2 million annual deaths and billions of cases of diseases are attributed to pollution. All over the world, people experience the negative effects of environmental degradation ... These facts clearly show the close linkages between the environment and the enjoyment of human rights, and justify an integrated approach to environment and human rights."[203]

Unfortunately, most of the anodyne international initiatives on human rights and the environment do little to promote either cause and, as noted in Chapter 3 with respect to business, succeed only in conflating internationally binding human rights norms with voluntary platitudes. The Inter-American Commission for Human Rights, for example, citing a 2008 resolution of the OAS General Assembly, opined in 2015 that

> climate change is a shared concern of all humankind, and ... its effects have an impact on sustainable development and could have consequences for the full enjoyment of human rights.
>
> Climate change affects human rights in different ways. The consequences of climate change lead to deaths, injuries, and displacement of individuals and communities because of disasters and events such as tropical cyclones, earthquakes, tornadoes, heat waves, and droughts. The Inter-American Commission has received hundreds of cases related to conflicts over land and water and threats to food sovereignty which evidence that climate change is a reality that is affecting the enjoyment of human rights in the region.
>
> The IACHR expresses concern regarding the existing evidence that climate change will increase poverty rates ...
>
> The IACHR urges the States Parties to fulfill their historical responsibility to humanity and achieve the level of ambition needed to ensure that the planet does not suffer greater damage from climate change.[204]

The Geneva Pledge for Human Rights in Climate Action, adopted by 15 states also in 2015, is little better:

We ... note that climate change-related impacts have a range of implications, both direct and indirect, for the effective enjoyment of human rights ...

We also note that human rights obligations and commitments have the potential to inform and strengthen international and national policymaking in the area of climate change, promoting policy coherence, legitimacy and sustainable outcomes ...

We will facilitate the exchange of expertise and best practice between our human rights and climate experts to build our collective capacity to deliver responses to climate change that are good for people and the planet.[205]

Law professor John H. Knox of Wake Forest University was the first special rapporteur on human rights and the environment; his term expired in 2018. His reports considered the human rights obligations of states that relate to the environment, best practices, climate change and human rights, biodiversity and human rights, and children's rights and the environment.[206] The careful formulation of the mandate and the legalistic approach of the rapporteur's work reflect ways in which the enjoyment (or violation) of human rights and environmental issues are linked, rather than identifying or advocating development of a free-standing *right* to a safe, clean, healthy, sustainable, beautiful, or species-protecting environment. Professor Knox's approach was graphically illustrated by his admission at one of his public presentations that his work did not extend to all problems related to the environment, as shown in his final slide of a lonely polar bear afloat on a small ice floe.

Knox's final report presents a set of 16 Framework Principles on Human Rights and the Environment and advocates formal recognition of a "human right to a healthy environment." It argues that the content of the proposed right has already been clarified through recognition by human rights bodies that a safe, clean, healthy, and sustainable environment is necessary for the full enjoyment of the human rights to life, health, food, water, housing, and so forth, similar to the rights to water and sanitation.[207] The comparison is a bit too facile, as ensuring a healthy environment is vastly more complex than the difficult, but manageable, obligations to provide access to water and sanitation. It is not just a question of what is healthy but a question of how best to accomplish the goal, bearing mind the competing human rights obligations discussed in Chapter 5 in the context of development. Knox believes that "States should accept the framework principles as a reflection of actual or emerging international human rights law,"[208] but he is careful not to overstate his case.

The framework principles and commentary do not create new obligations. Rather, they reflect the application of existing human rights obligations in the environmental context ... While many of the obligations described in the framework principles and commentary are based directly on treaties or binding decisions from human rights tribunals, others draw on statements of human rights bodies that have the authority to interpret human rights law but not necessarily to issue binding decisions.

The coherence of these interpretations, however, is strong evidence of the converging trends towards greater uniformity and certainty in the understanding of human rights obligations relating to the environment ...

An unusual aspect of the development of human rights norms relating to the environment is that they have not relied primarily on the explicit recognition of a human right to a safe, clean, healthy and sustainable environment – or, more simply, a human right to a healthy environment. Although this right has been recognized, in various forms, in regional agreements and in most national constitutions, it has not been adopted in a human rights agreement of global application, and only one regional agreement, the African Charter on Human and Peoples' Rights, provides for its interpretation in decisions by a review body ...

Treaty bodies, regional tribunals, special rapporteurs and other international human rights bodies have instead applied human rights law to environmental issues by "greening" existing human rights, including the rights to life and health.[209]

The principles themselves largely call for countries simply to respect and ensure human rights when considering environmental issues, such as rights to nondiscrimination and freedom of expression, association, and assembly.[210] Other recommendations include education on environmental issues, public access to environmental information, prior assessment of environmental impacts, and public participation in decision-making.[211] Vulnerable groups, including indigenous peoples and traditional communities, also should be consulted and protected.[212]

It is certainly possible to develop legal obligations applicable to states and private parties with respect to the environment, as evidenced by the environmental protection laws that already exist at both domestic and international levels. The question is whether it is possible to develop sufficiently precise and universally applicable norms to deal with this complex problem, particularly given the difficulties faced by countless international meetings in reaching agreement on even nonbinding commitments. As Knox concedes, the obligations owed to humans – the subjects of human rights – already include existing rights, such as to health and life, which are being recognized by human rights bodies, and I would argue that this is where our focus should remain. Perhaps there will be other options when rivers, mountains, and other lands can speak for themselves (conveniently through self-appointed representatives), but they are not present yet.[213]

Finally, a primarily human rights approach to the environment is likely to leave many legitimate environmental issues untouched (e.g., conservation of species, preservation of "natural" beauty, and the issue of sustainability itself), while inserting the environment into human rights without relatively specific norms may lead to little more than verbiage. Calling for Royal Dutch Shell to "clean up its human rights mess in the Niger Delta"[214] may be useful to an NGO looking for support and new sources of income, but confusing civil wrongs and damages with government obligations and people's rights is unlikely to help.

CORRUPTION

Scores of countries suffer from varying degrees of official corruption, and the resulting damage to the economy, government accountability, and the rule of law can be enormous. Former UN High Commissioner for Human Rights Navi Pillay called corruption "an enormous obstacle to the realization of all human rights ... Corruption violates the core human rights principles of transparency, accountability, nondiscrimination and meaningful participation in every aspect of life of the community."[215]

There can be little doubt that corruption impedes the enjoyment of many human rights, although it does not automatically prevent implementation of many of them. At the same time, merely including a concept as broad as corruption within international human rights law simply adds to the list of rights whose definition and implementation are extremely problematic.[216] The expert advisory committee to the HR Council observed in 2015 that "there is no single, consistent and recognized definition of corruption, at the international level."[217] It is simply not accurate to claim, as a recent article does, that "[c]orruption and rights violations, as actualized or implied corporal violence, are manifestations of the same root causes and produced by the same conditions."[218] Ensuring good governance is not the same as ensuring human rights, and the latter will never be sufficient to protect us fully from corrupt or ignorant government officials.

The United Nations adopted a Convention against Corruption in 2003,[219] and by late 2017 it had been ratified by 183 countries. It does not contain the words "human rights" and is classified by the UN treaty office with other treaties that concern "penal matters," not human rights.[220] This should make us wonder why there is "an urgent need to increase synergy between inter-governmental efforts to implement the United Nations Convention against Corruption and international human rights conventions," one of the "three key messages" of the OHCHR with respect to corruption.[221] We also should question whether "the battle against corruption, similar to human rights projects, is often a long-term process requiring profound societal changes, which include a country's institutions, laws and culture,"[222] as opposed to just a problem that requires serious efforts at law enforcement and ensuring the independence of the judiciary.

The danger of conflating corruption with human rights is exemplified by a 2018 declaration on the subject adopted by the Inter-American Commission on Human Rights, based in part on "two consultation meetings with justice operators [whoever they may be], experts and civil society."[223] The following extract from the resolution needs no comment, except to note that it is a prime example of the confusion and political babble that accompanies far too many discussions that purport to be relevant to universal human rights norms.

> Emphasizing that corruption has multiple causes and consequences and that numerous actors, both state and private entities and companies, participate in its

development, and therefore, the establishment of effective mechanisms to eradicate it in order to guarantee human rights is required ...

Reaffirming that victims of corruption should be kept at the heart of the fight against this phenomenon and form part of the analysis, diagnostic assessment, design and implementation of mechanisms, practices, policies and strategies to prevent, punish and eradicate corruption, bearing in mind the principles of non-discrimination and equality, accountability, access to justice, transparency and participation.

Recalling that the objective of any public policy to combat corruption should be focused on and implemented in light of the following principles: the central role of the victim; universality and inalienability; indivisibility; interdependence and inter-action of human rights; non-discrimination and equality; gender perspective and intersectionality; participation and inclusion; accountability; respect for the rule of law; and strengthening of cooperation between States. Consequently, the human rights-based approach must be applied transversally in all anti-corruption strategies and entities in the region ...

[States should] [s]trengthen their capacities to proactively guarantee access to public information, essential to the fight against corruption, and strengthen their active transparency and accountability mechanisms in relation to expenditures and investments in infrastructure, financing of election campaigns and transparency in the operations of political parties ...

The administration of assets seized from acts of corruption must incorporate an economic, social and cultural rights-based approach, in such a way that reparations for the rights of persons affected by these crimes must be contemplated ...

[States should generate] legal and public policy mechanisms that make it possible to clearly determine the impact of different forms of corruption on the effective enjoyment of economic, social, cultural and environmental rights by individuals and communities, especially those that live in poverty or extreme poverty, such as those historically discriminated against.[224]

It is difficult to imagine that "[r]eframing corruption as a rights violation sends an unequivocal message to both the victims of official corruption and the perpetrators: that corruption is neither cultural nor human nature; that the state might violate that right but cannot take it away; and that the vigorous enforcement of anti-corruption measures is not only possible, but essential."[225] It is much easier to imagine how delighted many countries must be to talk about human rights and corruption in the same breath ... and to devote equally ineffective efforts in dealing with both.

TECHNOLOGY

In February 2018, the Raoul Wallenberg Institute of Human Rights and Humanitarian Law, based in Lund, Sweden, announced the first episode of a new podcast series entitled, "Can Blockchain Technology Improve Your Human Rights?" Among the potential impacts discussed were limiting land grabbing by creating immutable ownership titles, stopping the use of fake drugs and tracking other supply chains, limiting voter fraud and other forms of corruption, providing swift and safe international cryptocurrency transfers to human rights advocates, and creating "blockchain courts."[226] An Amnesty International researcher suggested recently that technology can help solve other human rights challenges, such as "understanding how xenophobic, racist rhetoric from public figures affect attitudes towards refugees and migrants . . . tracking pollution and environmental damage . . . helping human rights researchers discover evidence of abuses in an ever-growing sea of often unstructured information shared through digital channels . . . [and] understanding public sentiment reliably and efficiently to more effectively mobilize people to advocate for their rights."[227] An estimated 100 technical experts worldwide are "teaching dissidents the skills they need to evade regime surveillance."[228] Entering the debate about artificial intelligence, the coordinator of Human Rights Watch's Campaign to Stop Killer Robots, which began in 2013, states, "Any killing orchestrated by a fully autonomous weapon is arguably inherently wrong since machines are unable to exercise human judgement and compassion."[229]

There is no doubt that modern communication technology has improved the capacity of human rights advocates to gather and transmit information about human rights violations, including detention or killings of human rights defenders and demonstrators.[230] Former High Commissioner for Human Rights Pillay said in a message on the eve of Human Rights Day in 2011 that "power shifted in the Arab world this year as ordinary men, women and even children used Facebook and other social media platforms to stand up to long-ruling dictators . . . 'In sum, in 2011, human rights went viral.'"[231] Of course, many violations, such as discrimination, unfair trials, or press censorship, do not require the immediacy of tweets and texts, although the consequences of violations can often be made more real when photos or videos document forced evictions, land seizures, police brutality, and similar events.

Unfortunately, just as the 2011 uprisings in Tunisia, Egypt, Syria, and Libya hailed by Pillay failed to create democratic rights-respecting governments (with the partial exception of Tunisia), the glow of the Internet and its guardians has faded.

> Cyberspace in the 1980s was a glorious sandpit for geeks: a world with no corporations, no crime, no spam, no hate speech, relatively civil discourse, no editorial gatekeepers, no regulation and no role for those meatspace masters whom [Grateful-Dead-lyricist-turned-essayist John Perry] Barlow called the "weary giants of flesh and steel." . . .
>
> Prying governments and giant companies have acquired the capacity to surveil our every move, both on the internet and, now that so many devices have built-in GPS, in the real world too. Through their ability to monitor our searches these companies – as well as the governments they co-operate with – are able to see our innermost thoughts and desires. (Yes, even our desires: what people search for on Google is incredibly revealing.)
>
> It all creates the potential for unprecedented manipulation . . .[232]

It also is important to be aware of the source of any electronic information concerning human rights, no matter how compelling, since authenticating information is more difficult as it becomes easier to manipulate that information.[233] Russia appears to have used "fake news" on Facebook, Twitter, and other social media in an attempt to influence the Brexit vote in the United Kingdom and the US presidential elections in 2016. "Police in Indonesia believe they … uncovered a clandestine fake news operation designed to corrupt the political process and destabilise the government" in early 2018.[234] In India, "false news stories have become a part of everyday life, exacerbating weather crises, increasing violence between castes and religions, and even affecting matters of public health. 'Common sense is extinct … People are ready to believe anything.'"[235]

Errors in reporting human rights violations have infrequently occurred, even by the most reliable NGOs, but publicizing potential or suspected violations has always been an important element of human rights advocacy, even when one lacks the proof that they have actually taken place. While the need for "early warning" is apparent, the possibility of deliberately misleading information infiltrating the human rights world is all too real.

In addition, technology is available not only to NGOs and individuals trying to document human rights abuses. As indicated above, governments also have made great strides in terms of surveillance and tracking; emails are easily compromised; and social media and instant messaging are no longer as reliable or safe as they were a few years ago for rallying supporters or coordinating demonstrations. In Cambodia, as Facebook became more popular, "authorities have increasingly co-opted it to spread propaganda and silence critics."[236] The massive data collection program by the US National Security Agency exposed in 2013 is perhaps simply the most expansive attempt by governments to collect data … with the possible exception of China.

> Since passing its broad new Cybersecurity Law in June [2017], the Communist Party has rolled out new regulations – and steps to enforce existing ones – that reflect its desire to control and exploit every inch of the digital world, experts say.
>
> Today, the Great Firewall is being built not just around the country, to keep foreign ideas and uncomfortable truths out, but around every individual, computer and smartphone, in a society that has become the most digitally connected in the world.
>
> Last month, the Cyberspace Administration of China effectively ended online anonymity here by making Internet companies responsible for ensuring that anyone who posts anything is registered with their real name.
>
> It has cracked down on the VPN (virtual private network) systems that netizens have used to jump the firewall and evade censorship, with Apple agreeing to remove VPN providers from its Chinese App Store in July and authorities detaining a local software developer for three days last month for selling similar services[237]

Perhaps even more unsettling is the developing "social credit" system in China, which works through close cooperation between the government and the private sector – a model that could certainly be transplanted elsewhere.

[T]he Chinese government has become convinced that a far greater degree of social control is both necessary and possible. It now has access to a set of tools for managing the complexity of contemporary life that it believes will deliver better, surer, and more reliable results than anything produced by the model of order from below.

Known by the anodyne name *social credit*, this system is designed to reach into every corner of existence both online and off. It monitors each individual's consumer behavior, conduct on social networks, and real-world infractions like speeding tickets or quarrels with neighbors. Then it integrates them into a single, algorithmically determined "sincerity" score. Every Chinese citizen receives a literal, numeric index of their trustworthiness and virtue, and this index unlocks, well, everything. In principle, anyway, this one number will determine the opportunities citizens are offered, the freedoms they enjoy, and the privileges they are granted ...

Citizens with higher social-credit scores enjoy discounts or upgrades on products and services, like hotel rooms or internet connectivity ...

But the system provides abundantly for sticks as well as carrots. Attend a "subversive" political meeting or religious service, for example, or frequent known haunts of vice, or do under-the-table business with an unregistered, informal enterprise, and the idea is that the network will know about it and respond by curtailing one's privileges.[238]

Whether we should welcome or fear today's ubiquitous cyber technologies, the real human rights issue is whether these innovations – such as the Internet, social media, artificial intelligence, blockchains, "big data," and modern surveillance capacities – should be treated simply as an expanded version of earlier communications technologies or whether they are, due to either the technology itself or its scale, something entirely different. Can technology today be judged by interpreting or extrapolating from existing human rights norms, particularly freedom of expression and the right to privacy? Are the current legitimate restrictions of these rights by governments — to protect "the rights or reputations of others ... national security or ... public order (*ordre public*) ... or public health or morals,"[239] or "promoting the general welfare in a democratic society"[240] – adequate? If not, what are the legal, moral, and ethical bases for the approaches that should be taken to these technologies?

The answers to these questions are too complex to be addressed sensibly here, as are the broader social, economic, and political implications of social media and diminishing privacy. However, it is clear that neither the facile arguments of the "free internet" libertarians who advocate an unregulated Internet, nor the self-serving promises of the rich and powerful companies to do no harm and guard our privacy and rights, are sufficient.

CONCLUDING REMARKS

The *enjoyment* of human rights may be influenced by a great many factors that affect how people see their society and themselves. Some of these factors are beyond the direct control of any single government or entity, such as natural disasters; the behavior of neighboring countries; and the complex interactions among international business, trade, and finance.

Respect for human rights will have an impact on some of these issues. Fulfillment of economic and social rights, such as affordable and available education, should make it easier for individuals to reach their potential as human beings, whatever they decide that they wish to achieve in life. Freedom of expression and the right to participate in governance might lead to greater accountability and equity. An efficient and functional justice system will promote equality and increase accountability of corrupt government officials.

Unfortunately, even the fulfillment of rights cannot guarantee that a society will function to the satisfaction of everyone within it or that those who govern will be wise rather than opportunistic or arrogant. It is no coincidence that many of the countries and societies that are seen to be most respectful of human rights or the happiest are relatively rich, small, homogeneous, and peaceful – but this is to a great extent due to history, geography, and circumstance, as well as conscious social and political choices.

As argued in the context of business in Chapter 3, overstating the ability of human rights to resolve the complex issues that every country and society face weakens their legitimacy and power. Conflating them with issues such as creating a sustainable environment, regulating trade, ending corruption, and dealing with rapid advances in technology reduces rights to mere tools to achieve other goals rather than laws to be followed and enforced.

In addition, substituting the adversarial absolutism of rights language for the often more fruitful path of disagreement and debate may make it *less* likely that society will be able to arrive at viable solutions to these problems. Finding solutions to climate change and sustainability, determining the most appropriate trade and immigration policies for a given country, or apportioning available resources among competing demands requires much broader, fact-based discussions than are likely to emerge if the only argument is whether my rights are superior to yours. Decoupling human rights from such debates does not diminish the importance of nondiscrimination, free expression and association, participation in public life, and education. Instead, it will enable the discussion to focus on the different political, economic, scientific, and ethical perspectives that must be reconciled if these issues are to be dealt with openly and successfully.

5

Undermining Old Rights with New Ones: You Can't Always Get What You Want

There are no doubt hundreds, if not thousands, of discrete human rights articulated in the Universal Declaration of Human Rights (UDHR) and the subsequent treaties developed since 1948 at both the global and regional levels. Both critics and some supporters of the human rights movement have expressed concern over this proliferation: "The more human rights there are, and thus the greater variety of human interests that are protected, the more that the human rights system collapses from an undifferentiated welfarism in which all interests must be taken seriously for the sake of the public good."[241] "[R[ights inflation – the tendency to define anything desirable as a right – ends up eroding the legitimacy of a defensible core of rights."[242] "[U]unbridled proliferation damages the very idea of international human rights by abandoning the notion of extraordinarily high priority norms in favor of an ever-expanding list of protected interests."[243]

These concerns are are not new, and criticism of the manner in which human rights were proliferating emerged only a decade after the entry into force in 1976 of the two fundamental UN conventions on human rights, the International Covenant on Economic, Social, and Cultural Rights (ESC Covenant) and the International Covenant on Civil and Political Rights (CP Covenant).[244] The UN General Assembly responded to these concerns in 1986, when it "invit[ed]" states and UN organs to take the following guidelines into account when they considered adopting new human rights norms:

(a) Be consistent with the existing body of international human rights law;
(b) Be of fundamental character and derive from the inherent dignity and worth of the human person;
(c) Be sufficiently precise to give rise to identifiable and practicable rights arid obligations;
(d) Provide, where appropriate, realistic and effective implementation machinery, including reporting systems;
(e) Attract broad international support.[245]

There is little evidence that anyone has paid attention to these guidelines, although the drafting of new UN human rights *treaties* has been serious and accompanied by a reasonable degree of deliberation. Alas, the same cannot be said for the UN Human Rights Council (and its predecessor, the UN Commission on Human Rights), other UN organs, nongovernmental orgizations (NGOs), governments, and various groups of "experts," both within and outside academia.

The occasional excesses of activists who misuse human rights norms to achieve social goals are matched by the attempts of some governments to use human rights as purely political tools to promote geopolitical strategies. The oft-decried politicization of human rights was obvious during the Cold War, as both West and East were guilty of selective assertions of rights and hypocritical condemnations of violations. Today, politics are only slightly more subtle, and governments that care little about rights have attempted to drown the whole concept by adding claims related to, e.g., economic development, solidarity, sustainability, peace, trade, defamation of religion, and the fight against real or imagined terrorism. Sociopolitical divisions remain, with European countries and the United States emphasizing in recent years the rights of women, sexual/gender minorities, and the environment, and developing countries, sometimes supported by China and Russia, emphasizing development, global economic issues, and respect for cultural and religious traditions.

Perfection was not achieved with the adoption of the Universal Declaration in 1948, nor with the adoption of the two covenants in 1966. There is a great deal of room for new rights, and there have been welcome advances in articulating new international norms for certain vulnerable or historically marginalized groups – women, children, racial minorities, and persons with disabilities, for example – through the adoption of treaties that made more concrete the covenants' focus on "everyone." The problem is therefore to better understand the process of expanding legal rights and to be aware of the potential downside of casting the rights net too widely.[246]

WHERE DO RIGHTS ORIGINATE?

First, it is important to distinguish the different ways in which "new" legal rights develop, leaving aside their ultimate origins in morality, religion, or notions of justice. While the categories are not water-tight, the most common means through which the content of rights can change are through interpretation, extension, and creation.

The basic rule of treaty *interpretation* is set out in the Vienna Convention on the Law of Treaties, which is widely held to reflect customary international law. Article 31.1 states, "A treaty shall be interpreted in good faith in accordance with the ordinary meaning to be given to the terms of the treaty in their context and in the light of its object and purpose."[247] This formulation in fact identifies a number of different methods of interpretation – the ordinary meaning, the treaty's context, and its object and purpose – but human rights tribunals and treaty bodies have been consistent in stating that their interpretation of human rights norms is guided by a progressive and evolutionary approach.

[The European Court of Human Rights] has never considered the provisions of the Convention as the sole framework of reference for the interpretation of the rights and freedoms enshrined therein. On the contrary, it must also take into account any relevant rules and principles of international law applicable in relations between the Contracting Parties.

The Court further observes that it has always referred to the "living" nature of the Convention, which must be interpreted in the light of present-day conditions, and that it has taken account of evolving norms of national and international law in its interpretation of Convention provisions.

... [I]t is not necessary for the respondent State to have ratified the entire collection of instruments that are applicable in respect of the precise subject matter of the case concerned. It will be sufficient for the Court that the relevant international instruments denote a continuous evolution in the norms and principles applied in international law or in the domestic law of the majority of member States of the Council of Europe and show, in a precise area, that there is common ground in modern societies.[248]

The Inter-American Court of Human Rights similarly states that

part of the transcendental function of an international court is to carry out a dynamic interpretation of the treaties within its competence ...

This guidance is particularly relevant in the case of international human rights law, which has made great headway thanks to an evolutive interpretation of international instruments of protection. That evolutive interpretation is consistent with the general rules of treaty interpretation established in the 1969 Vienna Convention ...

[H]uman rights treaties are living instruments whose interpretation must consider the changes over time and present-day conditions.[249]

A rather more critical view of the interpretative principles applied by the UN treaty bodies concludes that

... methodological weaknesses compromise the comprehensibility, consistency, rationality, and legitimacy of a committee's output ...

[D]isregard for rules of interpretation [in the Vienna Convention, quoted above] raises the question of where a committee draws the line between interpreting a treaty and developing new law for which it does not have a mandate. Although playing a general promotional role is part of a treaty body's overall mandate and contributes to the realization of human rights, a conflation of the promotion and the interpretation of rights and obligations endangers the credibility and significance of the treaty body monitoring system, which depends on the persuasiveness of its output.[250]

Thus far, interpretation has generally expanded the scope of human rights, for example by prohibiting the criminalization of homosexuality,[251] recognizing the rights of transsexuals to their identity,[252] and recognizing the right of indigenous peoples to their land,[253] despite the fact that none of these rights is explicitly mentioned in the treaties under consideration. However, not all interpretation is expansive. For example, human rights bodies have consistently refused to hold that there is an internationally recognized right to same-sex marriage, relying on the language of various treaties setting forth the right of "men and women" to marry. This is not unreasonable, but an equally persuasive interpretation might be that, while the texts refer to men and women, there is no specific language that implies that they can only marry one another.[254] However, the human rights bodies have been unwilling – understandably, at least from a political perspective – not to read into the treaties a result that clearly was not contemplated at the time of their adoption or of state ratifications.

Assertion of a human right of access to automatic teller machines (ATMs) might raise eyebrows, but just such a right was determined to fall within the scope of article 9.2.b of the Convention on the Rights of Persons with Disabilities.[255] In this context, the interpretation of ensuring "that private entities that offer facilities and services which are open or provided to the public take into account all aspects of accessibility for persons with disabilities" includes accessible ATMs seems perfectly reasonable.[256] Similarly, the UN Population Fund in 2012 declared that access to contraception and family planning is a human right, although it has no formal interpretative authority.[257] Indiana University law professor Lea Shaver usefully suggests that rights such as the right to read, the right to water, the right to sanitation, and the right to credit should be termed *intersectional rights*, which "are not truly demands for new human rights. Instead, they are demands for more focused attention to neglected issues within human rights."[258]

Most of the treaties adopted under the auspices of the United Nations have *extended* rights, by going beyond the universally applicable rights of everyone to proclaiming more specific rights of people in vulnerable categories, such as racial minorities, women, children, migrant workers, and disabled persons. New treaties also may clarify or deepen protection for particular rights, such as the prohibitions against torture and disappearances or the scores of treaties adopted by the International Labor Organization on workers' rights, health, and safety. These new treaties may clarify existing rights (e.g., specifying in the race and women's conventions that affirmative action is permissible or even required to redress past or present discrimination) or deliberately expand them (e.g., requirements in the same two treaties that governments criminalize advocacy of racial superiority and hatred or adopt measures "[t]o modify the social and cultural patterns of conduct of men and women, with a view to achieving the elimination of prejudices," respectively). Such extension through new treaties is not problematic, since a new treaty imposes obligations on countries only if they ratify the treaty, but a treaty's scope cannot be expanded merely through adoption of guidelines or recommendations per se, which would more properly be seen as a means of interpretation.

The attempted *creation* of new rights is best exemplified by the multitude of so-called soft law principles, guidelines, recommendations, and similar instruments, although there is a great deal of variation in their content and purpose. Some offer the kind of technical detail that would probably not be appropriate for a treaty; others articulate new directions or subjects of human rights, such as development, toxic waste, business, or a right to truth. It is these kinds of pronouncements, adopted either by governmental or nongovernmental bodies, groups of activists and/or academics, or by individuals serving as UN "special procedures" (usually denominated as special rapporteurs, experts, or representatives), that are often cited as examples of silly or over-the-top rights, although this is an unfair characterization of many serious efforts to address issues that proponents feel have been given too little attention. Of course, a new treaty also may create new rights, subject to the caveat that they apply only to states that ratify the treaty.

The discussion that follows considers what should perhaps be called "wannabe" rights, rights whose legitimacy has not been confirmed by their inclusion in a legally binding treaty or through wide political acceptance by states. The latter kind of acceptance may lead to a norm becoming part of customary international law, although most such norms were codified in treaties in the twentieth century. One of the few exceptions is the designation of crimes against humanity as international crimes, over which any country may exercise their own jurisdiction, which have been considered to be universally prohibited without the benefit of a treaty at least since the Nuremberg Tribunal that followed the end of the Second World War. A free-standing convention on crimes against humanity is currently under consideration by the UN's International Law Commission,[259] and the prohibition has been codified in the Rome Statute of the International Criminal Court, which is discussed in Chapter 2, since 1998.

Most of the other new rights have been articulated through soft law or simply by the assertions of human rights advocates, civil society, academics, or other experts. Advocating their acceptance as legal norms is certainly not inappropriate, and this is how most rights begin their existence. However, mere wishing or proclamation does not create law, and one of the most important arguments of the present book is that we should exercise care in seeking to expand the content of international human rights either too far or too quickly.

We first consider the right to development, before examining a potpourri of other would-be rights.

THE RIGHT TO DEVELOPMENT

One of the most questionable – yet almost universally accepted politically – of the new human rights was first set forth in the 1986 UN General Assembly Declaration on the Right to Development, the first article of which proclaims

1. The right to development is an inalienable human right by virtue of which every human person and all peoples are entitled to participate in, contribute to, and enjoy economic, social, cultural and political development, in which all human rights and fundamental freedoms can be fully realized.
2. The human right to development also implies the full realization of the right of peoples to self-determination, which includes, subject to the relevant provisions of both International Covenants on Human Rights, the exercise of their inalienable right to full sovereignty over all their natural wealth and resources.[260]

The conflation of development with inalienable human rights is evidence of the political character and importance of human rights even in the 1980s, and it reflects the concern of developing countries (and the United Nations in general) to create a more equitable international economic order. While there is no doubt that a country's level of development is relevant to its capacity to fulfill its human rights obligations, as explicitly recognized in the ESC Covenant, it is difficult to reconcile the myriad aspects of international development with the primary focus of human rights on the relationship between individuals and governments.

One of the better attempts to articulate the meaning of the right to development is by Arjun Sengupta, a former UN special rapporteur on the right to development from 1998 to 2004 and on extreme poverty and human rights from 2004 to 2008.

Recognizing the right to development as a human right raises the status of that right to one with universal applicability and inviolability. It also specifies a norm of action for the people, the institution or the state and international community on which the claim for that right is made. It confers on the implementation of that right a first-priority claim to national and international resources and capacities and, furthermore, obliges the state and the international community, as well as other agencies of society, including individuals, to implement that right . . .

The right to development refers to a process of development which leads to the realization of each human right and of all of them together and which has to be carried out in a manner known as rights-based, in accordance with the international human rights standards, as a participatory, nondiscriminatory, accountable and transparent process with equity in decisionmaking and sharing of the fruits of the process.

. . . Economic growth, attended by increased inequalities or disparities and rising concentrations of wealth and economic power, and without any improvement in indicators of social development, education, health, gender balance and environmental protection . . . cannot fulfill the human right to development.

. . . [W]hen human development is claimed as a human right, it becomes a qualitatively different approach. It is not just achieving the objectives of development, but also the way they are achieved that becomes essential to the process. The objective is fulfilling human rights and the process of achieving this is also a human right. That process must possess the features of all human rights, namely respecting the notion of equity and participation, not violating human rights, including a clear specification of obligations and responsibilities, establishing culpability and having a mechanism for monitoring and correcting the failures of the process.[261]

The multiple references to concepts such as accountability, transparency, equity, justice, sharing, gender balance, and environmental protection sound good, but interpreting the right to development as a synthesis of all other human rights (and more) sheds little light on its content. University of Denver professor Jack Donnelly, for example, calls the right to development "not just a charming delusion, but a threat to human rights, and a particularly insidious threat because it plays upon our fondest hopes and best desires, and diverts attention from more productive ways of linking human rights and development."[262]

Similarly, human rights law professor David Kinley of the University of Sydney observes that the declaration on the right to development

> is so riven with textual incoherencies as to be unworkable. Even the very idea of development as a human right is fundamentally problematic. It is ... an unattainable myth, the propagation of which endangers human rights precisely because such an empty promise devalues their currency. Alas, however, none of this has deterred ongoing attempts to flog this particular dead horse ... and the textual and political problems facing the idea remain as insurmountable today as they were thirty years ago.[263]

The dead horse was resurrected in 2012 by the OAS General Assembly, which approved a 35-article nonbinding Social Charter of the Americas that did little to improve our understanding of development as a human right.[264] Among its chapter headings are Social Justice, Development with Equity, and Democracy; Cultural Development, Diversity, and Pluralism; and Solidarity and Collective Endeavor in the Americas.

Despite its obvious flaws, the rhetoric of the right to development enjoys broad political support, and the resolution that created the position of UN High Commissioner for Human Rights specifically mandates that the High Commissioner shall "promote and protect the realization of the right to development."[265] A few years later, the Commission on Human Rights created a working group on the right to development,[266] and the HR Council added a special rapporteur to the suite in 2016.[267] Among the latter's simple tasks is to "engage and support efforts to mainstream the right to development among various United Nations bodies, development agencies, international development, financial and trade institutions, and to submit proposals aimed at strengthening the revitalized global partnership for sustainable development from the perspective of the right to development."[268]

The UN Development Program introduced the concept of *human development* in 1990,[269] and the phrase has stuck. No one today measures development solely by referring to Gross Domestic Product or infrastructure or growth rates; rather, "the human development approach focuses on improving the lives people lead rather than assuming that economic growth will lead, automatically, to greater opportunities for all. Income growth is an important means to development, rather than an end in itself."[270] This is a sound statement of what the goals of development should be, and it is perfectly consistent with international human rights law. Indeed, one can rightly view development as often an essential component of economic, social, and cultural rights. However, development is a concept that falls within the domains of business, economics, trade theory, and finance, and that is reflected in government policy in many different and often contradictory ways. Its breadth and complexity make it simply impossible to define a right to development coherently within international human rights law, which explains why the right to development has not yet been proclaimed in any UN human rights treaty and is unlikely to be in the future.[271]

In trying to make human rights more relevant to development, a *human rights–based approach* has been promoted by a number of actors, including the United Nations, governments, and many NGOs. As defined by UN Organization for Education, Science, and Culture (UNESCO), for example, it is "a conceptual framework for the process of human development that is normatively based on international human rights standards and operationally directed to promoting and protecting human rights. It seeks to analyze inequalities which lie at the heart of development problems and redress discriminatory practices and unjust distributions of power that impede development progress."[272] In essence, however, the approach calls simply for ensuring that human rights – particularly the rights to participate in public affairs, nondiscrimination, and free expression – are respected in considering and implementing development projects. This is certainly a principle to be welcomed, but it does not help us understand just what the inalienable human right to development means in either theory or practice.

Similarly, there have been frequent calls for international development institutions, such as the World Bank and other international financial institutions, to incorporate human rights into their operations.[273] A recent report by a special rapporteur on human rights and extreme poverty, Philip Alston, offers a more acerbic tone than most, but it is typical of many of the criticisms. After noting that "[f]or most purposes, the World Bank is a human rights–free zone,"[274] Alston continues:

> The key question then is whether it actually matters if the Bank uses the language of human rights or opts instead for surrogates which are perceived to be less politically loaded or contentious ...
>
> [T]he use of a human rights framework and discourse actually makes an enormous difference, which is of course precisely why the Bank is so resistant to using it and so attached to the never-ending search for surrogate language that enables it to get at the same concerns. Human rights provides a context and a detailed and balanced

framework; it invokes the specific legal obligations that States have agreed upon in the various human rights treaties; it emphasizes that certain values are non-negotiable; it brings a degree of normative certainty; and it brings into the discussion the carefully negotiated elaborations of the meaning of specific rights that have emerged from decades of reflection, discussion and adjudication. Even more importantly, the language of rights recognizes the dignity and agency of all individuals (regardless of race, gender, social status, age, disability or any other distinguishing factor) and it is intentionally empowering.[275]

Unfortunately, what follows offers no real indication of what the "enormous difference" might entail. Alston notes, for example, that recognizing the human rights of those living in extreme poverty "does not guarantee them food, education, or health care, but it does acknowledge their dignity and agency, empower them and their advocates and provide a starting point for a meaningful debate over the allocation of societal resources in contexts in which their interests have been systematically ignored."[276] While asserting that "it makes a huge difference if education reforms are premised on the right to education,"[277] there is no explanation of what this means. Alston is a well-respected academic and has held a number of positions as an independent expert within the UN human rights system, and his failure to move beyond rhetorical incantations in this instance is disappointing. As might be expected, his report also seems to have had no visible impact on the World Bank's policies, and the tone of the report ensures that little attention will be paid to the valid concerns that Alston raises.

The World Bank's general resistance to any mention of human rights obligations formally relies on language in its Articles of Agreement, which state that the bank and its officers "shall ... [not] be influenced in their decisions by the political character of the member or members concerned. Only economic considerations shall be relevant to their decisions, and these considerations shall be weighed impartially in order to achieve the purposes stated in Article I."[278] Human rights have fairly consistently been deemed to be "political" and therefore not to be considered during the process of making loans.

Nonetheless, the bank has adopted a number of policies and safeguards over the years that address issues closely related to human rights, although without using the term itself. "Gender equality for development is a core theme" of the bank's impact evaluation process, at least with respect to "reducing gender gaps in four key areas: (i) human capital, (ii) economic productivity, (iii) access to finance, and (iv) empowerment."[279] In 2016, the bank adopted a number of environmental and social standards to guide development projects, which were applied to loan agreements beginning in 2018. The standards include labor conditions, community health and safety, pollution prevention, restrictions on land use and involuntary resettlement, indigenous peoples, biodiversity conservation, and cultural heritage. Human rights are mentioned only three times in the bank's 120-page Environmental and Social Framework, which does state that the World Bank's activities support the realization of human rights expressed in the Universal Declaration of Human Rights. Through the projects it finances, and in a manner consistent with its Articles of Agreement, the World Bank seeks to avoid adverse impacts and will continue to support its member countries as they strive to progressively achieve their human rights commitments.[280]

The only commitment to substantive human rights is found in the bank's objective "[t]o ensure that the development process fosters full respect for the human rights, dignity, aspirations, identity, culture, and natural resource–based livelihoods of Indigenous Peoples/Sub-Saharan African Historically Underserved Traditional Local Communities."[281]

As Alston rightly observed, "an inconsistent, ad hoc and opaque policy of the type that exists today [in the World Bank] is in no one's interests."[282] The bank's continuing position that human rights are political and therefore beyond the bank's mandate to consider is questionable, but its attempt to consider not only human rights-related issues but broader relevant matters is difficult to fault – if, indeed, the commitments are implemented in practice. It is also difficult to argue with the bank's insistence on the obligation of *states* to ensure human rights, and advocates should follow and attempt to influence the conduct of both donor and recipient countries in their fashioning of bank policies and their implementation of development projects.

Finally, there has been a persistent attempt to introduce human rights into the discussions among governments and the United Nations about the Millennium Development Goals for 2015[283] and the Sustainable Development Goals for 2030[284]; the latter, in particular, are frequently invoked by NGOs and regularly appear on the agendas of human rights meetings. The eight earlier Millennium Goals did not address rights directly, and the summary description of the seventeen 2030 goals is to "end poverty, protect the planet and ensure prosperity for all. For the goals to be reached, everyone needs to do their part: governments, the private sector, civil society and people like you."[285] Goal 16 "is dedicated to the promotion of peaceful and inclusive societies for sustainable development, the provision of access to justice for all, and building effective, accountable institutions at all levels."[286]

All of the sustainable development goals are worthy, although they are neither rights nor legal commitments, and there are indications that many governments have taken their political promises to achieve the goals seriously.[287] The goals call for attention to most of the pressing issues that face the world today, including poverty, environmental degradation, climate change, technology, energy, infrastructure, the challenges facing cities, and many more. Effective implementation of existing human rights norms would no doubt facilitate achieving many of these goals, but sustainability in all its incarnations remains a goal, not a right.

The battle against recognizing a human right to development was lost long ago, but its proclamation attests to the importance of meaningful development in the lives of billions of people around the world. Designation as a right remains unfortunate, however, not because development is not integral to improving the lives of people but because the right itself is incomprehensible. While human rights must guide the process of determining development priorities (as they should guide other decision-making processes), they cannot determine what the outcome of that process will be or even define with any precision what it should be. The question of how best to ensure development is vital, but the primary result of its rhetorical designation as a human right is only to blur the distinction between obligatory respect for rights and laudable goals.

THE HUMAN RIGHTS COUNCIL AND ITS SPECIAL PROCEDURES

Nearing the end of her time as UN High Commissioner for Human Rights, Navi Pillay observed that "all [states] argued that she should avoid creating new rights. 'That came up again and again,' she said."[288] It is not clear whether Pillay thought that it was, indeed, her role to "create" new rights, or whether she was reacting to the objections of non-rights–supportive states to even the slightest broadening interpretation or expansion of rights.

Any philosopher or political activist can claim that his or her particular concern is or should be considered to be a human right. As suggested throughout this book, however, wishing it to be so does not create reality, and there is a real danger of undermining the universal legal rights that most states have formally accepted if they are constantly confused with mere aspirations that are neither legally based nor widely accepted. This section will mention only briefly some of the rights that advocates, UN officials or special rapporteurs, and others have claimed in recent years.

The list of topics today addressed by the most important UN human rights body, the Human Rights Council, puts in sharper perspective the rights-inflation criticism. Beginning in 1980, the Council (then Commission) has created working groups and individual experts (collectively known as "special procedures") on an ad-hoc basis to address a number of thematic issues, as well as the human rights situation in specific countries. The early thematic special procedures were concerned with physical security (such as disappearances, torture, arbitrary execution and detention) and civil rights (such as independence of judges and lawyers, freedom of religion and belief, racism). Consideration of a number of socioeconomic rights followed, including the rights to health, food, water, education, and housing.

By the end of 2017, the list of special procedures had grown to 44,[289] and the issues addressed now include even narrower categories (e.g., minorities, indigenous peoples, African descendants, persons with albinism or leprosy, human rights defenders), as well as a number of what might be termed "rights and" issues (discussed in the preceding chapter). Many, however, do seem to chart new ground, and they might be judged against the guidelines adopted by the General Assembly in 1986 and quoted at page 57 above, particularly those related to fundamental character and precision. Among these relatively recent special procedures are those on the implications for human rights of the environmentally sound management and disposal of hazardous substances and wastes (created in 1995); extreme poverty and human rights (1998); effects of foreign debt and other related international financial obligations of States on the full enjoyment of all human rights, particularly economic, social, and cultural rights (2000); human rights and international solidarity (2005); the use of mercenaries as a means of violating human rights and impeding the exercise of the right of peoples to self-determination (2005); human rights and transnational corporations and other business enterprises (2011); human rights obligations relating to the enjoyment of a safe, clean, healthy and sustainable environment (2012); the promotion of a democratic and equitable international order (2011); the promotion of truth, justice, reparation and guarantees of nonrecurrence (2011); the negative impact of unilateral coercive measures on the enjoyment of human rights (2014); the right to development (2016); and violence and discrimination based on sexual orientation and gender identity (2016).[290]

The scope of these mandates affects the normative content of human rights, which is the primary focus of this chapter. However, it also has an insidious effect on the practice and monitoring of human rights within the United Nations, as detailed in a recent article evaluating the special procedures.

> It is ... apparent from the research findings and our analysis that proliferation of mandates is having a negative impact upon the special procedure system. At the most basic level, because there have not been increased resources to match the increasing number of mandates, those mandate holders focusing on tangible violations of tangible rights are able to conduct fewer country visits, produce fewer reports and recommendations, and have less time to discuss their findings at the Human Rights Council ... The newer mandates are designed in such a way as to be able to criticize countries for policy programs or interstate relations, or to criticize international institutions. The focus is being shifted away from the relationship between states and individuals and toward examining state policies and foreign relations.[291]

These mandates are normally adopted by a reasonable degree of consensus among the 47 members of the HR Council, although that is not always the case. For example, creation of the special procedure on sexual orientation and gender identity received only a plurality of 23 votes in 2016, primarily from developed states; resolutions on unilateral coercive measures (economic sanctions), a democratic and equitable international order, and the impact of foreign debt each received approximately 30 affirmative votes, with most of the proponents being from developing countries.

The Human Rights Council Advisory Committee is a body of 18 individual experts described as a think-tank for the Council; its work is directed by the council, and its advice is limited to "thematic issues pertaining to the mandate of the council, namely promotion and protection of all human rights."[292] Its past and current mandates from the council have at times seemed only vaguely relevant to the promotion and protection of human rights and have included the better understanding of traditional values of humankind, terrorist hostage-taking, the right of peoples to peace, missing persons, unilateral coercive measures, international solidarity, unaccompanied migrant children and adolescents, the impact of vulture funds on human rights, and the negative impact of the nonrepatriation of funds of illicit origin.[293]

The special procedures have provided a needed, relatively informal approach to a range of human rights, including the possibility of contacting states directly to request information on alleged rights violations.[294] Within the terms of their mandates, however, the experts are free to pursue whatever they think appropriate. They are frequently referred to by the press as simply "UN experts," thus giving the misleading impression that they speak on behalf of the organization, but their creativity in terms of interpreting rights offers more than a few surprises.

For example, the special rapporteur in the field of cultural rights has raised concerns about the impact of commercial advertising and marketing practices "on cultural diversity and the right of people to choose their own ways of life."[295] In a report on her visit to Vietnam, she expressed concern about the "folklorization" of the playing of traditional Vietnamese gongs, which "are now being played on demand for tourists in some places, thus clearly losing its original cultural significance."[296] On the other hand, the same rapporteur stressed the limits of culture in a report devoted to determining "how to arrive at a point at which women own both their culture (and religion and tradition) and their human rights."[297] The last-mentioned raises legitimate issues concerning power, inferiority, and social constraints, but the report seems to stray far beyond women's *rights* to include the following:

> From a human rights perspective, participation must ensure decision-making . . .
>
> [T]here is a need to understand universality as a transformative dialogue in which disparities in power are acknowledged . . .
>
> The positing of cultural diversity and the universality of human rights as either irreconcilable or mutually exclusive must be unequivocally rejected. Whenever "gender-biased social arrangements are defended in the name of culture, the purported cultural norms need to be challenged" . . .
>
> Cultural diversity is not to be confused with cultural relativism. The cultural diversity within a community and within each individual is at least as important as diversities across communities. These diversities must be vigorously respected, protected and promoted, for they are the kernels of a democratic order . . .
>
> The reality of intra-community diversity makes it vital to ensure that all voices within a community are heard without discrimination in terms of representing the interests, desires and perspectives of that particular community. Women must be equally empowered to decide the criteria for, and conditions of, belonging to communities of shared cultural values, and to decide the normative content of values and the contours and context of practices that respect, protect and promote their human dignity.

Women's cultural rights provide a new framework for promoting all other rights. The realization of equal cultural rights for women would help to reconstruct gender in ways that transcend notions of women's inferiority and subordination, thereby improving conditions for the full and equal enjoyment of their human rights in general.[298]

A special rapporteur on the right to health stated that the criminalization of sex work violates human rights by, inter alia, "creating barriers to access by sex workers to health services and legal remedies."[299] Again, a perfectly legitimate position, but one that does not reflect existing rights and that most states reject.

As discussed briefly in the note on technology in Chapter 4, human rights norms will need to address realties of the Internet, social media, and other technological changes that were simply unknown when the norms were being developed. However, when a special rapporteur on freedom of opinion and expression called on governments "to develop effective policies to attain universal access to the Internet" for their populations,[300] journalists widely, breathlessly – and inaccurately – reported that "the United Nations" had declared broadband access to be "a basic human right, right up there with the right to healthcare, shelter and food."[301]

Other special procedures cannot resist the temptation to address broader issues, no matter what their particular mandate might be. For example, here is an extract from comments by a special rapporteur on the rights to freedom of peaceful assembly and of association, at the conclusion of his 2017 visit to the United States:

> ... [T]he new administration of President Trump has talked of taking a radically different approach on all fronts: its engagement with the United Nations, its promotion of human rights abroad and even its attitude towards fundamental rights domestically. The signals coming from the current administration, including hateful and xenophobic rhetoric during the presidential campaign, threats and actions to lock out and expel migrants on the basis of nationality and religion, a dismissive position towards peaceful protesters, the endorsement of torture, intolerance of criticism and threats to withdraw funding from the United Nations, are deeply disturbing ...
>
> While the Special Rapporteur's focus is the status of the rights to freedom of peaceful assembly and of association, he necessarily situates his assessment within the context of several overarching concerns. It is impossible to discuss those rights, for example, without issues of racism pervading the discussion. Racism and the exclusion, persecution and marginalization that come with it, affect the environment for exercising the rights to freedom of peaceful assembly and of association. Understanding that context means looking back at 400 years of slavery, the Civil War and the Jim Crow laws, which destroyed the achievements of the reconstruction era, enforced segregation and marginalized the African-American community, condemning it to a life of misery, poverty and persecution. It means looking at what happened after the Jim Crow laws, when the old philosophies of exclusion and discrimination were reborn, cloaked in new and euphemistic terms. A stark

example is the so-called war on drugs, which has resulted in a situation where 1 in every 15 black men is currently in jail and 1 in every 13 African-Americans has lost their right to vote owing to a felony conviction.

In contradistinction, Wall Street bankers looted billions of dollars through crooked schemes, devastating the finances of millions of Americans and saddling taxpayers with a massive bailout bill. Meanwhile, crimes against workers, including wage theft, sexual abuse, union busting and more, remain rampant; yet we do not hear of a "war on Wall Street theft" or a "war on abusive employers." Instead, criminal justice resources go towards enforcing a different type of law and order, targeting primarily African-Americans and other minorities. As a result, there is justifiable and palpable anger in the black community that needs to be expressed. This is the context that gave birth to the non-violent protest movement Black Lives Matter and the context in which it must be understood.

The Special Rapporteur also recognizes that his visit coincided with a tumultuous election period marked by divisive and corrosive rhetoric. The election period sharply exposed the intolerance, inequality and exclusion that had been building up without being adequately addressed.[302]

Many of the special rapporteur's observations are well founded, and, as an independent expert, he speaks for himself. While his recommendations were offered "in the spirit of constructive engagement,"[303] there appears to have been no official US response to the report.

At least when it declared 20 August to be the International Day of Happiness, the UN General Assembly did not declare that happiness was also a human right, although it did include a reference to "the need for a more inclusive, equitable and balanced approach to economic growth that promotes sustainable development, poverty eradication, happiness and the well-being of all peoples."[304] Interestingly, the Global Happiness Council in its annual policy report does distinguish between the goal of being happy and the scope of human rights, an approach that social justice activists would be well advised to follow:

> Societies that are more inclusive generally achieve better results on health and happiness. Also, the social inclusion approach should address need or alienation wherever it exists. Such an approach means going beyond enforcing human rights, to reducing poverty and barriers to social connection in the city ...
>
> Social work is a practice-based profession and an academic discipline that promotes social change and development, social cohesion, and the empowerment and liberation of people. Principles of social justice, human rights, collective responsibility and respect for diversities are central to social work.[305]

OTHER COUNCIL INITIATIVES

Since 2010, the HR Council has considered "the need to protect human rights and ensure accountability for violations and abuses relating to the activities of private military and security companies."[306] A new intergovernmental working group was created in 2017 to elaborate the content of an international regulatory framework, "without prejudging the nature thereof," on the issue.[307] As of mid-2018, the initial session of the working group had not yet been held.

In 2016, the HR Council adopted a resolution on the right to peace, which was subsequently endorsed by the UN General Assembly. While the UDHR and the two human rights covenants were cited in the second of the 36 preambular paragraphs in the GA resolution, the right itself was fortunately not described as a "human" right. Article 1 of the declaration states simply, "Everyone has the right to enjoy peace such that all human rights are promoted and protected and development is fully realized."[308]

Another human rights–related movement taken up by the council has focused on the rights of peasants and rural farmers. The Geneva-based Le Centre Europe – Tiers Monde (CETIM) and an international movement of peasants and farmers, La Via Campesina, have advocated adoption of a human rights instrument on the rights of peasants and food sovereignty for over a decade.[309] The movement gained the support of a UN special rapporteur on the right to food, Olivier de Schutter, and a special session of the Human Rights Council was called in May 2008 to consider what was then a world food crisis. In 2010, the council asked its advisory committee of experts to prepare a study on "on ways and means to further advance the rights of people working in rural areas, including women, in particular smallholders engaged in the production of food and/or other agricultural products." This led to two reports,[310] which were followed by creation of an intergovernmental working group to draft a declaration on the rights of peasants.[311]

It now appears that the final draft of a declaration will be prepared by the chair of the working group and submitted to the HR Council in 2019. In many respects, this might be seen as only an extension of human rights to another vulnerable group rather than the creation of new rights, similar to the specific attention paid to groups such as minorities, indigenous peoples, women, and people with disabilities. However, the 2018 draft declaration goes far beyond existing human rights norms, and it epitomizes how norm development within the United Nations has changed over the past two decades. For example, the 1981 UN Declaration on the Elimination of All Forms of Intolerance and of Discrimination Based on Religion or Belief is two or three pages long, with eight substantive articles;[312] the 1992 Declaration on the Rights of Persons Belonging to National or Ethnic, Religious and Linguistic Minorities is slightly longer and has nine articles.[313] In contrast, the 2007 Declaration on the Rights of Indigenous Peoples is several times longer, with forty-six articles,[314] and the revised draft Declaration on the Rights of Peasants and Other People Working in Rural areas is fourteen pages long, with twenty-eight detailed articles.[315]

The draft declaration states that countries "shall respect, protect, and fulfil" the rights of peasants set forth in the declaration, which include "the right to determine and develop priorities and strategies to exercise their right to development" (article 3.2); the right to "enjoy physical and economic access at all times to sufficient and adequate food that is produced and consumed sustainably and equitably, respecting their cultures, preserving access to food for future generations, and that ensures a physically and mentally fulfilling and dignified life for them, individually and collectively, responding to their needs" (article 15.2); the individual and collective right "to have access to, use and manage land ... to achieve an adequate standard of living, to have a place to live in security, peace and dignity and to develop their cultures" (article 17.1); the right to benefit from "redistributive agrarian reforms where there is lack of broad and equitable access to land and other natural resources necessary to ensure that peasants and other people working in rural areas enjoy adequate living conditions, particularly young people and landless persons" (article 17.6); the right to seeds, including the right "to equitably participate in sharing the benefits arising from the utilization of plant genetic resources for food and agriculture" (article 19.1.b); and the right to biological diversity (article 20).

There is no doubt that peasants (who are defined in article 1.4 of the draft declaration as including "hired workers, including all migrant workers, regardless of their legal status, and seasonal workers, on plantations, agricultural farms, forests and farms in aquaculture and in agro-industrial enterprises") continue to suffer systematic human rights violations, discrimination, and economic marginalization in most countries. However, this is quite a list, and implementing the declaration would entail complicated political, economic, social, trade, and other measures. It also appears, somewhat problematically, to single out for special protection rural communities and individuals, as opposed to those engaging in work other than agriculture or living in poverty in urban areas or elsewhere.

Since the working group is open-ended, it is difficult to determine the degree of support for the 2018 draft. At the working group's 2018 session, the nonaligned movement and the African group spoke in favor of the declaration; a number of countries were supportive but expressed concerns over various provisions; and the United Kingdom and United States objected to the mention of collective rights.[316] The European Union adopted the following position:

> The EU has constructively engaged in the four sessions of the Working Group. We thank you for taking on board some of our proposals. We recognize that there are improvements to the text, however we note that problems in the text remain, especially with regard to notions of extra-territoriality, rights to seeds, land, means of production, food sovereignty and biological diversity.
>
> We remain concerned that this draft attempts to create new rights, while we are negotiating a Declaration, which by definition, will not constitute a legally binding document and, thus, cannot create new rights. Attention must be paid to adopt a consistent approach regarding to the existing human rights framework ...
>
> For the reasons outlined above, the EU as a whole is not in the position to support the Declaration in this present version.[317]

In all likelihood, the declaration will be adopted by a divided vote in the HR Council in the near future, thus giving it some political legitimacy and allowing it to be used by NGOs as an advocacy tool. Whether its wide-ranging recommendations will be accepted by states, even gradually, or whether it will remain largely unimplemented is yet to be seen. Also unknown is whether this initiative will be seen as providing an overdue focus on a disadvantaged category of people or as just another unwarranted political expansion of the concept of rights.

REGIONAL BODIES, GOVERNMENTS, AND NGOS

Regional bodies and experts have been equally creative. An OAS convention on the rights of the elderly calls upon states to "take steps to ensure that public and private institutions offer older persons access without discrimination to comprehensive care, including palliative care; avoid isolation; appropriately manage problems related to the fear of death of the terminally ill and pain; and prevent unnecessary suffering, and futile and useless procedures, in accordance with the right of older persons to express their informed consent."[318] Professor Victor Abramovich argues that "reinterpretation of the principle of equality has allowed the ISHR [inter-American system of human rights] to involve itself with social issues."[319] Elsewhere, in the context of economic regulation and the protection of foreign investment, Abramovich purports to identify an "emerging right to social communication ... [that] reinforces the state's duty to prevent undue media concentration and to guarantee the access of historically marginalised groups or sectors to expression in the public sphere ... [T]he human rights regime ... broaden[s] the public sphere ... and demand[s] greater state intervention in the economy and the markets."[320]

In Europe, the 2000 European Landscape Convention[321] is said to contribute "to the exercise of human rights and democracy with a view to sustainable development." [322] A Council of Europe publication on the convention includes chapters on "landscape and human rights" and "landscape and democracy," although the convention itself does not mention human rights.[323]

A Chinese government official claimed that it was a human right of the Chinese people to host the 2008 Olympic Games in Beijing.[324] The Foreign Minister of Ecuador reportedly argued that there was a "fundamental right" to sunbathe for Julian Assange, founder of WikiLeaks, who has been granted refuge in the embassy of Ecuador in London since June 2012 in order to avoid extradition.[325]

Even mainstream human rights NGOs are not immune. As expressed recently by a Programme Officer of the Raoul Wallenberg Institute.

> The human rights field needs to catch up with a swiftly developing world, and the emerging challenges this world poses. This includes everything from globalization to advancements in science and technology (e.g. biomedicine, robotics, etc.) Unfortunately, too often International Human Rights Law is too slow to see and address emerging issues.[326]

In early 2018, Amnesty International (AI) began a campaign against Twitter, including a "Troll Patrol" of supporters: "Every day, women face violent threats, sexism, racism and more on Twitter. This abuse is flooding Twitter, forcing women out of public conversations – and at times, driving them off the platform."[327] At a panel discussion during a Human Rights Council session in 2018, a group of NGOs, the Women Human Rights Defenders International Coalition, "stressed that the first step towards addressing online violence is to recognise that it is a legitimate and harmful manifestation of gender-based violence."[328] While Twitter deserves to be called to account if such allegations are true, does being driven off Twitter constitute a human rights violation? Even more egregious have been AIUSA's fund-raising appeals for "emergency donations for Syrian families," which promise not humanitarian relief (which AI does not provide) but merely to "continue to document the horrific abuses and demand that governments and armed groups stop attacking civilians."[329] AI's expansion beyond internationally recognized human rights actually goes back to 1980, when the organization added abolition of capital punishment to its mandate – a worthy and moral campaign but one which reflected Amnesty's own beliefs as opposed to international human rights norms. The move also had the unfortunate consequence of alienating many of AI's more conservative supporters, a situation that is still true today.

New York–based Human Rights Watch (HRW), probably the largest and most influential human rights NGO, also has a broad range of interests, some of which go beyond traditional human rights issues. Based on the programs for which there are staff directors, these include emergencies/humanitarian law, international justice, refugee rights, business and human rights, arms control, international financial institutions, terrorism and counterterrorism, and environment and human rights.[330]

Finally, a recent book from Oxford University Press argues that "all human beings have rights to the fundamental conditions for pursuing a good life; therefore, as human beings, children have human rights to the fundamental conditions for pursuing a good life. Since being loved is one of those fundamental conditions, children thus have a right to be loved."[331]

Is it any wonder that people are sometimes confused about the meaning of human rights?[332]

A BRIEF NOTE ON MIGRATION

The worldwide debate over migration is a prime example of stretching the concept of human rights law in order to advance advocates' own views of how society should respond to a significant issue with wide social, economic, and political ramifications.

Both the UDHR and CP Covenant explicitly deal with freedom of movement, both within countries and between them. Both instruments proclaim, "Everyone shall be free to leave any country, including his own."[333] In the CP Covenant, this language is followed by the standard recognition that the right to leave may be limited, but only when "necessary to protect national security, public order (*ordre public*), public health or morals or the rights and freedoms of others."

The UDHR also states in article 14.1, "Everyone has the right to seek and to enjoy in other countries asylum from persecution." While there is no comparable provision in the covenant, there is a well-developed international law of refugees and asylum-seekers that prevents anyone from being sent back to a country from which he or she is fleeing, if the asylum-seeker's "life or freedom would be threatened on account of his race, religion, nationality, membership of a particular social group or political opinion."[334] This principle of *non-refoulement*, the right not to be returned, is now customary international law, and it has been applied in a number of cases before international human rights tribunals to prevent countries from returning people to places where they were likely to be killed, tortured, or arbitrarily detained.

The UN High Commissioner on Refugees (UNHCR) has expanded the working definition of refugee to include "people who cannot return to their country of origin because of a well-founded fear of persecution, conflict, violence, or other circumstances that have seriously disturbed public order, and who, as a result, require international protection."[335] This concept of temporary protection for displaced persons has been formally adopted by the African Union and European Union.[336] While UNHCR also is involved with many aspects of migration, it cautions that "[t]he tendency to conflate refugees and migrants, or to refer to refugees as a subcategory of migrants, can have serious consequences for the lives and safety of people fleeing persecution or conflict."[337]

A convention on the rights of migrant workers was adopted under UN auspices in 1990. It had only 51 parties as of early 2018, almost all of which are sending rather than receiving countries; none of the major receiving countries in Europe or North America has ratified it.[338] While the convention refers to workers who are "nondocumented or in an irregular situation," it specifically provides that nothing in the treaty "shall be interpreted as implying the regularization of the situation of [such] migrant workers or members of their families or any right to ... regularization of their situation, nor shall it prejudice the measures intended to ensure sound and equitable conditions for international migration," which is mentioned elsewhere in the convention.[339]

The European Union adopted a regulation that identified the criteria for determining which of its member states is responsible for examining claims for asylum or international protection,[340] but its implementation was largely ignored during the European refugee/migration crisis of 2015. In 2016, in response to the crisis and the widely publicized deaths of many of those seeking entry to Europe, the UN General Assembly adopted a consensus resolution on migrants and refugees.[341]

None of these instruments includes an explicit right for any person to *enter* a country not his or her own. All people have the right to *leave* a country, and those fleeing persecution (and perhaps violence, at least in Africa and the EU) have the right to *seek* protection or asylum in another country. However, there is no guarantee that they will be admitted, only that they will not be returned to the country where they fear persecution or widespread violence. Migrants who seek to enter a country for economic or other reasons are subject to the domestic laws of that country that govern admission, residency, etc.

Everyone within a country's jurisdiction, including asylum-seekers and migrants, whether documented or undocumented, must be guaranteed the human rights to which everyone is entitled, including having a fair determination of any claims to asylum that they may present and to be treated humanely if they are detained. However, states have zealously guarded their sovereign right to control who may or may not enter their territory, and human rights law does not prohibit governments from deporting or expelling those who attempt to enter illegally or without proper documentation (subject only to the norms related to refugees).

There is no doubt that anti-immigrant fears in Europe, the United States, and elsewhere are driven in part by racial prejudice and ill-informed assumptions about the economic and social impact of migrants, but adopting a highly restrictive approach to potential immigrants does not violate international human rights law – although it may be immoral, unwise, and economically misguided. By framing migration in human rights terms, advocates of liberal immigration policies misstate what human rights law does provide, and they contribute to popular perceptions of nationalists that human rights are part of the problem.

In such a situation, everyone loses. Migration must be addressed in all of its social, economic, cultural, and political complexity, not simply swept beneath the invented tent of a human right to enter another country, no matter how understandable that desire might be. The failure to deal with the crisis is not to be found in gaps in human rights law but in the refusal of politicians and populations to engage more directly and honestly with important social and ethical issues.

CONCLUDING REMARKS

International human rights law in the early twenty-first century is not perfect, and it would be foolish and counterproductive to pretend that it is. For the past 50 years, since the entry into force of the two UN covenants, international rights have expanded dramatically, both regionally and globally. Much of human rights advocacy in the past 20 years, in particular, has been directed toward expanding existing rights and/or focusing attention on discrimination against particular groups and individuals.

While the situation of human rights has improved in the world, there is little evidence that expanding the quantity of human rights has played much of a role in this improvement. With the possible exception of the early treaties calling for the end of discrimination against members of racial groups and women, identifying new categories at risk seems rarely to have led to an increase in their protection. While attention to vulnerable categories is often a necessary first step to greater understanding and tolerance, "new" rights often originate in response to the denial of well-established rights, often through discriminatory practices. In such circumstances, it may be a wiser course to ensure enforcement of existing antidiscrimination and other human rights norms, rather than creating a whole new set of rights or simply defining new categories of victims.

Full respect for existing civil, cultural, economic, political, and social rights would vastly improve the situation of all members of society, rich and poor, elites and marginalized, majority and minority. Ignoring the fact that compliance with existing norms is often weak and hoping that the articulation of new norms will somehow help is unrealistic and may reduce resources needed to combat existing human rights violations.

When advocates believe that expanding existing rights or creating new ones is warranted, those who are asked to support or fund such appeals should ask a number of questions. Beginning with the recommendations of the UN General Assembly quoted at the beginning of this chapter, new rights should be *consistent* with existing norms, although by definition they will be new in either substance or scope. They should be *fundamental* and also *sufficiently precise* so that both the right itself and the obligation on government to ensure the right are understandable. Most importantly, they should "attract broad international support."

International support can be manifested in a number of ways, but it cannot be demonstrated simply by winning a special rapporteur over to your point of view or successfully adopting a resolution in the Human Rights Council that does not even enjoy majority support among the Council's members. Both pro- and anti-human rights governments have utilized this tactic, often in the context of creating a new special procedure to either expand or detract from existing norms. Open-ended governmental working groups offer a wonderful excuse to sideline the need to protect existing rights while conjuring up new ones.

> There is of course a tension between the concern with diluting human rights currency and the call to expand the human rights remit, and between the suggestion that human rights becomes more modest and that it should become more radical. Such tensions may be inevitable and could be resolved – or managed – only in the context of concrete, practical, questions.[342]

This tension will continue, and advocates should not be dissuaded from pursuing the causes that they believe to be most deserving. However, governments, foundations, celebrities, donors, and international organizations need to recognize that sympathy for a cause is not a sufficient reason to turn its advancement into an international human rights norm.

On the other hand, new or expanded rights should be welcomed at the domestic level, given that international human rights law sets only a minimum standard for social justice and equity. Domestic rights are in general more readily enforceable, and they can be deliberately designed to reflect national situations and priorities, with no pretense of applying to the entire world. For example, France in 2018 adopted a law recognizing the right of citizens to "make mistakes" when dealing with officials and the French bureaucracy, based on a presumption of good faith.[343] Another European example is the "right to be forgotten," i.e., to have certain information about oneself erased from the Internet and social media.[344] Entire classes of people, such as students, consumers, property owners, peasants, and others may be granted rights to promote the situation of such groups directly or as a means of implementing broader goals of equity and inclusion. While international human rights provide the democratic and participatory context for advocating the adoption of such laws, they do not, in most cases, determine their content.

"To use human rights as a measure for the quality of life possible within community is like using minimum health standards as a universal index on the quality of restaurants."[345] Attempting to regulate ever more narrow slices of life under ever more diverse circumstances through promoting new rights runs a serious risk of undermining both the legitimacy of human rights and their universality. The result may be simply to expand the number of rights that are routinely ignored rather than to bring real help to those whose rights, no matter how narrowly construed, are already being violated.

6

Women, Sex, and Gender

Among the most controversial and difficult issues faced by "universal" human rights today are those concerned with sex, gender, and the degree to which human rights norms should govern relations between men and women in the private, as well as public, realm. For example, when Amnesty International voted to support full decriminalization of the sex trade, the decision came only after "days of emotional debates and intense lobbying" by those supporting and opposing the decision.[346] AI's Secretary General Salil Shetty said, "We recognise that this critical human rights issue is hugely complex and that is why we have addressed this issue from the perspective of international human rights standards," but it was still left up to national AI sections to determine whether or not they would support the new position.[347]

While the concepts are related, the three subtopics of this chapter have been addressed quite differently in international human rights law, both in terms of the texts themselves and the manner in which they have been interpreted by advocates, opponents, and international human rights bodies. Whether one takes an expansive or a restrictive view of how these three categories should be treated, even the "easy" norm of nondiscrimination against women remains woefully unimplemented in many countries and societies.

WOMEN

The United Nations Charter does not define what human rights are, but it does declare in Article 1.3 that they must be recognized for "all without distinction as to race, sex, language, or religion." Article 2 of the Universal Declaration of Human Rights extends this principle of nondiscrimination to "distinction of any kind, such as race, colour, sex, language, religion, political or other opinion, national or social origin, property, birth or other status." Both the ESC and CP Covenants contain a similar broad nondiscrimination clause, as well as an almost identical Article 3, which declares that states "undertake to ensure the equal right of men and women to the enjoyment of all ... rights set forth in the present Covenant." Regional human rights treaties in Europe, the Americas, and Africa have similar provisions.

The goal of nondiscrimination on the basis of sex was clearly problematic at the time of the Charter's adoption in 1945, when women around the world faced widespread legal, as well as social, restrictions on their activities. One of the first human rights treaties adopted under the UN's auspices was the 1953 Convention on the Political Rights of Women,[348] a short treaty that simply provides that women have the rights, without discrimination, to vote, be eligible for election, and hold public office. Implementation of these simple norms took decades: generally rights-respecting Switzerland did not grant women the right to vote until 1971; Liechtenstein was the last European country to do so, after a referendum in 1984 in which only men voted; and it was only in 2015 that women finally became eligible to vote in municipal elections in Saudi Arabia.

There has been no lack of attention to women's rights in recent decades. The Convention on the Elimination of All Forms of Discrimination against Women (CEDAW), which entered into force in 1981, vastly expands the rights of women and is discussed in greater detail below.[349] In addition to CEDAW, there are regional treaties that specifically address women's rights in Africa[350] and Europe.[351] A UN Commission on the Status of Women, now under the umbrella of UN Women, was established in 1946. Among the thematic procedures created by the UN Human Rights Council (discussed in Chapter 5), three concern women: a special rapporteur on violence against women, its causes, and consequences (created in 1994); another rapporteur on trafficking in persons, "especially women and children" (2004); and a working group on the issue of discrimination against women in law and in practice (2010).

The mantra that "women's rights are human rights" thus came as no surprise to human rights advocates – no one doubted that this had always been the case – but the contemporary focus on women's rights reflects the fact that not only the legal rights of women but the much broader social, economic, cultural, political, psychological, and power aspects of women's role(s) in society are still being contested. In some respects, the debates about women, men, and the relationships between the two reflect a paradigmatic question about the nature of human rights themselves: Do human rights articulate the highest, most inclusive, egalitarian standards and aspirations of half of the world's population in a meaningfully universal way? Or do human rights set forth only a minimum standard of true nondiscrimination and at least formal equality, and leave it to countries, societies, and even local communities to determine what is fair, just, and desirable beyond that international minimum?

By early 2018, 189 countries were parties to CEDAW, nearly every country in the world; the nonparties include Iran, Palau, Somalia, Sudan, Tonga, and the United States. While many of the parties to CEDAW have entered reservations limiting the obligations that they have accepted (an issue discussed further in Chapter 7), this quasi-unanimous acceptance of the basic norms of nondiscrimination and equal treatment is still impressive, given the subordinate roles imposed upon women throughout history. It also is important to note the primary scope of CEDAW, i.e., the elimination of discrimination, defined as "any distinction, exclusion or restriction made on the basis of sex which has the effect or purpose of impairing or nullifying the recognition, enjoyment or exercise by women, irrespective of their marital status, on a basis of equality of men and women, of human rights and fundamental freedoms in the political, economic, social, cultural, civil or any other field."[352]

Despite its title, some of the subsequent articles of CEDAW go well beyond formal nondiscrimination. For example, states agree

> To embody the principle of the equality of men and women in their national constitutions or other appropriate legislation ... and to ensure ... the practical realization of this principle;
>   To take all appropriate measures to eliminate discrimination against women by any person, organization or enterprise; [and]
>   To take all appropriate measures, including legislation, to modify or abolish existing laws, regulations, customs and practices which constitute discrimination against women ...[353]

The last paragraph is amplified in article 5, which is perhaps the most relevant to the principles of universality and flexibility that inform many of the discussions in this book.

> States Parties shall take all appropriate measures
>   (1) To modify the social and cultural patterns of conduct of men and women, with a view to achieving the elimination of prejudices and customary and all other practices which are based on the idea of the inferiority or superiority of either of the sexes or on stereotyped roles for men and women;
>   (2) To ensure that family education includes a proper understanding of maternity as a social function and the recognition of the common responsibility of men and women in the upbringing and development of their children, it being understood that the interest of the children is the primordial consideration in all cases.[354]

It is worth noting the contrast between CEDAW and the similarly titled Convention on the Elimination of All Forms of Racial Discrimination (CERD), which was adopted and entered into force just over a decade prior to CEDAW.[355] Both treaties deal with endemic discrimination against significant numbers of people that has been present in almost every society in the history of humankind. However, race and women are dealt with quite differently in at least a couple of important respects.

First, CERD's definition of discrimination extends only to the impairment of human rights "in the political, economic, social, cultural or any other field of *public life*" (emphasis added), a limitation not found in CEDAW.[356] CEDAW deliberately ignores the distinction between public and private life and adopts an all-encompassing vision of equality between men and women that demands not just equal results but special treatment to "modify social and cultural patterns of conduct."

Second, similar to CEDAW, CERD in article 4 condemns propaganda based on ideas or theories of racial superiority or that "attempt to justify or promote racial hatred and discrimination in any form . . ." It also calls for punishing such conduct by law and prohibiting organizations that promote and incite racial discrimination. Unlike CEDAW, however, there is no reference to social and cultural patterns, customary practices, or stereotyped roles, even though the position of racial minorities[357] in society is often governed by exactly such patterns and roles, as is true for women. The CEDAW language greatly increases the scope of states' obligations.

This broad scope is well illustrated by a case involving the discriminatory dismissal of a female hairdresser by her male employer in Turkey. The CEDAW Committee that oversees the treaty found a violation of CEDAW because Turkish courts "failed to give due consideration to the claim of gender-based discrimination . . . and hence revealed their lack of gender sensitivity" – despite the fact that the Turkish courts provided the woman two separate remedies for her dismissal: they agreed that the woman had been unlawfully dismissed and awarded her compensation, and she also brought and won a libel suit against her employer.[358]

Stereotypes exist everywhere, based on nationality, occupation, geography, political affiliation, income, age, and many other qualities, including sex. Stereotypes are often offensive to those who are their object, and they vary depending on the perspective and experience of the person using the stereotype. The problem with eliminating conduct grounded in "stereotyped roles for men and women," as required by CEDAW, is that in some instances it is difficult to distinguish stereotypes from inherent (if not necessarily universal) attributes, whether the latter originate from traditional roles assigned by society or from DNA.

For example, if women are *not* more likely to seek consensus rather than confrontation, more concerned than men with family issues, more compassionate, and less aggressive, why should they necessarily be included in legislatures, peace negotiation or conflict resolution teams, or corporate boards of directors? Their absence may be evidence of discrimination, which must be eliminated, but many proponents of such inclusion view the goal not as temporary affirmative action or positive discrimination, but rather as a means of bringing the needed – and different – perspectives of women to these tasks. For example, the Harvard Women and Public Policy Program states that "[p]ast research has found that in business and negotiation, women hold higher ethical standards and are less prone than men to engage in unethical practices such as deception."[359] A country director for UN Women stated, "While women and girls are suffering disproportionately, they also bring unique experiences and skills to disaster risk reduction and climate adaptation as active agents of change."[360] Should we understand these to be stereotypes to be eliminated, as demanded by article 5, or an inherent attribute? Is the implicit finding that men are *more* likely to engage in unethical conduct evidence of an inherent attribute or a stereotype, along with other (generally negative) assumptions about male aggressiveness, competitiveness, and penchant for violence and confrontation?

We have now gone well beyond the realm of human rights, and answers to these questions depend more on sociologists, psychologists, and scientific research than on the musings of lawyers. The questions are raised to illustrate the ambiguities in a universal legal regime that is designed to ensure the same rights for everyone, without discrimination based on sex or other status. Of course, discrimination is not the same as difference or distinction, and law is in essence about drawing distinctions based on behavior (criminal law), ability (requirements for certification for certain professions), wealth (progressive taxes that fall more heavily on the rich than the poor), residence (geographical restrictions on voting), and other status. However, under human rights law, the burden is on the state to justify any such distinctions, by showing that they are necessary and proportional to achieving a pressing social need. For example, according to the World Bank, women are legally barred from certain jobs in 104 countries.[361] Most of these prohibitions no doubt constitute discrimination against women and should be repealed, but it would be open to a government to try to justify some of them on specific grounds (for example, limiting women's access to jobs that might expose them to substances that would be harmful if a woman became pregnant or restricting women's role in armed combat – although neither of these limitations would be without controversy).

These observations do not diminish the fact that women have been treated not only differently than men throughout history, but that this difference is, indeed, based on discrimination and assumptions of subservience, obedience, and weakness – in a word, patriarchy. Truly eliminating discrimination against women in all fields – legal, social, economic, political, and everywhere else – is mandated by international human rights law and may be achievable. However, broader social change in all public and private relationships is much more difficult to impose through international norms that are supposed to be universal. For example, CEDAW mandates "[t]he right to equal remuneration, including benefits, and to equal treatment in respect of work of equal value, as well as equality of treatment in the evaluation of the quality of work."[362] If "equal" means "the same," there should be little problem in implementing this provision, and a man and a woman performing the same job should receive the same compensation. However, if equal implies measuring the value to society of particular occupations, how do we determine whether the (traditionally female) occupations of primary school teaching and nursing are equal to the (traditionally male) occupations of construction and policing? How do we even understand these questions in the context of the alleged universality of human rights, when such comparisons would certainly expose different values for different types of work in different societies?

Women face daunting realities in every society, including violence (both within and outside the family), blatant discrimination based solely on their sex in work and public life, and male attitudes of control over women that stem from millennia of human social history. Human rights can certainly assist in changing the first two elements; the last will require much more than law, as evidenced from the following account of efforts to improve the lives of women in Afghanistan.

> The clash between Western ideals and Afghan realities means a program established to promote women [in the Afghan police forces] has all too often backfired, subjecting the recruits themselves to abuse and retribution ...
>
> "It's the absurdity of imposing our liberal Western beliefs," said a Western diplomat who has spent many years in Afghanistan and asked not to be named because of the sensitivity of the subject for governments that have invested heavily in training Afghan women for the security forces. "It's easy for us to put these women out there and tout their accomplishments, but then we leave, cut them loose, and what happens to them?"[363]

Of course, this criticism may be more relevant to the tactics of ensuring equality than to the long-term goal, the achievement of which is likely to depend as much on education and economic advancement as on immediately putting women into situations where their presence can be expected to create resentment and resistance, without meaningful preparation or protection.

Religious beliefs and sacred texts are often cited to oppose equal treatment of women, but human rights bodies in recent years have frequently relied upon principles of equal treatment and integration into society to uphold the state's refusal to permit religious practices to undermine these principles. For example, in addition to the well-known cases involving bans on public face coverings, such as the niqab and burqa,[364] the European Court of Human Rights has upheld a Swiss prohibition on separating boys and girls in school swimming pools, agreeing with the government's argument that "school plays a special role in the process of social integration, one that is all the more decisive where children of foreign origin are concerned."[365] The UK court of appeal found that a co-educational Muslim school in Birmingham caused unlawful discrimination by separating boys and girls,[366] although single-sex schools are still permissible.

A UN special rapporteur on freedom of religion or belief, Heiner Bielefeldt, devoted one of his reports to the relationship between freedom of religion and belief and equality between men and women.[367] Noting that "freedom of religion or belief protects 'believers rather than beliefs',," Bielefeldt warns that state protection or enforcement of "the doctrinal and normative contents of one particular religion as such ... will almost inevitably lead to discrimination against adherents of other religions or beliefs, which would be unacceptable from a human rights perspective."[368] The broad pronouncement that "as a human right, freedom of religion or belief can never serve as a justification for violations of the human rights of women and girls"[369] begs the question of just what those rights are. The observation that "[i]ntegrating a gender perspective into programmes designed for protecting and promoting freedom of religion or belief is a requirement that ultimately follows from the universalistic spirit of human rights"[370] seems to prioritize women's rights automatically over religion, a conclusion not easily justified in light of the general possibility of limiting rights in order to protect the rights of others. Bielefeldt's report does emphasize the need to analyze perceived conflicts between religion and equality with as much precision as possible, suggesting that there can be different responses in different situations. For example, there is no suggestion that segregation of the sexes within the context of religious rituals violates international human rights norms, although it certainly contradicts the principle of equality. The extent of government interference with religious preferences also may be less acceptable with respect to adults, as opposed to children, whose welfare was at issue in the cases cited above.

A related question that has not yet been adequately addressed by human rights bodies is whether equality considerations should always outweigh religious or cultural values sincerely held by minority communities within a state, whose rights are articulated in article 27 of the CP Covenant, UN declarations on minority[371] and indigenous rights,[372] and the European Framework Convention on Minorities.[373] In Europe, at least, the soft law standard is clear:

> Member States should ensure equality between women and men in culturally diverse societies and the systematic integration of the gender equality dimension in the framework of securing human rights and fundamental freedoms. Gender equality should be ensured regardless of traditional or cultural attitudes.[374]

Whether this standard requires the state to *compel* minority communities to alter their attitudes toward women, as opposed to encouraging them to do so, seems open to debate.

In sum, even the relatively straightforward norm that women should not be subject to discrimination, as defined in CEDAW is not as clear as it appears to be, although progress toward that goal has been considerable and is continuing. As the accompanying norm of equality takes shape in widely different social contexts, however, we should not expect that this malleable term will lead to the same results everywhere, as women and men within societies determine, paradoxically on the basis of equality, just what that entails. These issues are explored more fully in Chapter 7, in the discussion of the flexibility of human rights.

SEX

It is doubtful that many people imagined during the drafting of human rights instruments in the 1940–1960s that they encompassed persons other than men and women who might want to marry or who engaged in heterosexual sex. Nonetheless, human rights bodies have given a broad interpretation to the prohibition against discrimination based on sex, often in conjunction with the right to privacy that is also included in most human rights texts.

Beginning with the landmark 1981 case of *Dudgeon v. U.K.*,[375] the European Court of Human Rights has consistently held that the right of adults to engage in consensual sexual activity is protected by their right of privacy, even where, as in *Dudgeon*, there is "a strong body of opposition stemming from a genuine and sincere conviction shared by a large number of responsible members of the ... community" against the legalization of such conduct.[376] The court has upheld prohibitions against sex with minors, but only where there is no distinction drawn based on either homosexual versus heterosexual behavior or women and men.[377] The court also has upheld the rights of transsexuals to change their names and identification to correspond to their "new" or appropriate sex.[378]

The Inter-American Court of Human Rights did not rule until 2012, in a case that concerned denying a lesbian custody over her children based on her sexual orientation, that discrimination against homosexuals violated the American Convention on Human Rights prohibition against sex discrimination.[379] Prior to this judgment, the Inter-American Commission on Human Rights in 2011 had decided "to give special thematic emphasis to the rights of lesbian, gay, bisexual, trans and intersex persons," and the commission subsequently appointed one of its members to be a rapporteur on the topic.[380]

Many African governments remain generally hostile to LGBT rights, and an estimated two-thirds of them still criminalize homosexual acts. In 2014, the African Commission on Human and People's Rights adopted its first resolution on the topic, although its scope was limited to "Protection against Violence and other Human Rights Violations against Persons on the basis of their real or imputed Sexual Orientation or Gender Identity."[381] The resolution makes no reference to the jurisprudence of the European, inter-American, or UN human rights regimes, although the commission frequently includes such references in its opinions on communications submitted to it alleging human rights violations.

The situation in Asia with respect to sexual orientation has been described as "broadly negative and repressive, although developments are complex and mixed."[382] Informally, many Asian societies tolerate a wide range of sexual behavior and do not overtly discriminate against individuals based on their sexual orientation. However, during drafting of the ASEAN Human Rights Declaration, Malaysia, Brunei, and Singapore strongly objected to any reference to rights of sexual orientation or gender identity.[383] Similarly, the 2004 Arab Charter on Human Rights, adopted in 2004, prohibits discrimination in general but does not mention sexual orientation or refer to "other status," the phrase found in most other human rights instruments.

UN human rights treaty bodies and other mechanisms have followed the European approach of including discrimination based on sexual orientation within the general prohibition of discrimination based on sex and/or protected under the right to privacy. More than two decades ago, in a communication concerning Australia, the Human Rights Committee declared that "it is undisputed that adult consensual sexual activity in private is covered by the concept of 'privacy'" and concluded that "the provisions [of the challenged law] do not meet the 'reasonableness' test in the circumstances of the case, and that they arbitrarily interfere with [the applicant's] right ..."[384] The Australian government did not contest this conclusion nor did it defend the Tasmanian law at issue, since consensual homosexual behavior was at the time permitted in the rest of Australia.

It is not surprising that, given the wide variations in law, practice, and opinion among countries on these issues, the intergovernmental organs of the United Nations (as opposed to the human rights bodies composed of individual experts rather than diplomats) have preferred to avoid rather than confront them. The Security Council mentioned sexual orientation for the first time only in 2016, when its members "condemned in the strongest terms the terrorist attack in Orlando, Florida, on 12 June 2016, targeting persons as a result of their sexual orientation, during which 49 people were killed and 53 injured."[385]

While there have been frequent references to discrimination based on sexual orientation during the Human Rights Council's debates and its Universal Periodic Review of individual countries, the council did not adopt a resolution directly on the subject until 2011.[386] Again, the focus was narrow, and the short resolution expressed "grave concern at acts of violence and discrimination, in all regions of the world, committed against individuals because of their sexual orientation and gender identity."[387] The resolution merely requested that the High Commissioner for Human Rights undertake a study of the issue and that a panel discussion be convened subsequently "to have constructive, informed and transparent dialogue on the issue of discriminatory laws and practices and acts of violence against individuals based on their sexual orientation and gender identity."[388] Nonetheless, the resolution was controversial and was adopted by a narrow vote of 23 to 19, with five countries abstaining or not voting. Most of the opponents were from African and Asian countries, many of them Muslim, and the Organization of Islamic Cooperation, the Arab Group, and a majority of the African Group opposed any mention of the "controversial notion of sexual orientation."[389]

As noted in Chapter 5, a special rapporteur on sexual orientation and gender identity was appointed by the council in 2017, again by a deeply divided vote, with a plurality of 23 votes out of the 47 council members. All EU and Latin American members of the council voted in favor; all Arab and African countries voted against or abstained; and all Muslim countries (except Albania), China, and Russia voted against. The opponents even took the unusual step of attempting to overturn the decision in the UN General Assembly, although this ultimately failed.[390] While some of the opposition appeared to stem from resentment at the heavy-handed tactics of the American and British delegations, there is no doubt that the votes also reflected substantive disagreements.

A major barrier against widespread acceptance of LGBT rights is the fact that the two largest religions in the world, Islam and Catholicism, condemn homosexuality as sinful, although there is no way of knowing how many believers agree with this formal position. With respectively 1.8 billion and 1.3 billion adherents, roughly 40% of the world's population,[391] governments that reflect these beliefs are understandably loath to oppose what they believe to be the wishes of their constituents. However, these beliefs do not mean that there cannot be a universal legal right to engage in same-sex sexual activity without being attacked, imprisoned, or discriminated against. Recent comments by Pope Francis welcoming homosexuals into the church also may indicate that even long-held doctrines are shifting.[392]

Being accused of committing a sin or acting unethically is entirely different from being legally required or prohibited from engaging in certain conduct. Laws frequently stem from and reflect moral values, but attempting to align a state's laws with exclusively one religion or belief (including secularism) will inevitably clash with a government's obligation to guarantee the rights of *all* its citizens and residents, not just most of them.

A comprehensive analysis by Nottingham law professor Dominic McGoldrick of international legal developments with respect to sexual orientation perceptively observes:

> Supporters of the prohibition on ... discrimination [based on sexual orientation] have sought to subsume it within established human rights—such as non-discrimination, privacy, family, expression and association—and within established human rights procedures and institutions. Opponents of the prohibition have, to various degrees, rejected these arguments. They see the prohibition as a 'new' additional right to which they have not and are not going to consent. Approached from a positivist perspective, State practice appears to reveal fundamental divisions on this issue ...
>
> [T]he variations in State practice are such that there is no credible argument for such an existing prohibition as a matter of general or universal customary international law. There is either no customary rule or there are a very large number of persistent objectors ...
>
> The widespread and significant opposition from States ... has created a situation in which there is a very serious tension between what is asserted to be clear international human rights law and what are clearly the practices of a large number of States from all regions of the world and marked regional differences.[393]

If discrimination based on sexual orientation itself remains an issue – although it should be remembered that a state violates its human rights obligations if it does not adequately protect individuals, including LGBT persons, from threats and violence against them – what about the more difficult question of same-sex marriage?

Until 2017, no international human rights body had specifically declared that same-sex marriage was a human right. Most of them rely on the references to "the right of men and women" to marry that appear in various treaties and interpret that phrase as meaning the right of marriage "between a man and a woman."[394] In the case of Europe, the ECtHR has not found a common European standard on marriage, unlike its reliance in *Dudgeon* on the fact that the rest of Europe and the UK had decriminalized homosexual behavior. However, the court recently held that it was a violation of the convention not to provide for some kind of legally recognized partnership for same-sex couples, although not necessarily marriage.[395]

In 2017, the Inter-American Court delivered an advisory opinion that broke new ground, no doubt reflecting the legalization of same-sex marriage in a number of Latin American countries and the United States in the preceding decade.

> ... [T]he presumed lack of consensus within some countries regarding full respect for the rights of sexual minorities cannot be considered a valid argument to deny or restrict their human rights or to reproduce and perpetuate the historical and structural discrimination that such minorities have suffered.
>
> The establishment of a differentiated treatment between heterosexual couples and couples of the same sex regarding the way in which they can form a family – either by a de facto marital union or a civil marriage – does not pass the strict test of equality because, in the Court's opinion, there is no purpose acceptable under the Convention for which this distinction could be considered necessary or proportionate ...
>
> [T]he evolution of marriage evidences that its current form responds to the existence of complex interactions of, inter alia, cultural, religious, sociological, economic, ideological and linguistic aspects. The Court also notes that, at times, the opposition to the marriage of same-sex couples is based on philosophical or religious convictions. The Court recognizes the important role that such convictions play in the life and dignity of those who profess them. Nevertheless, these convictions cannot be used as a parameter of conventionality because the Court could not use them as an interpretative guide when determining the rights of [a] human being. In that sense ... such convictions cannot condition what the Convention establishes in relation to discrimination based on sexual orientation. As such, in democratic societies there must exist a peaceful coexistence between the secular and the religious spheres, implying therefore that the role of the States and of this Court is to recognize the sphere inhabited by each of them, and never force one into the sphere of the other.[396]

Since the advisory opinion is technically not binding even on the countries that have accepted the court's jurisdiction, it remains an open question whether the opinion will be widely or quickly embraced. However, the court is certainly likely to maintain its position when challenges to the prohibition of same-sex marriage are raised in individual cases presented to the court in the future.

We should also be careful of overly generalizing when discussing regional or even religious tendencies. For example, according to the International Lesbian, Gay, Bisexual, Trans, and Intersex Association (ILGA), same-sex sexual acts are legal in 124 countries, including 22 in Africa and 19 in Asia.[397] Approximately 20 Muslim majority countries have legalized homosexuality.[398] Iran legally tolerates transexuality but outlaws homosexuality.[399] Latin American countries, most of whose populations are Catholic, have generally been supportive of LGBT rights in UN human rights forums. Nonetheless, the differences between pro-LGBT advocacy in Europe and the Americas and anti-LGBT attitudes in Africa, Arab countries, and much of Asia are striking, and they reinforce the long-standing (although often hypocritical) argument that human rights are nothing more than an attempt to impose "Western" norms on the rest of the world.

A related problem is the tendency by some LGBT activists to encompass much more in their advocacy than nondiscrimination. For example, Andrew Sullivan, a well-known, openly gay, conservative political commentator, complains that

> no one seems to notice the profound shift in the tone and substance of advocacy for gay equality in recent years, and the radicalization of the movement's ideology and rhetoric . . .
>
> The movement is now rhetorically as much about race and gender as it is about sexual orientation ("intersectionality"), prefers alternatives to marriage to marriage equality, sees white men as "problematic," masculinity as toxic, gender as fluid, and race as fundamental . . . Above all, they have advocated transgenderism, an ideology that goes far beyond recognizing the dignity and humanity and civil equality of trans people into a critique of gender, masculinity, femininity, and heterosexuality . . .[400]

Unfortunately, increased attention also seems to have led to increased risks for LGBT people in many countries, rather than their protection. According to Amnesty International, "Many of the recent advances made by brave activists are now under threat . . . At the highest levels, some governments are listening to [well-funded, organized interest groups, including powerful religious institutions] . . . and questioning sexual and reproductive rights and gender equality . . ."[401] Deutsche Welle observed in 2016, "Across Africa, LGBT people are increasingly afraid of violence, persecution and discrimination."[402] In 2017, the president of Gambia publicly threatened to "slit the throats" of gay people.[403] In early 2018, Human Rights Watch commented, "Looking back over a tumultuous year, for lesbian, gay, bisexual and transgender (LGBT) people in many parts of the world, 2017 was grim by any standard."[404] Of course, there are other perspectives, and a contrasting summary of 2017 in an online LGBT news site opined that, "in many ways 2017 was a banner year for LGBT progress," particularly with respect to same-sex marriage.[405] As of early 2018, roughly 70 countries still criminalize same-sex sexual activity between consenting adults, while approximately two dozen are at the opposite extreme and now recognize same-sex marriage.

Governments frequently react with repression to unwanted assertions of rights, particularly when they come from marginalized groups within society. NGOs and activists cannot be blamed for such reactions, but it is at least worth considering whether the extremely vocal espousal of LGBT rights by the United States (at least until the advent of President Trump), the United Kingdom, and other governments

has unintentionally fanned the flames of prejudice, rather than encouraging tolerance and acceptance through quieter or more subtle means. *The Economist*
observes, for instance, that "the rise of Islamic fundamentalism in the 1980s coincided with that of the gay-rights movement in America and Europe, hardening
cultural differences. Once homosexuality had become associated with the West,
politicians were able to manipulate anti-LGBT feelings for their personal gain."[406]
The primary goal of human rights advocacy should be to protect all individuals, no
matter what their sexual orientation, in the real world, not simply to support one's
own sincere convictions or seek broad social change in very different societies
through the narrow lens of human rights law.

GENDER

Then there is the question of gender.

> The word *gender* has been used since the fourteenth century as a grammatical term,
> referring to classes of noun designated as masculine, feminine, or neuter in
> some languages. The sense denoting biological sex has also been used since the
> fourteenth century, but this did not become common until the mid twentieth
> century. Although the words gender and sex are often used interchangeably, they
> have slightly different connotations; sex tends to refer to biological differences,
> while gender more often refers to cultural and social differences and sometimes
> encompasses a broader range of identities than the binary of male and female.[407]

Gender has been used by feminists and others for decades to describe a socially
constructed sense of what is "male" and what is "female"; because it was constructed, it also could be deconstructed, as a means to overcome gender stereotypes
and patriarchy.

In her groundbreaking 1970 book, *Sexual Politics*, Kate Millet quotes UCLA
psychiatry professor Robert J. Stoller, who observes that, "while *sex* and *gender* seem
to common sense inextricably bound together, one purpose of this study will be to
confirm the fact that the two realms (sex and gender) are not inevitably bound in
anything like a one-to-one relationship, but each may go into quite independent
ways."[408]

Today, concerns about gender have morphed into concerns about "gender
identity." The latter appears to be infinitely fluid, and, unlike gender, it is no longer
socially constructed. Instead, it is now often presented as innate, something to be
discovered rather than created. This shift has caused considerable confusion in
understanding what "gender" is or implies, and the term remains highly contested
both in its meaning and its implications.

> ... [I]n recent years "gender identity" has come to mean how people feel or present
> themselves, as distinct from biological sex or sexual orientation. Growing numbers
> of young people describe themselves as 'non-binary'. Others say gender is a

spectrum, or that they have no gender at all. Facebook offers users a list of over 70 gender identities, from "agender" to "two-spirit", as well as the option to write in their own . . .

[T]ransgender identities raise more general questions, and not only for those cultural conservatives who regard them as transgressing the natural, perhaps God-given, order. There is a tension between believing that it is possible to feel, act or look so much "like a woman" that you should be acknowledged as one, and believing, as feminists do, that a woman can act in any way she wishes without casting doubt on her womanhood.[409]

The Lesbian, Gay, Bisexual, Transgender, Queer, Intersex, Asexual Resource Center at the University of California, Davis, states that the terms and definitions in its online glossary (which range from "ability" and "ableism" to "Ursula" and "womyn/womxn") "are always evolving and changing and often mean different things to different people. They are . . . a starting point for discussion and understanding."[410]

Perhaps the broadest definition of gender identity is found in the Yogyakarta Principles on sexual orientation, which were proclaimed in 2006 by a group of approximately 30 individual experts. Gender identity is defined as referring "to each person's deeply felt internal and individual experience of gender, which may or may not correspond with the sex assigned at birth, including the personal sense of the body (which may involve, if freely chosen, modification of bodily appearance or function by medical, surgical or other means) and other expressions of gender, including dress, speech and mannerisms."[411] A decade later, the principles were expanded to include categories of "gender expression" and "sex characteristics."[412] While the principles have not been adopted by any intergovernmental body, they have been referred to by, for example, the Inter-American Court of Human Rights in its 2017 advisory opinion on gender identity.[413]

The second Yogyakarta document describes itself as "*an affirmation of existing international legal standards* as they apply to all persons on grounds of their sexual orientation, gender identity, gender expression and sex characteristics. States must comply with these principles both as a legal obligation and as an aspect of their commitment to universal human rights."[414] As cogently demonstrated by McGoldrick's analysis above, this is simply not true or, at best, is highly debatable. While many of the Yogyakarta Principles are concerned with protecting individuals from violence, criminalization, and discrimination in exercising their rights, protections that are certainly included within existing international human rights norms, other provisions go much further. Examples of the latter include the right to recognition and to change "gendered information" in official documents[415]; "the right to protection from all forms of poverty and social exclusion associated with sexual orientation, gender identity, gender expression and sex characteristics;"[416] and a state obligation to provide "gender affirming healthcare."[417]

Given the relevantly recent appearance of the concept of gender identity, distinct from the constructed concept of gender as articulated by feminists since the 1960s, it is not surprising that many countries claim vociferously that there is no such thing. Recalling the discussion in Chapter 5, protecting and recognizing gender identity in the terms found in the Yogyakarta Principles and elsewhere seem to go well beyond interpretation and into the realm of creation. This statement does not imply that "each person's deeply felt internal and individual experience of gender" is not protected by freedom of conscience and belief, the right to privacy, and the prohibition of discrimination based on this feeling, as well as being encompassed within the government's obligation to protect everyone against threats, violence, or discrimination. However, it would be mistaken to assume that the extent and relevance of this identity is automatically congruent with human rights provisions relating to women and "sex." If we are to respect the principle of universality in a meaningful way, as argued in Chapter 7, we cannot simply dismiss the consistently expressed opposition of countries when they believe that rights are being unjustifiably expanded or created.

CONCLUDING REMARKS

As indicated at the beginning of this chapter, no area of human rights (with the possible exception of religion) is more contested than that relating to the rights of women and the wider issues of sexual orientation and gender identity. The reason cannot be simply because discrimination based on these categories has been pervasive in most societies for most of their history; the same could be said about the use of torture, racial and religious discrimination, or the nonrecognition by governments of any obligation to ensure economic, social, and cultural rights. The often fierce opposition from major religious groups is certainly significant, but there are differences of opinion between liberal and conservative factions within religious institutions and among believers.

One plausible difference between "sex rights," if I may call them that, and most of the other rights in the international human rights panoply is that sex intrudes much more deeply into the intimate and private lives of individuals in a way that fair trials, freedom of association, and the right to education simply do not. The traditional and usually conservative moral beliefs of many societies are an additional impediment to the recognition that sex and gender are personal, malleable, and fall largely fall within an individual's right to privacy.

The recognition of LGBT rights has increased dramatically in the relatively recent past, but significant differences in state practice remain. For example, "Council of Europe standards and mechanisms seek to promote and ensure respect for the human rights of every individual ... including lesbian, gay, bisexual and transgender (LGBT) persons."[418] Since 1998, all schools in Sweden have been required to work against gender stereotypes.[419] Belgium and France have laws against sexism or verbal sexual harassment in public places, which have already led to convictions for abuse of a female police officer and a woman on a bus.[420]

On the other hand, while the Heads of State of the African Union adopted a Declaration on Gender Equality in Africa in 2004, its terms refer only to women, not to sexual orientation or gender identity.[421] A decade later, as noted above, the African Commission on Human and Peoples' Rights adopted a broader resolution that condemned violence committed against people based on "their real or imputed sexual orientation or gender identity" but not calling directly for the recognition of gender identity or legalization of same-sex conduct.[422]

One option in the face of such disagreement is simply to quarantine the issue and agree to disagree about everything having to do with sex. This would be unhelpful, given the constant and natural evolution of human rights protections, and it would unjustifiably ignore a fundamental provision on nondiscrimination that has been consistently proclaimed since 1945. Another option is to accept that there are regional or country-specific variations in states' interpretation of the prohibition against discrimination on the basis of "sex" that appears in global instruments, such as the two UN covenants. A third option is to attempt to distinguish, at least for the purpose of informed activism, between the rights on which there is substantial consensus in theory, if not always in practice, and possibly emerging rights on which countries remain in clear conflict.

This last approach could confidently assert that prohibition of discrimination on the basis of sex is prohibited under international human rights law, subject to the same possibility that exists with respect to most other rights of being restricted for specific reasons, including the rights of others, that are spelled out in treaties. Vague assertions of conflict with religious laws or community morals are insufficient to limit this fundamental principle of nondiscrimination, particularly when considered in conjunction with the right to private life, and it must be a touchstone for advocacy efforts.

The Human Rights Committee and human rights institutions in Europe and the Americas have consistently protected at least three distinct groups (although there may be some overlap) – women, persons with non-heterosexual sexual orientations, and transsexuals – against discrimination and invasions of their privacy. This provides a basis for continuing to push countries within these regions to include protection and recognition for people in these categories, including, for example, the right to marry.

Beyond this, universal acceptance of rights for persons of any sexual orientation or gender identity is more problematic. At a minimum, there is explicit recognition in all regions of the world of the right of *all* persons, specifically including those identified by their sexual orientation or gender identity, to be protected by the state from violence and threats of violence. This minimal government obligation must be reasserted and prioritized, even where nontraditional sexual identity and/or relationships are discouraged or even criminalized.

The next step is to work against criminalization of private sexual behavior and legal or public discrimination against individuals based on their sex or gender.

Even this small step goes well beyond the situation in a majority of the countries in the world today, and advocates should not expect that the extensive legal protections that exist in Europe and most highly developed countries will be easily exported to other regions.

The final steps – eliminating stereotypes as mandated by CEDAW, expanding acceptance of those traditionally viewed as different, and altering social expectations so that male and female roles disappear entirely in private life as well as in public – are unlikely to lead every society to view issues of women, sex, and gender identically. As discussed further in the next chapter, the universality of human rights does not require creating uniform societies everywhere, whether we are considering sex, social preferences, family values, economic equity, fair trial procedures, or ethical behavior.

Sex rights are neither more nor less important than other rights, and they cannot be ensured in a vacuum. As education for everyone expands, meaningful economic development occurs, and modernization (not necessarily Westernization) spreads, it is likely that tolerance of diversity within societies will increase. The increasing support for legalization of same-sex marriage is evidence that change has already come to Europe and many countries in the Americas, much more rapidly than most would have imagined.

However, not every community or family will warmly embrace sexual diversity on the personal level, and mandating such acceptance is beyond the reach of mere international law. No law requires parents to embrace their children's choice of career, religion, or partner, and international norms explicitly protect many beliefs that run counter to modern principles of tolerance and inclusion. Human rights activists should not hesitate to advocate new or expanded rights, and they should not be discouraged from seeking social change through activity at the domestic level. At the same time, however, they should be honest enough to admit that not all change can be imposed from above and that universal human rights norms will never reflect everything good that they would like to see in the world.

7

The Flexibility of Human Rights Norms: Universality Is Not Uniformity

Most human rights advocates and governments talk about human rights in summary fashion, referring simply to *freedom of expression* or the *right to housing*. Few human rights are absolute, however, and the drafters of the Universal Declaration of Human Rights and subsequent instruments understood that rights may be legitimately limited by other competing rights or interests. Among the reasons identified in treaties that may justify such limitations are protection of the rights and freedoms of others, public order (*ordre public*), public health, public morality, national security, and the general welfare.

Of course, these terms are frequently advanced by governments to justify violating rights, not simply limiting them, but their mere invocation does not free a state from upholding its human rights obligations. Rights may be limited only if the limitations are necessary (not merely convenient or desirable), imposed by law (not just at the whim or discretion of government officials), and for purposes that are essentially democratic (an authoritarian government cannot limit rights merely to keep itself in power). In addition, human rights treaties subject countries to at least a degree of international oversight, and it is up to these international bodies, not the states themselves, to render a judgment or opinion as to whether a particular limitation is justified and proportionate.

Restrictions on rights imposed in good faith, for legitimate purposes, enable states to adapt universal human rights norms to specific local conditions. Fair trials must be possible under both common law and civil law jurisdictions. Humane prison conditions can vary from country to country, although there may be a universal floor of minimum treatment. Priorities need to be set when fulfilling many economic, social, and cultural rights, as anticipated by the obligation of progressive realization found in the ESC Covenant.

Jack Donnelly, a political scientist who has written frequently and persuasively about the "relative universality" of human rights, adopts a useful three-tiered description to explain what I refer to as the inherent flexibility of human rights.

In Donnelly's analysis, the broadest level is that of the *concept* of human rights, where there is near universal consensus on broad principles such as the liberty and security of person and the right to social security.[423] At the second level, these concepts have multiple and defensible *conceptions* of the rights they articulate, in which factors such as history, *ordre public*, and culture may play a role.[424] The lowest level is that of *implementation*, when specific norms are translated into national law and practice.[425] Donnelly offers as a particularly good example of the implementation phase the myriad forms of electoral systems that have been adopted in order to implement the right "to take part in the government of his country, directly or through freely chosen representatives."[426]

Donnelly's tiered analysis is not precise, and the distinction between concept and conception may beget a certain degree of confusion, if only linguistic. However, the schema accurately portrays in a general sense the way in which international human rights law is translated into practice by states. Thus, universality does not, cannot, and should not be equated with uniformity in a world of diverse societies, differing government structures, and sovereign states.

The Covenant on Economic, Social, and Cultural Rights makes explicit the distinction between acceptance of legally binding international norms and their implementation.[427] Article 2.1 of the covenant provides as follows:

> Each State Party to the present Covenant undertakes *to take steps*, individually and through international assistance and co-operation, especially economic and technical, to the maximum of its available resources, *with a view to achieving progressively* the full realization of the rights recognized in the present Covenant by all appropriate means, including particularly the adoption of legislative measures.[428]

The Optional Protocol to the ESC Covenant, which was adopted only in 2008 and entered into force in 2013, specifically provides that, in its examination of individual communications, the ESC Committee "shall consider the reasonableness of the steps taken by the State Party ... [and] shall bear in mind that the State Party may adopt a range of possible policy measures for the implementation of the rights set forth in the Covenant."[429] In this respect, the obligation on countries is an obligation of result, i.e., to adopt whatever legitimate means that they deem appropriate to achieve the goals set forth in the treaty.

Because of the broad language employed in the ESC Covenant and the progressive nature of implementation, some commentators (particularly in the United States, which has signed but not ratified the treaty) question whether these are rights at all, but this is very much a minority position.[430] The vast majority of countries have ratified both the ESC and CP Covenants; as of March 2018, while approximately two dozen states have ratified neither treaty, only seven (Andorra, Botswana, Brazil, Comoros, Cook Islands, United States, and Vanuatu) had ratified only the CP Covenant and three (China, Congo, and Solomon Islands) had ratified only the ESC Covenant. Of course, many of the rights in the covenants are repeated in the more specific treaties subsequently adopted by the United Nations. For example, every state in the world, except the United States, has ratified the UN Convention on the Rights of the Child, which guarantees to children under the age of 18 freedoms of expression, association, peaceful assembly, thought, conscience, and religion, and the rights to privacy, health, social security, education, an adequate standard living, and participation in cultural and artistic life.

Early in its existence, the ESC Committee noted that, "while the Covenant provides for progressive realization and acknowledges the constraints due to the limits of available resources, it also imposes various obligations which are of immediate effect," among which is the obligation "to take steps."[431] These steps "must be taken within a reasonably short time ... [and] should be deliberate, concrete and targeted as clearly as possible towards meeting the obligations recognized in the Covenant."[432] In addition, states have "a minimum core obligation to ensure the satisfaction of, at the very least, minimum essential levels of each of the rights" in the covenant.[433]

There is no comparable reference to progressive realization in the CP Covenant, and states are "to respect and to ensure" the covenant's rights and "ensure that any person whose rights ... are violated shall have an effective remedy."[434] In practice, however, it is difficult not to conclude that civil and political rights also are implemented flexibly, if not explicitly progressively. For example, article 10's requirement that detainees "shall be treated with humanity and with respect for the inherent dignity of the human person" is likely to be interpreted differently if one is examining prison conditions in Denmark, Brazil, or Chad; the norm is the same, but implementation in such different countries will vary according to both capabilities and differing notions of "dignity." Even given the fairly specific "minimum guarantees" set forth in article 14.2 that apply to anyone charged with a criminal offence, the basic obligation in article 14.1 to ensure "a fair and public hearing by a competent, independent and impartial tribunal" in any civil or criminal proceeding is a relatively broad concept whose precise interpretation and implementation may vary from country to country and as judicial systems within countries develop. The prohibition against "arbitrary or unlawful" interference with one's privacy or reputation in article 17 surely must be balanced by article 19's protection of freedom of expression, and that balance is likely to vary with cultural, social, and political norms. In addition, countries' interpretations of what permissible restrictions might be placed on rights for the purpose of, for example, protecting the rights and freedoms of others or for reasons of public morality, will no doubt vary depending on the specific historical circumstances and socio-cultural values of their societies.

Variation in interpretation and implementation is evident for many rights, perhaps none more so than freedom of expression. As set forth in article 19.2 of the CP Covenant, the right includes "freedom to seek, receive and impart information and ideas of all kinds ..." However, the subsequent paragraph notes that the exercise of the right "carries with it special duties and responsibilities" and that it may be restricted, where necessary, in order to respect the rights or reputations of others, national security, public order (*ordre public*), public health, or public morals.[435]

International human rights bodies recognize flexibility in many ways. For example, the European Court of Human Rights does not act as a "fourth instance" by serving as a de facto appellate court from decisions of national courts applying national law.[436] It also is a fundamental principle of international law, including human rights law, that an alleged victim must have exhausted all domestic remedies before an international body will admit a formal communication or complaint. While the available remedies must be adequate and effective, not illusory or overly prolonged, the purpose is to ensure that the government has the first opportunity to provide a remedy for any human rights violation.[437]

Restrictions on rights justified by public order (*ordre public*) often refer to a state's historical circumstances and cultural, religious, or political foundations. The French phrase *ordre public* has a different connotation from its English equivalent; it refers to the underlying constitutional and political structure of a country, including its history, not just to keeping public order as a matter of policing. This *ordre public* necessarily includes respect for human rights, which makes it a bit tautological, but it allows human rights bodies to recognize the differences among, for example, the secularism of France or pre-Erdogan Turkey, the religious foundations of Israel or Saudi Arabia, or the communist past and current concerns of the Baltic states. This can be significant in determining whether a particular limitation on a right serves a legitimate purpose.

In the jurisprudence of the European Court of Human Rights, the flexible interpretation of rights is often achieved through reference to the "margin of appreciation" that is accorded to states in their interpretation of treaty rights.[438] "By reason of their direct and continuous contact with the vital forces of their countries, state authorities are in principle in a better position than the international judge to give an opinion on the exact content" of human rights, when they determine what limitations are "necessary."[439] This state discretion is not unlimited, and it is accompanied by international supervision, but it correctly reflects the subsidiary role of human rights bodies and the fact that "the initial and primary responsibility for the protection of human rights lies with the contracting parties" to human rights treaties.[440] Proposed Protocol No. 15 to the European Convention on Human Rights, adopted in 2013, adds an explicit reference to the "primary responsibility" of states to secure human rights and affirms that "in doing so they [the states] enjoy a margin of appreciation, subject to the supervisory jurisdiction of the European Court of Human Rights."[441]

Of course, such deference to a government can be dangerous, and it is often difficult to discern the criteria upon which states are determined to have exceeded or acted within their margin of appreciation.[442] Differences of opinion over whether an act falls with the margin of appreciation frequently depend on one's view of the outcome of the case – confirming or rejecting a state's arguments for limiting the exercise of a right – rather than on the application of well-articulated criteria. Nevertheless, some discretion in interpretation and implementation of human rights norms is essential, unless one believes that every right must mean exactly the same thing in every country at all times.

For example, prohibitions on questioning the historical accuracy of the Holocaust (whose primary victims were Jews) before and during World War II have been upheld by international human rights bodies as necessary for the protection of the rights and freedoms of others, on the ground that the particular historical reality of France justifies the equation of Holocaust denial with anti-Semitism and threats to the rights of Jews.[443] However, a number of concurring opinions among members of the HR Committee stressed the potential danger of the impugned law and emphasized the particular facts on which the decision was based. Notwithstanding this opinion, the committee's general comment on freedom of expression more than a decade later seems to repudiate this nuanced view: "Laws that penalize the expression of opinions about historical facts are incompatible with the obligations that the Covenant imposes on States parties in relation to the respect for freedom of opinion and expression."[444]

Similar country-specific deference has been shown by the ECtHR in permitting Turkey to limit the wearing of headscarves[445] and to retain an electoral system that resulted in effectively marginalizing regional parties.[446] The court upheld the controversial ban by France of the public wearing of the niqab or burqa (through a law outlawing face coverings in most circumstances), stating that it "has a duty to exercise a degree of restraint" in assessing "a democratic process within the society in question."[447] It accepted France's argument that the ban served the legitimate goal of ensuring respect for the values of an open and democratic society and "seeking to protect a principle of interaction between individuals . . . essential for the expression of . . . pluralism . . . tolerance . . . [and] broadmindedness . . ."[448]

Similarly, the court allowed Italy to hang crucifixes on the walls of all public school classrooms, finding that the crucifixes were religious symbols but also a tradition that the court should protect.[449] Since the educational atmosphere was open and tolerant, the impact of the crucifixes was not deemed to be significant, even though crucifixes gave "the country's majority religion preponderant visibility in the school environment."[450] Similarly, the court accepted that it was permissible to give Christianity a special place in the Norwegian school curriculum, given Norway's "national history and tradition."[451] However, it found a violation of the convention by a 9–8 vote due to the "not only quantitative but even qualitative differences applied to the teaching of Christianity as compared to that of other religions and philosophies."[452]

Concern for the rights of others was expressed by the court in each of these cases, but the specific circumstances of each state – and the open, democratic manner in which the challenged restrictions had been adopted – led the court to allow the concerned states in most situations their "margin of appreciation" and to recognize the historical realities of each.

In a case concerning the UK about the right of a prisoner to wear a political symbol, which may well have applicability outside Europe, the court continued its relatively permissive approach.

> The Court recognises that in the present case the significance of the Easter lily will be relevant to any assessment of the necessity of the interference. It notes that in Northern Ireland many emblems are not simply an expression of cultural or political identity but are also inextricably linked to the conflict and can be viewed as threatening and/or discriminatory by those of a different cultural, political or religious background. Consequently, the public display of emblems can be inherently divisive and has frequently exacerbated existing tensions in Northern Ireland. Therefore, as cultural and political emblems may have many levels of meaning which can only fully be understood by persons with a full understanding of their historical background, the Court accepts that Contracting States must enjoy a wide margin of appreciation in assessing which emblems could potentially inflame existing tensions if displayed publicly.[453]

A former president of the European Court of Human Rights has observed that "essentially the Convention guarantees are applied in a context defined by the democratic society in which they function. This is just common sense. Human rights cannot be and should not be divorced from the practical day-to-day functioning of society."[454] Domestic laws are frequently founded, if only implicitly, on a society's moral beliefs, and international human rights law permits a great deal of discretion to states in legislating such beliefs. Even in a relatively homogeneous region such as Europe, for example, the European Court of Human Rights has consistently been unable to identify a common European morality.

> [I]t is not possible to find in the legal and social orders of the Contracting States a uniform European conception of morals. The view taken of the requirements of morals varies from time to time and from place to place, especially in our era, characterised as it is by a far-reaching evolution of opinions on the subject. By reason of their direct and continuous contact with the vital forces of their countries, State authorities are in principle in a better position than the international judge to give an opinion on the exact content of these requirements as well as on the "necessity" of a "restriction" or "penalty" intended to meet them.[455]

The recognition of such moral diversity does not imply that any restriction that a state democratically adopts is automatically acceptable, and human rights bodies are often very protective of freedom of expression, in particular. For example, the general comment adopted by the Human Rights Committee in 2011 declares

> Prohibitions of displays of lack of respect for a religion or other belief system, including blasphemy laws, are incompatible with the Covenant, except in the specific circumstances envisaged in article 20, paragraph 2, of the Covenant.

Such prohibitions must also comply with the strict requirements of article 19, paragraph 3, as well as such articles as 2, 5, 17, 18 and 26. Thus, for instance, it would be impermissible for any such laws to discriminate in favour of or against one or certain religions or belief systems, or their adherents over another, or religious believers over non-believers. Nor would it be permissible for such prohibitions to be used to prevent or punish criticism of religious leaders or commentary on religious doctrine and tenets of faith.[456]

For some human rights advocates, even this is not enough. Eschewing relative universality, they implicitly assert that morality should be defined by a country like The Netherlands, fair trial procedures by the convoluted US criminal justice system, social security by France, and women's rights by Iceland or Sweden. In this view, all traditional (and perhaps non-Western) social customs must fall, as exemplified by the fact that the most widely publicized human rights violation under the Taliban in Afghanistan was forcing women to wear the all-covering burqa, rather than the pervasive violation of other rights – despite that fact that many Afghan women hadn't taken off the burqa for centuries. Of course, this is precisely the view that is most widely criticized by governments that claim to represent national "culture" or "values."[457]

A recent, not entirely satisfactory, UN attempt to balance traditional values and human rights concluded somewhat lamely, but perhaps accurately, that "States should respect the cultural diversity and pluralism that exist within communities and societies as a source of enrichment and value added . . . this should not, however, justify any breach of universal human rights and fundamental freedoms."[458]

Societies and cultures are constantly changing, and evolving conditions make resisting any change whatsoever both impossible and undesirable. In particular, outsiders should be allowed to support domestic efforts to foster social change that is consistent with modern values of tolerance and nondiscrimination. However, a focus on what are seen by many cultures as particularly "Western" rights, such as the rejection of gender stereotypes, advocacy of same-sex marriage, or prohibiting corporal punishment for children,[459] may undermine efforts to guarantee or restore equally important rights on which one may be able to find a wider degree of agreement. International human rights law does not lend itself well to the concept of "best practices" that often finds its way into UN documents; even if it did, it is foolish to assume that what is "best" is to be found solely in liberalism or capitalism, as those terms are understood in the United States and much of Europe.

Assailing the Taliban for violating women's rights was accurate and appropriate, but it missed the point – the Taliban regime violated *everyone's* rights. However, activists might have had a better chance of advocating changes that would improve human rights while the Taliban were still in power if their campaigns had not been primarily directed at practices that were grounded in entrenched social customs, no matter how distasteful those customs are to modern liberal societies and even though they violated international norms. Similarly, while the sometimes violent rejection by crowds in Cairo in March 2011 of attempts to raise women's rights issues was reprehensible,[460] there was perhaps some justification for the feeling that the broader goals of regime change and democracy were more important than high-lighting the concerns of any particular subgroup of the population, no matter how large or how well-founded its complaints.

Even legitimate complaints about rights violations may be lost if the context is muddied. For example, members of the Russian punk protest group Pussy Riot, who were sentenced to several years' imprisonment for interrupting a religious service to protest Russian government policies, were certainly victims, but they were hardly human rights heroes or defenders. Performance art is certainly protected under the guarantee of freedom of expression, even when it deliberately offends political or cultural sensitivities, but interfering with the rights of others under the guise of free expression can be legitimately restricted. It was the excessive sentence of the group that violated human rights norms, not the refusal to allow them to violate the equally legitimate rights of the Russian Orthodox clergy and parishioners in the church.

The New York Times claimed that the imprisonment of Pussy Riot's members "elevated their stature into global symbols of human rights and freedom in Russia,"[461] and the Boston Globe enthused that Pussy Riot had become "synonym-ous with a new style of activism, one that knew no boundaries and traveled at the speed of social media."[462] One wonders how this star-struck glamorization of the group resonated with ordinary Russians suffering from daily rights violations that are far removed from excessive punishments for punk artists.

The result of such overly enthusiastic endorsement by primarily young Western advocates is often to stoke the fires of nationalism and parochialism, for it is easy (and convenient) for populists to contrast such irreverent fervor for snubbing one's nose at authority with the often religious and usually conservative tendencies of those elements of society to which the populists are trying to appeal. If human rights are too often dressed in the clothing of celebrities or breathless campaigns to raise money or join the "movement," there is a real chance that the seemingly drab reality of international human rights law and norms will be too easy to ignore.

For example, an unidentified Amnesty International staff member who disagreed with the organization's plans to decentralize in the early 2010s observed, "But it's more than that. They [AI's senior management] seem to be moving Amnesty into campaigning mode with big stunts and branding exercises designed to boost mem-bership – at the expense of the detailed research on which our credibility depends. We will launch a campaign on Pussy Riot because it's fashionable, chasing the energy, lurching from one issue to the next."[463] While celebrities and the causes that they support are often sincere and well-meaning, what happens if a cause can't attract one?[464] A recent analysis of the activities of US actor Ben Affleck in the Democratic Republic of Congo concluded that "however well-intentioned this A-list entertain-ment professional may be, the conclusion is that Affleck's human rights advocacy for Congo holds the promise of an alternative narrative for a neglected issue area, but, in the process, celebrity engagement outweighs the prospects for increasing the power, influence, and voice of the Congolese people."[465]

Shorthand references to rights and rights violations also frequently ignore the content of the obligations that states have actually assumed. For example, over 40% of the 189 parties to the Convention on the Elimination of All Forms of Discrimination against Women (CEDAW) have filed reservations or declarations that qualify their acceptance of particular provisions. While it may be surprising that Saudi Arabia has ratified CEDAW, for example, it has done so with a telling reservation that limits its acceptance of the convention's provisions to those that do not contradict "the norms of Islamic law."[466] Other states have objected to this reservation on the grounds that it is incompatible with the object and purpose of the convention and should therefore be ignored,[467] but it is no doubt an accurate reflection of just how far Saudi Arabia is willing to go to comply with international norms. No state has refused to treat Saudi Arabia as a party to the treaty, despite the arguably impermissible Saudi reservation. This and similar reservations have not prevented Muslim countries from improving women's status and equality, albeit unevenly and sometimes almost imperceptibly, but neither do they represent a sincere legal commitment to conceptions of gender equality as they are generally perceived in Western societies.

A variation on this theme is the domestic debate over multiculturalism that is now occurring within many societies and that is a shared concern within Western states (over the political and cultural influence of Islam) and within many Muslim and developing countries (over the political and cultural influence of the West and, to a lesser extent, Christianity). It has been said many times that human rights are, in their essence, about protecting the rights of minorities, since majorities can protect themselves through political processes. Freedoms of thought, religion, association, and expression implicitly reject the possibility of forced assimilation or, indeed, any campaign by a government (whether chosen democratically or not) to impose a monolithic cultural or spiritual pattern on those under its jurisdiction. At the same time, minorities cannot demand that every aspect of their culture or every belief that they hold must be tolerated by the majority, even if, at the very least, human rights norms set a floor of rights that governments representing the majority not only may but must protect.

This is not the place for a detailed discussion of minority–majority relations, legally or politically. It suffices to say that neither has unlimited authority to impose its beliefs, social practices, or morality on the other. But if this is true within countries, then surely some of this same tolerance for cultures or beliefs with which we disagree must extend to the international level of human rights interpretation, as well.

This observation returns us to a fundamental principle of international law alluded to in Chapter 1: no state may be bound to an international legal norm without its consent. There are a few exceptions to this rule, as in cases where a specific norm is peremptory (*jus cogens*) and therefore deemed by the international community to bind every state, even if it has not explicitly consented to being bound. In the realm of human rights, such a rule may extend to the commission of international crimes, when they involve government authority, such as genocide, war crimes, crimes against humanity, and torture. (As discussed in Chapter 2, government involvement is not necessary for individual criminal responsibility to attach to these crimes, but a direct or indirect government nexus is required for human rights norms to be engaged.)

Customary international law is binding on states if they do not explicitly object to it when it is in the process of being formulated; if a country does object, it is known as a *persistent objector*. Today, a conservative reading of customary international law in the area of human rights would include prohibitions against slavery; institutional racial discrimination, as exemplified by apartheid; indefinite arbitrary detention; murder or causing the disappearance of individuals; and torture; and the right to recognition as a person before the law.[468] It also might include some elements of economic, social, and cultural rights, subject to resource constraints, such as the right to free primary education and the obligation, when resources are clearly available, to provide a minimum core of other socio-economic rights, such as the rights to health, housing, food, culture, and an adequate standard of living.

Discussions of custom and *jus cogens* are hardly necessary today, given the thousands of ratifications to global and regional human rights treaties. The issue is whether a state may undermine the essential character of an international norm through a reservation to a treaty, as exemplified by the general reference to Islamic norms in the Saudi reservation to CEDAW, quoted above. The legal answer is no, since a reservation may not be contrary to the "object and purpose" of a treaty, but this does not mean that reservations cannot ever limit a state's obligations; indeed, that is their very purpose.

The deliberate flexibility contained within formulations of international norms does not excuse blatant or politically motivated discrimination, but it does permit differing definitions of morality and political priorities to guide a government. Sexual mores are different in Sweden than in rural areas of the United States; the social roles of women are different in Morocco and Japan than in Germany and France; the preference for consensus over confrontation is stronger in Cambodia than in the United Kingdom. In each of these countries, cultural norms are changing, and human rights norms mandate that those within each society be free to argue for or against such change. However, advocates should bear in mind that there is a difference between social pressure and law, and human rights as articulated since 1948 are concerned primarily with the latter. They are not intended to create a single social and moral order throughout the globe, unless by that single moral order we mean respect for the indefinable concept of human dignity[469] or the somewhat more manageable commitment to nondiscrimination and equal treatment.

France and many other European countries allow women to go topless on beaches. Germany bans Nazi salutes, even by tourists who may have no idea that the gesture is not just offensive, but illegal. In Myanmar, individuals have been charged with the crime of insulting Buddhism for using a depiction of Buddha wearing headphones to promote their business. Insulting the monarchy is a crime in a number of countries, including Spain and Thailand; the European Court of Human Rights has upheld such laws in theory,[470] while the UN Human Rights Committee has criticized them in its general comment on freedom of expression.[471] The European Court has upheld requiring Sikhs to remove their turbans for identity photos,[472] while the UN HR Committee reached exactly the opposite conclusion[473] and has explicitly rejected the concept of margin of appreciation.[474]

Article 20 of the CP Covenant prohibits "[a]ny advocacy of national, racial or religious hatred that constitutes incitement to discrimination, hostility or violence." Most countries do not find this limitation problematic, and criminal sanctions against so-called hate speech are not uncommon. Even here, however, there will be different interpretations in different countries of what restrictions may be appropriate. The United States, for example, entered a reservation to its ratification of the covenant stating that article 20 cannot justify any act "that would restrict the right of free speech and association protected by the Constitution and laws of the United States."

There can be no doubt that publication of cartoons of the Prophet Mohammed in various European newspapers in 2006 offended most, perhaps all, Muslims, for whom even the depiction of Mohammed is unacceptable. The outrage was compounded by the fact that many of the cartoons were disrespectful or satirical; perhaps the most infamous is one that pictured Mohammed wearing a bomb as a turban.

Denmark (where the cartoons were first published) and many other countries apologized for the insult caused by the cartoons, but they also vigorously defended the right of journalists in a free society to publish them, no matter how upsetting. The reaction among Muslims varied greatly; Western embassies were attacked, violent protests killed dozens, and a rally of children reportedly organized by the largest Islamic group in Pakistan chanted, "Hang those who insulted the prophet!" and burned a coffin draped in American, Israeli, and Danish flags.[475] The South China Morning Post reported that Malaysia's de facto law minister threatened criminal prosecution for any non-Muslim who insults Islam, although his suggestion was criticized by the daughter of long-time Malaysian premier Mahathir Mohamad, who complained that soon no one other than Muslim men with religious backgrounds would be allowed to speak about Islam.[476] Other individual Muslims and Muslim organizations called for restraint and nonviolence, although condemnation of the cartoons' publication was universal.

Similarly, when eleven people in the office of the satirical and provocative French magazine *Charlie Hébdo* were attacked and killed in January 2015 by gunmen who professed to be offended by the magazine's cartoons of Mohammed, the world rightly rallied around the right of *Charlie Hébdo* to publish the offensive material.[477] However, defense of the magazine was complicated by the fact that, while Christian and Muslim religious figures were rhetorically insulted by the magazine on a fairly regular basis, there were few similar attacks on Jews or Judaism. The explanation is simple: France has laws specifically prohibiting hate speech and anti-Semitism,[478] pursuant to article 20 of the Covenant on Civil and Political Rights.[479]

What guidance does human rights law offer us in these situations? Should freedom of expression always trump religious sensibilities? Does respect for the principle of freedom of religion require that religions be protected from any criticism, even by nonbelievers? Does public criticism or rejection of the religious beliefs of a particular group automatically constitute "incitement to discrimination, hostility or violence," which is prohibited under international law? Should publication of an offensive article or cartoon be prohibited, solely on the grounds that those who are offended threaten violence?

Let us first separate two different aspects of the controversy. One argument against the insulting cartoons is that, because depiction of Mohammed is prohibited under the tenets of Islam and harms Muslim sensibilities everywhere, such depiction should be illegal everywhere in the world. On its face, this proposition is ludicrous, just as extending the Jewish prohibition against eating pork to non-Jews or extending the Catholic prohibition on abortion to all people is unacceptable. If religious tolerance means anything, it surely means that it is wrong to impose one's own religious beliefs on others, no matter how strongly felt.

The second aspect of the controversy – that publication of the cartoons constitutes an incitement to religious hatred and should therefore be punished – deserves to be taken more seriously. As many Muslim commentators have noted, anti-Semitic speech is punishable in many European countries, and the United Kingdom retains laws against blasphemy against the Church of England. A British historian was sentenced in Austria to three years' imprisonment for denying the existence of the Holocaust. In France, the Catholic church succeeded in obtaining an injunction against a fashion ad campaign that parodied Christ's Last Supper. In the 1990s, the European Court of Human Rights upheld a ban on screening a film in Austria that was deemed offensive to Catholics, as a reasonable exercise of the state's power to limit rights in order to protect the rights and freedoms of others.[480]

Is this evidence of a double standard, in which Islam is treated with less respect in Europe than Christianity or Judaism? Perhaps, but one finds a parallel double standard in Muslim countries, where anti-Semitic expressions are frequent, even in government-controlled publications. Does this entire controversy undermine the claim that human rights norms are universal?

In short, not really, so long as one accepts the principle of flexibility that is advocated in this chapter. Of course, discretion is open to abuse, and one of the primary tasks of human rights lawyers and institutions is to look behind the rhetoric of those governments that seek to mask intolerance and despotism behind a veil of cultural values or religious purity. While many people would prefer an open climate in which criticism of all beliefs is permitted, we must recognize that what is acceptable free expression in one country may be unacceptable provocation in another. This should come as no surprise; even within the United States, for example, standards of what constitutes obscenity are based on "contemporary community standards," not on a single national norm.[481]

What cannot be defended is the suppression of all dissent and criticism on the vague grounds of promoting solidarity, ensuring communal peace, or combating terrorism – history has shown us that blasphemy, lèse majesté, and sedition laws have been used much more often to suppress legitimate dissent than to prevent the outbreak of communal or other violence.

REGIONAL VARIATIONS

International lawyers frequently express concern about the fragmentation of international law, now that so many international legal regimes operate at the same time, including the potential overlaps between human rights law and criminal, humanitarian, trade, and finance law. Fragmentation also would seem to be inimical to one of the fundamental principles of human rights, their universality. Nonetheless, regional norms and institutions have multiplied, and this book has already offered examples of instances where interpretations of human rights norms differ between global/UN institutions and regional bodies.

The three regional human rights regimes in Europe, the Americas, and Africa have adopted somewhat different approaches to both the substantive law of human rights and its implementation, although none is widely divergent from the others or from global human rights norms.[482] Each system began in a similar manner, based on a treaty that provided purely optional mechanisms to permit individual complaints against states and/or the possibility of accepting the jurisdiction of a court whose judgments would be legally binding. Today, acceptance of the legally binding authority of the European Court of Human Rights is mandatory for all 47 members of the Council of Europe, and states generally (though not always) comply with the court's decisions in good faith. The comparable (but still optional) jurisdiction of the Inter-American Court of Human Rights has been accepted by 20 members of the Organization of American States.[483] Thirty states have accepted the jurisdiction of the African Court of Human Rights, which has been in operation only since 2006, although only eight have accepted the optional jurisdiction of the court to receive complaints from individuals and NGOs.

The oldest and most active of these regional courts is that in Europe.[484] In 2017 alone, the European Court of Human Rights considered more than 60,000 applications, roughly 11% of which were formally referred to governments for a response; it delivered over 15,000 judgments and 70,000 decisions, and over 50,000 cases were pending at the end of the year. Approximately 60% of the court's case load is made up of complaints against four countries: Russia, Ukraine, Turkey, and Italy. The court also has delivered a number of judgments in cases brought by one state against another, which have considered situations as varied and politically charged as Northern Ireland, Cyprus, the 1967 military coup in Greece, allegations of widespread killings and torture by Turkey in its campaign against Kurdish rebels, and disputes between Russia and Ukraine and Georgia, respectively.

The European convention deals primarily with civil and political rights, and it was not until 2005 that a broad prohibition against discrimination was added to it. The European Social Charter sets forth a number of labor rights and some other social and economic rights. A number of other European institutions (for example, the European Union, European Parliament, and other bodies within the Council of Europe) deal with economic and social issues, discrimination, racism, and the situation of the Roma, but, unlike the court, any recommendations that they may make are not legally binding. Europe also has taken the lead in formulating a new catalogue of minority rights, although, again, the oversight bodies concerned only have the power to offer recommendations.

The widespread acceptance of the European Court does not mean that the court has been uncontroversial.[485] It has issued difficult judgments on sexual orientation, abortion, corporal punishment, the rights of persons suspected of terrorism, prisoners' voting rights, freedom of expression, trade unions, and political rights, and it has created a vast jurisprudence on fair trials, both civil and criminal.[486] Instances of noncompliance and delays in paying compensation appear to be increasing, and in recent years the court and the body responsible for overseeing implementation of its judgments, the Council of Europe's Committee of Ministers, have attempted to deal more directly with systemic violations, in part through a new "pilot judgment" procedure.[487]

In the Western hemisphere, the inter-American system remains a hybrid.[488] The Inter-American Commission on Human Rights is empowered to examine complaints against all 35 members of the Organization of American States, but it has only the power of recommendation when it ultimately acts on those complaints. Twenty-three countries have ratified the American Convention on Human Rights, which created an Inter-American Court of Human Rights. Twenty of the twenty-three parties to the convention have accepted he court's optional jurisdiction; like the European court, its judgments are legally binding. In its nearly forty years of existence, the court has issued approximately 350 decisions and judgments and 25 advisory opinions. While that is an impressive number, the court remains a part-time body of only seven judges. The commission has been much more active, particularly prior to establishment of the court in 1979, and it has published dozens of politically significant reports on the human rights situations in individual countries and thousands of decisions on individual complaints.

Both the commission and court have adopted an activist, progressive approach to interpreting and expanding the rights that they protect, which is discussed briefly in the context of accountability and impunity in Chapter 2. It is not uncommon for both institutions to identify violations of several rights in a single case, including a violation of the general obligation of states in article 1 to respect and ensure the rights in the American Convention on Human Rights.[489] The inter-American system has adopted a wide variety of additional instruments, including treaties or declarations on democracy, freedom of expression, access to information, racism and discrimination, women's rights, children, corruption, and asylum. Although the commission also has only seven members, it has been given responsibility for considering complaints concerning treaties on violence against women, disappearances, racism, discrimination and intolerance, and older persons.

Some of the commission's recent press releases sound more like political congratulations or criticisms than they do like the pronouncements of a quasi-judicial international body, such as those concerning the impeachment process that led to the removal from office of the president of Brazil;[490] US immigration policies regarding the fate of illegal migrants brought to the country when they were children;[491] a pejorative reference by Paraguay to "gender ideology";[492] gun control laws in the United States;[493] and the failure of Brazil to appoint to its cabinet of ministers any women or members of ethnic minorities.[494]

A former president of the commission observes

> ... [T]he Inter-American human rights system, for a variety of historical and institutional reasons, is, in its history, at present, and increasingly a system heavily influenced by the legal and political culture of the Latin countries of the region ...
>
> A common law court would not normally insert a new claim or cause of action based on the alleged facts in the event that the plaintiff fails to do so. Yet, this is exactly what happens in the Inter-American system, with great frequency and to extreme levels. Under the banner of iura novit curia, the Commission routinely inserts new claims into cases, finding violations never asserted by the petitioners ...
>
> The uses of prior case law and precedent, from a common law point of view, is [sic] extremely weak and inconsistent in the Inter-American institutions. That is, prior cases are frequently cited without any serious analysis of how they are the same or different or what the relevant prior case actually holds and whether it is applicable in the same way. The end result is that a line of cases on a particular question can be substantially inconsistent and lacking in coherence ...
>
> [T]he Commission and Court [make] ... extremely broad use of a wide range of norms that would be unrecognized as formal sources of international law in general – soft law, unratified treaties, expansive assertions of custom, and a putatively normative "corpus juris" in one area or another. This is probably less a reflection of any Anglo-Latin divide than it is a divide between the Inter-American practice and the classically accepted standards of public international law more generally.[495]

The following comments by a Harvard law professor and former US member of the UN Human Rights Committee Gerald Neuman are consistent with the above extract, but they are somewhat more critical:

[T]he Court has come to undervalue the consent of the relevant community of states as a factor in the interpretation of a human rights treaty. This neglect distorts the Court's elaboration of human rights norms, and risks damage to the effectiveness of the regional human rights system ...

The rate of compliance with the remedial orders in the inter-American system is lower than in the European system. In part, however, that fact reflects the wider remedial powers of the Inter-American Court and its enthusiastic exercise of those powers.

The Court should not bow to the will of individual violators, but it needs to induce, and not merely exhort, the support of the regional community of states.[496]

The African system is the youngest of the three regional systems, and it is probably the least effective whether measured in terms of influence, number of cases addressed, budget, or level of state compliance.[497] The African Commission on Human and People's Rights issues nonbinding recommendations in individual cases, and it generally adopts a broad perspective in its opinions that, like that of the Inter-American Commission, calls on states to adopt detailed measures to redress violations. For example, it adopted a very broad interpretation of article 24 of the ACHPR ("All peoples shall have the right to a general satisfactory environment favourable to their development.") in one of its earlier cases, in which the allegations of violations were not contested by the successor government that responded to them:

> The right to a general satisfactory environment, as guaranteed under Article 24 of the African Charter or the right to a healthy environment, as it is widely known, therefore imposes clear obligations upon a government. It requires the State to take reasonable and other measures to prevent pollution and ecological degradation, to promote conservation, and to secure an ecologically sustainable development and use of natural resources.
>
> Government compliance with the spirit of Articles 16 and 24 of the African Charter must also include ordering or at least permitting independent scientific monitoring of threatened environments, requiring and publicizing environmental and social impact studies prior to any major industrial development, undertaking appropriate monitoring and providing information to those communities exposed to hazardous materials and activities and providing meaningful opportunities for individuals to be heard and to participate in the development decisions affecting their communities.[498]

The commission also found violations of the rights to housing and food, although neither is explicitly provided for in the convention.[499]

The African Court on Human and People's Rights was similarly expansive in a case involving indigenous rights, which had been forwarded to it by the commission on behalf of the Ogiek people, who had been denied recognition of their right to their traditional communal homeland.[500] Drawing on the commission's own working group on indigenous peoples and the work in the 1980s of a UN special rapporteur on minorities, the court "recognise[d] the Ogieks as an indigenous population that is part of the Kenyan people having a particular status and deserving special protection deriving from their vulnerability."[501]

> The Court observes that, although addressed in the part of the Charter which enshrines the rights recognised for individuals, the right to property as guaranteed by Article 14 may also apply to groups or communities; in effect, the right can be individual or collective ...
> [T]o determine the extent of the rights recognised for indigenous communities in their ancestral lands as in the instant case, the Court holds that Article 14 of the Charter must be interpreted in light of the applicable principles especially by the [2007 Declaration on the Rights of Indigenous Peoples adopted by the] United Nations.[502]

The court found violations of the prohibition against discrimination and the Ogieks' rights to land, religion, culture, control over natural resources, and development.

On a scale of more limited to more expansive catalogues of human rights, the European Convention lies at the limited extreme and the African Charter on Human and People's Rights at the other end; the inter-American system is closer to the African. One cannot, of course, dismiss the many economic, social, and political differences among Europe, Africa, and Latin America, but a partial explanation for the greater acceptance by states of the European Convention may lie precisely in its relatively limited formulation of rights, as well as its longer history. European human rights law has become "thicker" through decades of often technical jurisprudence, and this has allowed the development of a greater consensus on the content of human rights and a greater willingness to acquiesce in their enforcement by an international legal body. While some expansion of rights has occurred, particularly in the areas of property rights and, more recently, nondiscrimination, the European catalogue of rights subject to the binding jurisdiction of an international court remains relatively restrained.

Human rights activists often seek to conflate the legally sophisticated judicial model of the ECHR with the expansive substantive scope of rights set forth in the Americas, Africa, and some UN instruments. This leap is often unwarranted, however, and European human rights standards on sensitive issues such as sexuality, abortion, and judicial procedures cannot automatically be applied to regions with different legal and social systems. It is worth noting that there is no international human rights body with judicial powers in Asia or the Pacific, although subregional bodies without the authority to issue legally binding judgments do exist.

Advocates should continue to promote universal and, within the regions that have adopted them, regional norms, but they should be wary of merely transplanting interpretations of those norms from one region to another. Particularly problematic is the idea that an international court is capable of mandating compliance with a vast range of rights, the implementation of many of which are dependent on economic capabilities and political willingness.

While he is speaking specifically in the context of the European doctrine of margin of appreciation that is enjoyed by states, McGoldrick's conclusions are more broadly relevant:

> Although human rights are universal in the sense of imposing some minimum fundamental standards, universalism does not operate by means of uniform, harmonized rules which cannot be varied ...
>
> It is submitted that when properly understood the MoA [margin of appreciation doctrine] is a complex, sophisticated and defensible intellectual instrument for international bodies supervising polycentric rights claims ... But if it represents a sensible pragmatic legal doctrine for a [European] system applying to 47 States and over 820 million people, then why not to a system applying to 168 States and something close to six billion people ... The MoA could assist ... to mediate between the idea of universal human rights and leaving space for reasonable disagreement, legitimate differences, and national or local cultural diversity. It would thus represent a principled response to many of the Third World critiques of Eurocentrism and universalism.[503]

A WORLD COURT OF HUMAN RIGHTS?

Elements of both over-legalization and over-Westernization are evident in various proposals that have been advanced to create a World Court of Human Rights. The most fully articulated proposal for such a court was launched by a panel of human rights notables, supported by the governments of Switzerland, Austria, and Norway, in 2011.[504] The panel included, among others, former UN High Commissioner for Human Rights Mary Robinson, former Deputy High Commissioner Bertrand Ramcharan, and former New York University law professor and president of the Appeals Chamber for the International Criminal Tribunals for both Yugoslavia and Rwanda, Theodor Meron. The proposed court would be "a permanent court with professional full time judges to be established by a multi-lateral treaty under the auspices of the United Nations. It should be competent to decide in a final and binding manner on any complaints brought by individuals, groups or legal entities alleging a violation of any human right found in an international human rights treaty binding on the duty-bearer."[505]

The theoretical and practical problems of such a proposal are addressed pithily and persuasively by Philip Alston, who believes the basic assumptions behind the court to be "problematic and misconceived."[506] His conclusion, with which I agree, is that "the notion that there should be a single, universally valid answer to complex questions involving competing rights, and that those answers should be uniformly and strictly enforced, both by domestic law enforcement agencies and by the Security Council, goes far beyond the assumptions that have been carefully built into the existing system."[507]

CONCLUDING REMARKS

Cultural, moral, and political values and legal norms will continue to vary from country to country, as well as within countries, and human rights are not designed to eradicate them. Of course, the very intent of universal human rights norms is to prevent some of the worst excesses of government and to assert basic principles of fairness, nondiscrimination, equal treatment, and meaningful socio-economic progress. However, governments that truly represent their people (and many that don't) will rarely be willing to alter fundamental traditions or beliefs just because international law demands it. The relatively weak implementation mechanisms for human rights – note the term *implementation* rather than *enforcement* – were created deliberately, and their purpose is to goad, shame, and encourage governments to obey higher standards, standards to which those same governments have themselves consented.

In addition, human rights norms are directed at governments, not at cultures or societies. While laws adopted to implement human rights will often have an impact on cultures, the latter are not static, and law is only one of the many factors that influence cultural change.

Cultural and regional differences are a strength of humanity itself, not a weakness, and the inherent flexibility of human rights is also one of their strengths. It is not pandering to backward or repressive cultures to recognize that different concepts of justice and fairness can exist alongside meaningful international norms. As suggested in the following extract, even concepts such as fairness and justice can imply very different results in specific circumstances:

> The educated Westerner chases ideals, founded on principles and discourse. For the Chinese, an ideal does not fill stomachs with food, bank balances with assets or brains with education. Confucius still stands as the paragon of Chinese philosophy because he is seen as advocating a practical, sensible and often successful way of living ...
>
> To me one of the clearest examples of how difficult it is to reconcile the different approaches rests in the idea of fairness. For a long time now in the West, that word and the ideal behind it have been invested with such power that it has started revolutions ...
>
> In Chinese philosophy, there is no popular word or attitude that really captures what fairness means in the West; it does not seem to be a part of Chinese culture.
>
> These approaches are almost irreconcilable. But I believe there are signs of a change and there is now an increasing awareness in China, outside of academic circles, of the rise of ideals like fairness ...[508]

National identity – understood as membership in a political grouping, such as a state, not necessarily as having an ethnic component – is real, and human rights advocates should not ignore this fact. The challenge is to distinguish between true moral and cultural differences and attempts by authoritarian or repressive leaders to equate themselves with this national identity, as a means of justifying their rule or discriminating against those within the country who are viewed as not "belonging" sufficiently to the nation.

Toward the end of his term in office, former French President Nicolas Sarkozy proposed creating a Museum of French History, "to distill centuries of Gallic gloire into a chronological display, supplemented by lectures, seminars and temporary shows borrowing materials from the country's already plentiful local and regional history museums . . . The problem? It boils down to a few issues: What does it mean to be French in the twenty-first century? And whose 'history' should be celebrated? In an increasingly fractious and multicultural nation, the questions have no simple answers."[509] These fundamental questions about identity cannot be resolved simply by invoking human rights, and they were properly decided in this instance by politics, when Sarkozy's successor abandoned the project.

Luzius Wildhaber, former president of the European Court of Human Rights, observes that "it has to be acknowledged that in developing the law it is difficult to avoid value judgments, whether on domestic or on international law. This applies especially to human rights, which, anchored as they are in the concepts of constitutionalism, democracy and the rule of law, are value judgments *par excellence*."[510] These value judgments are part of human rights; they are reflected not only in concepts such as the margin of appreciation utilized in the European regional system but in the very language of human rights treaties. The ESC Covenant refers to "progressive" implementation and permits rights to be interpreted or limited "to promote the general welfare in a democratic society." The CP Covenant is somewhat more rigorous, but it, too, permits limitations on rights and refers occasionally to arbitrariness or for the need for states to "take appropriate steps" to ensure rights. CEDAW requires states to take "appropriate" measures and adopt "appropriate" legislation to implement many of its provisions; the almost universally ratified Convention on the Rights of the Child uses the word "appropriate" more than forty times.

These terms are designed to allow countries flexibility in implementing human rights, although they cannot utilize this flexibility to undermine the essence of the rights themselves. If Europe cannot identify a "uniform European conception of morals" and the US Supreme Court cannot define obscenity without a reference to "community standards," it is unreasonable to insist that the nearly 200 countries in the world are obliged to interpret and implement international human rights law in exactly the same manner.

Not only differing value judgments but even differing language renders it impossible always to translate universal norms into uniform understanding. Concepts such as democracy and rule of law may have quite different meanings in different contexts. "Rule of law 'is not an attractive concept,' said U Pe Myint, a [Burmese] commentator and columnist. 'We do not usually equate the rule of law with justice. It has connotations of pacifying, subjugating people. I think most people don't really understand what it means."[511]

Democracy implies a system of government in which the governed exercise ultimate control over those who govern them, but it need not manifest itself in a way that is immediately familiar to the UK or France, let alone South Africa, Brazil, or Nepal. Electoral regulations, money, geography, ethnic ties, economic status, language and a multitude of other circumstances contribute to creating the political differences that arise during the electoral process, and they vary from country to country. We need not accept the legitimacy of elections purposely designed to keep incumbents in power or thwart the will of the electors, but the "democratic" means of governing a country may still vary considerably.

Ignoring the flexibility inherent in interpreting rights or attempting to define rights primarily through the lens of liberal western Europeans misrepresents the goals that human rights have set for themselves. Whether or not to permit countries to require that public school students shake hands with their teachers (Switzerland), kindergartens include pork on their lunch menus (Denmark), and immigrants accept local laws and customs (Germany) are not human rights issues.[512] They may be good or bad ideas, but they remain primarily within the domain of the country and society concerned.

The reality of this flexibility is illustrated by the varying approaches taken by international human rights bodies themselves regarding the sensitive issue of abortion. Without entering into a detailed discussion of cases that are often very fact-specific, the European Court of Human Rights has rejected extreme arguments (1) that there is an unlimited right to abortion, dependent solely on the wishes of the pregnant woman, or (2) that abortions may be prohibited absolutely, ignoring the life or health of the mother. A great deal of deference, usually citing the court's understanding of a state's margin of appreciation, has been granted to countries in their determination of the conditions under which abortions are permitted.[513]

Article 4 of the American Convention on Human Rights states that the right to life "shall be protected by law and, in general, from the moment of conception;" six states in Latin America prohibit abortion under all circumstances; nine allow abortion only to protect the life of the mother.[514] Neither the Inter-American Court nor Commission had addressed abortion definitively as of April 2018,[515] although the latter did issue a press release in 2017, in which it stated that "[t]he absolute criminalization of abortion, including in cases where the woman's life is at risk and when the pregnancy results from a rape or incest, imposes a disproportionate burden on the exercise of women's rights and creates a context that facilitates unsafe abortions and high rates of maternal mortality."[516]

Africa has the only treaty-based right to abortion in the world. Article 14.2.c of the Maputo Protocol requires states to "take all appropriate measures . . . [to] protect the reproductive rights of women by authorising medical abortion in cases of sexual assault, rape, incest, and where the continued pregnancy endangers the mental and physical health of the mother or the life of the mother or the foetus."[517] The African commission issued a general comment on this provision in 2014, to provide "interpretative guidance" to countries.[518]

The UN Human Rights Committee concluded in 2013 that the restrictive abortion law then in effect in Ireland violated the CP Covenant's prohibition against torture or inhuman or degrading treatment or punishment, privacy, and equality before the law. It recommended that Ireland amend its law and constitution to ensure "effective, timely and accessible procedures for pregnancy termination in Ireland, and take measures to ensure that health-care providers are in a position to supply full information on safe abortion services without fearing they will be subjected to criminal sanctions."[519] The constitutional provision at issue in the case was repealed in a May 2018 referendum, by a vote of 66% to 34%, which will lead to adoption of a less restrictive law on abortion by the Irish parliament.

No one would disagree that the "right to life" proclaimed in every major human rights treaty is fundamental; obviously, we cannot enjoy any human right if we are dead. However, issues such a abortion, assisted suicide, regulation of in-vitro fertilization and surrogacy, and capital punishment demonstrate that even fundamental rights can be subject to differing interpretations.

To some extent, of course, worrying too much about flexibility and relative universality is irrelevant to what human rights advocates and NGOs do most of the time: discover and publicize violations and appeal to governments to stop obvious abuses. Nuances of interpretation, such as those addressed in this chapter, are hardly problematic when governments are accused of torture, electoral fraud, widespread suppression of free expression, forced evictions, discrimination against women in education and employment, or other situations in which defining the rights in question is easy.

No human rights advocate, NGO, academic, or donor has a monopoly on truth. What the best approach is to equality, respect, tolerance, individual liberty, equity, and achieving the proper balance between the rights of the individual and the legitimate requirements of the community will vary from country to country. Accepting this reality does not undermine human rights; perhaps somewhat ironically, it strengthens their universality.

8

Human Rights Hawks

It is almost impossible not to "do something" in the face of widespread suffering, particularly if a country or international organization publicly proclaims its commitment to human rights and humanitarianism and accepts as a general principle that one should help those in need. European and US leaders, in particular, are regularly caught in what appear to be hypocritical situations, if they do not respond to the world's tragedies. For example, on a single day in 2015, the print version of *The New York Times* carried a full page ad calling for help for the Syrian people; it was headlined, "President Obama, What are you waiting for?"[520] On one-third of the opposite page was a story headlined, "U.S. Doing Too Little to Rein in President of Sudan, Critics Say."[521] For good measure, another third of that page warned, "Dominican Republic Set to Deport Haitian Migrants."[522] The lead story on the front page of the same issue reported that 60 million people were displaced from their homes at the end of 2014, according to the UN High Commissioner for Refugees.[523] This is only one day, three pages.

Nothing in international human rights law authorizes the use of force by outsiders to protect rights. However, it has been argued or proposed that severe or mass human rights violations *should* justify the use of force by one state or a group of states against another, as part of a so-called humanitarian intervention. Such a justification would modify or serve as an exception to the prohibition against the threat or use of force "against the territorial integrity or political independence of any state," which is contained in Article 2(4) of the United Nations Charter.[524]

In addition, the simultaneous application of international human rights law and international humanitarian law (IHL, also known as the law of war) in armed conflicts may modify one or the other body of law. The first issue involves *jus ad bellum*, or the legality of the use of force. The second implicates *jus in bello*, or the modalities of using force once hostilities have begun. These two issues will be discussed separately in the following pages.

GOING TO WAR: *JUS AD BELLUM*

In his book *Freedom on Fire*, John Shattuck proudly proclaims, "I am a human rights hawk."[525] A well-respected human rights lawyer and activist for decades, Shattuck served as assistant secretary of state for democracy, human rights, and labor under US President Bill Clinton in the challenging years of 1993–1998; he was subsequently the US Ambassador to the Czech Republic. Citing the rise in chaos and repression that followed the end of the Cold War, along with the mass killings during the conflicts in Bosnia and Herzegovina, Haiti, Rwanda, and Kosovo, Shattuck argues that international security must be redefined "to include the global protection of human rights, as we face an ever increasing threat of instability and terror emanating from failed states."[526] In fact, the "human rights wars" of which Shattuck speaks are often cases of genocide or massive crimes against humanity, and his use of the much more expansive notion of human rights wars is unfortunate; the confusion is increased when he defines humanitarian intervention as "a combined military and civilian effort by a coalition of countries to protect a civilian population *from severe human rights abuse* at the hands of their own government."[527]

While Shattuck supports multilateral action, comparative law professor of New York Law School Ruti Teitel observes that the "drumbeat for humanitarian intervention" after Bosnia and Rwanda also was supported by "human rights activists [who] were unabashed unilateralists, arguing for humanitarian intervention with or without procedural authorization or multilateral political backing."[528] Michael Glennon, international law professor at the Fletcher School of Law and Diplomacy, notes the "veritable cottage industry [that] has sprung up [after the 1999 NATO bombing in Kosovo] among manufacturers of new sets of rules concerning humanitarian intervention."[529]

Anne-Marie Slaughter, former Director of Policy Planning in the US Department of State under Hillary Clinton, is another well-known hawk, who supported the use of force in Kosovo in 1999, Iraq in 2003, and Libya in 2011. Complaining that international law has been too slow to legalize humanitarian intervention, she, too, goes well beyond genocide and crimes against humanity when she defines an intervention as "legitimate … when it responds to a 'gross and systematic violation of human rights that offends our common humanity.'"[530] Aware of the danger of "aggression masquerading as humanitarian intervention," she argues that "it is necessary to keep the requirement of collective authorization" for the use of force, on the assumption that, once we "spell out the global conditions for legitimacy over legality … the law will catch up with the reality of state practice."[531] Like so many other theoretical justifications for force, however, the devil is in the details: despite Slaughter's recognition that "[i]t is impossible to strike Syria legally … ," she advocated US attacks on Syria and urged US President Obama "to demonstrate that he can order the offensive use of force in circumstances other than secret drone attacks or covert operations ... To lead effectively, in both the national and the global interest, the US must demonstrate its readiness to shoulder the full responsibilities of power."[532]

THE RESPONSIBILITY TO PROTECT

For nearly two decades, the debate over humanitarian or human rights intervention referenced by Slaughter has largely evolved in the context of the doctrine of the "responsibility to protect" (R2P). Unfortunately, the vagueness, hyperbole, and neocolonial undertones of R2P may have the consequence of making it more, not less, difficult to reach consensus on criteria for humanitarian intervention in the future. As R2P continues to evolve within the labyrinthine corridors of the United Nations, what little potential the concept might have had as a catalyst for action is diminishing rather than increasing.[533] Finally, it may make it even more difficult to promote and protect human rights, properly understood, if a clear distinction is not maintained between the humanitarian-political aspirations of R2P and the legally binding norms of international human rights law.

After the West "won" the Cold War, human rights and democracy were supposed to break out everywhere; after all, we had reached Fukuyama's "end of history," and liberalism had won. Unfortunately, two events almost immediately reflected how far the world had yet to go to reach the golden future of the post-Cold-War era: the war in the former Yugoslavia in 1991–1995, on the doorstep of Europe, and the genocidal killing of perhaps 800,000 people in the small central African country of Rwanda in April–July 1994.[534] The failure of anyone (particularly Europe and the United States) to intervene to stop the slaughter led to renewed cries of "never again" and ultimately to the bombing campaign by NATO air forces in 1999 to end what, at the time, was said to be another potential genocide, this time in Kosovo.

Unfortunately, neither Kosovo nor Rwanda presents a very attractive example of how armed intervention might have been the answer to whatever question was being asked. The situation in Kosovo was regularly exaggerated by politicians and the media, although repression and killings by Serb forces certainly occurred in the context of the on-going low-intensity conflict between Serbia and rebels of the Kosovo Liberation Army. The conclusions of subsequent investigations by bodies sympathetic to the stated humanitarian goals of the 1999 bombing reflect the difficulties. For example, the Independent International Commission on Kosovo (an initiative of the then-Prime Minister of Sweden) concluded that the NATO bombing was "illegal, but legitimate," although "[t]he rationale for military intervention by NATO ... rested not on the immediate scale of humanitarian catastrophe in early 1999, but rather on a weaving together of past experiences and future concerns ... [Abuses in Kosovo] were comparable with those of numerous other recent counter-insurgency wars, for example, Colombia or Turkey."[535] The monitoring mission of the Conference on Security and Cooperation in Europe, which was present in Kosovo from October 1998 until just before the bombing began in March 1999, characterized the massacre of 45 people in the town of Racak in January 1999 as "indicative of what was to follow" *after* the bombing began, but it stated that "[t]he more frequent occurrence in the period of . . . [its] presence in Kosovo was, however, killings on an individual basis."[536]

Estimates for total deaths during the NATO campaign, most of them Albanians killed by Serbs, range from 5,000 to 10,000.[537] However, NATO was widely criticized for its high-altitude bombing tactics – there was not a single NATO casualty during the 78-day campaign – and Human Rights Watch estimates that approximately 500 civilians were killed by NATO air strikes.[538]

One year after the end of the NATO campaign, the UN's special rapporteur on the former Yugoslavia, former Czech foreign minister Jiri Dienstbier, stated that "[d]ozens and perhaps hundreds of individuals have been killed since June 1999 on account of their ethnicity" – this time, almost all the victims were Serbs or other minorities.[539] UNHCR reported that approximately 500 persons were killed from June 1999 to June 2000. [540] In March 2000, the special rapporteur stated at the UN Commission on Human Rights that most of Kosovo was "ethnically-cleansed of non-Albanians, divided, without any legal system, ruled by illegal structures of the Kosovo Liberation Army and very often by competing mafias."[541]

In contrast, there was little initial exaggeration of the situation in Rwanda, where approximately 800,000 people died in little over three months. A subsequent UN inquiry found that "[t]he systematic slaughter of men, women and children . . . will forever be remembered as one of the most abhorrent events of the twentieth century. Rwandans killed Rwandans, brutally decimating the Tutsi population of the country, but also targeting moderate Hutus. Appalling atrocities were committed, by militia and the armed forces, but also by civilians against other civilians . . . The failure by the United Nations to prevent, and subsequently, to stop the genocide in Rwanda was a failure by the United Nations system as a whole."[542]

There is disagreement as to who knew what when, whether the genocide was foreseeable, and what the impact of armed intervention might have been, given the short duration and ferocity of the countrywide killing. One also cannot ignore the international geopolitical and chronological context in which the massacres occurred: the killing of US marines in Mogadishu and subsequent withdrawal of US forces from Somalia occurred in October 1993 and March 1994, respectively; an estimated 50,000 people were killed in neighboring Burundi immediately after the October 1993 assassination of the first Hutu president of that country, and 200,000 to 300,000 Burundians subsequently have died in Hutu-Tutsi violence; Haitian President Aristide was deposed in September 1991, and the Security Council authorization for the use of force to restore him to power came in July 1994; and the conflict in former Yugoslavia did not end until late 1995. Nonetheless, there is a minimum consensus that at least 100,000–200,000 lives might have been saved in Rwanda, even with a relatively minimal intervention strategy.[543]

Yugoslavia and Rwanda continue to color the views of many liberal internationalists and human rights activists with respect to the desirability of and criteria for using
force to prevent atrocities and/or ensure respect for human rights. The comment of
Susan Rice, former US ambassador to the United Nations, national security adviser
to President Obama, and a member of President Clinton's National Security
Council at the time of the Rwandan genocide, perhaps sums up the prevailing view
among many government officials and diplomats in the 1990s: "I swore to myself
that if I ever faced such a crisis again, I would come down on the side of dramatic
action, going down in flames if that was required."[544] Hillary Clinton had similar
feelings: "[W]hen the choice is between action and inaction, and you've got risks in
either direction, which you often do, she'd rather be caught trying."[545] President
Obama, on the other hand, "would say privately that the first task of an American
president in the post-Bush international arena was 'Don't do stupid shit.'"[546]
Even after the debacle in Libya discussed below, Hillary Clinton maintained,
"Great nations need organizing principles, and 'Don't do stupid stuff' is not an
organizing principle."[547]

The genesis of R2P lies in the 2001 report of the International Commission on
Intervention and State Sovereignty (ICISS), which was created a year earlier by the
Canadian government after the Kosovo bombing, to consider how the international
community "should respond in the face of massive violations of human rights
and humanitarian law."[548] The commission began by accurately observing that
"'[h]umanitarian intervention' has been controversial both when it happens, and
when it has failed to happen."[549]

> For some, the international community is not intervening enough; for others it is
> intervening much too often. For some, the only real issue is in ensuring that
> coercive interventions are effective; for others, questions about legality, process
> and the possible misuse of precedent loom much larger. For some, the new
> interventions herald a new world in which human rights trumps state sovereignty;
> for others, it ushers in a world in which big powers ride roughshod over the smaller
> ones, manipulating the rhetoric of humanitarianism and human rights. The con-
> troversy has laid bare basic divisions within the international community. In the
> interest of all those victims who suffer and die when leadership and institutions fail,
> it is crucial that these divisions be resolved . . .[550]

The commission argued that substituting the concept of the "responsibility to
protect" for that of "humanitarian intervention" better reflected the desired focus
on victims, rather than the intervener, and was more likely to be acceptable to states.
It appears that the hope was to have the report considered by the UN Security
Council in autumn 2001, but the Al-Qaeda attack on the United States on 11 September quashed that plan.

While the primary public arguments for the invasion of Iraq in 2003 by the United
States and its "coalition of the willing" (which included such European human

rights stalwarts as the United Kingdom, Netherlands, Spain, Portugal, Italy, and Denmark) initially rested on illusory claims of weapons of mass destruction and support for terrorism, the case for invasion also included Saddam Hussein's record of heinous violations of human rights and the need to establish democracy by over-throwing the regime. In December 2002, for example, prior to the invasion, President George W. Bush cited the UN Commission on Human Rights' finding that

> Iraq continues to commit extremely grave violations of human rights, and ... the regime's repression is all pervasive ... Events can turn in one of two ways: If we fail to act in the face of danger, the people of Iraq will continue to live in brutal submission ... The regime will remain unstable – the region will remain unstable, with little hope of freedom, and isolated from the progress of our times ... If we meet our responsibilities, if we overcome this danger, we can arrive at a very different future. The people of Iraq can shake off their captivity. They can one day join a democratic Afghanistan and a democratic Palestine, inspiring reforms throughout the Muslim world.[551]

Whatever the true motives for invading Iraq, the mantra that emanated from Washington during the George W. Bush administration, at least, was that the United States should assist in replacing dictatorships with democracy – implicitly, anywhere it can. With democracy would come tolerance and open societies, although the path to achieve these goals in Iraq is strewn with thousands of dead Americans and hundreds of thousands of dead Iraqis.[552] The overuse of *democracy* and *freedom* by President Bush sounded suspiciously like "human rights" to many beyond Washington, DC, although the Bush administration's understanding of the latter term was myopic, at best.

R2P did not disappear after 2001, but reactions to the ICISS proposals were decidedly mixed. The so-called Group of 77 (which now includes 133 developing states) explicitly rejected the notion that unilateral humanitarian intervention is permissible under international law.[553] With the support of UN Secretary-General Kofi Annan, R2P was addressed in two subsequent UN documents, written to prepare the way for significant reform of the United Nations during 2005–2006. The first is disingenuous in observing, "The Charter of the United Nations is not as clear as it could be when it comes to saving lives within countries in situations of mass atrocity."[554] In fact, the Charter's prohibition of the use of force is straightforward; it just isn't the position that the drafters of the report desired. The second document, the "outcome document" of the discussions of UN reform, sets forth what remains the core international consensus around R2P, although it came as a disappointment to those who favored a more robust approach to intervention.

> Each individual State has the responsibility to protect its populations from geno-cide, war crimes, ethnic cleansing and crimes against humanity. This responsibility entails the prevention of such crimes, including their incitement, through appro-priate and necessary means. We accept that responsibility and will act in

accordance with it. The international community should, as appropriate, encourage and help States to exercise this responsibility and support the United Nations in establishing an early warning capability.

The international community, through the United Nations, also has the responsibility to use appropriate diplomatic, humanitarian and other peaceful means, in accordance with Chapters VI and VIII of the Charter, to help to protect populations from genocide, war crimes, ethnic cleansing and crimes against humanity. In this context, we are prepared to take collective action, in a timely and decisive manner, through the Security Council, in accordance with the Charter, including Chapter VII, on a case-by-case basis and in cooperation with relevant regional organizations as appropriate, should peaceful means be inadequate and national authorities are manifestly failing to protect their populations from genocide, war crimes, ethnic cleansing and crimes against humanity. We stress the need for the General Assembly to continue consideration of the responsibility to protect populations from genocide, war crimes, ethnic cleansing and crimes against humanity and its implications, bearing in mind the principles of the Charter and international law. We also intend to commit ourselves, as necessary and appropriate, to helping States build capacity to protect their populations from genocide, war crimes, ethnic cleansing and crimes against humanity and to assisting those which are under stress before crises and conflicts break out.[555]

In 2009, the General Assembly convened a two-day debate on the responsibility to protect, at which proponents and skeptics offered their views. There was no support for expanding the concept beyond the international crimes of genocide, war crimes, ethnic cleansing, and crimes against humanity, nor was there significant support for developing more specific criteria or legitimizing the use of force by states outside the context of the United Nations.[556] The General Assembly has taken no formal action on R2P since then, although it does hold an "annual informal interactive dialogue" based on reports submitted by the Secretary-General. Since 2007, there has been a Special Advisor to the UN Secretary General on the responsibility to protect, whose primary task is "conceptual development and consensus-building,"[557] and a UN website on the topic, although no further formal action has occurred.[558]

Despite the circumspect manner in which the General Assembly delineated R2P, a 2009 report on R2P by the UN Secretary-General curiously added the phrase "and violations" to most mentions of the four crimes, apparently as a means of tying the 2005 Summit Outcome's version of the responsibility to protect against specific international crimes to the broader responsibility of states to respect, ensure, and recognize international human rights.[559] The newly coined phrase of *crimes and violations* provides a context for the broad discussion of human rights that makes up the bulk of the 2009 report.[560] Among many wide-ranging recommendations related to the protection responsibilities of the state are preventing sexual and gender-based violence,[561] ending impunity,[562] "[c]andid self-reflection" and "searching dialogue,"[563] training,[564] and fostering individual responsibility[565] – all of which are supposed to contribute to preventing the mass atrocity crimes that actually do fall within R2P.[566]

By linking the new concept of R2P to the long-standing and widely accepted principle of state responsibility for human rights, the Secretary-General and others risked undermining the latter for no apparent reason. Fortunately, the platitudes that infused the Secretary-General's 2009 report have not been expanded or given more specific content in subsequent iterations of R2P, although the linkage of R2P with "gross" or "severe" or "systematic" human rights violations continues. Implementing human rights is difficult enough without the baggage of the responsibility to protect, and linking the concept of R2P with the law of human rights is unlikely to help either gain adherents.[567] Then-Senator Barack Obama opposed the Iraq invasion in 2003, but his subsequent presidential administration was not immune to resolving human rights dilemmas by force, although it seemed relatively reluctant to do so. A 2014 op-ed article went so far as to conclude that "some of the most outspoken warmongers in Washington are self-proclaimed human rights advocates," citing arguments for the use of US military power "to capture a warlord in Uganda, impose order in the Ivory Coast, crush rebels in South Sudan, and locate kidnap victims in Nigeria."[568]

The New-York based Global Center for the Responsibility to Protect was founded in 2008; the co-chairs of its International Advisory Board remain Gareth Evans and Mohammed Sahnoun, who were co-chairs of ICISS, which invented the R2P concept. The center was founded by a number of supportive governments,[569] "leading figures from the human rights community," and International Crisis Group, Human Rights Watch, Oxfam International, Refugees International, and the World Federalist Movement. It has offices in Geneva, one of whose goals since 2015 has been "advancing the institutionalization of R2P within the UN in Geneva, particularly at the Human Rights Council."[570]

Prior to the birth of R2P, the UN Security Council did authorize the use of force on occasion, although the protection of civilians was only part of the mandates that the council approved. In 1991, the council insisted that Iraq allow access by humanitarian organizations to Kurds in northern Iraq, which France, United Kingdom, and United States interpreted unilaterally as authorizing the creation of no-fly zones in the region.[571] Use of force was explicitly authorized in Somalia, "in order to establish a secure environment for humanitarian relief operations in Somalia as soon as possible."[572] Later in 1992, the council commended the Economic Community of West African States (ECOWAS) "for its efforts to restore peace, security and stability in Liberia," but this occurred two years after ECOWAS had intervened militarily in the country.[573] In 1993, the council demanded somewhat cryptically that "all concerned" facilitate access to "safe areas" established in Bosnia and Herzegovina.[574] An intervention in Rwanda led by France was authorized only in June 1994, after most of the killings had ceased, and was supposed to contribute "to the security and protection of displaced persons, refugees and civilians at risk."[575] A resolution on Haiti, whose adoption was supported by recognized Haitian president Jean-Bertrand Aristide, mentions "the significant further deterioration of the humanitarian situation in Haiti, in particular the continuing escalation by the illegal de facto regime of systematic violations of civil liberties," but it authorized the use of "all necessary means" primarily "to facilitate the prompt return of the legitimately elected President [Aristide] and the restoration of the legitimate authorities of the Government of Haiti."[576] Many, but not all, of these resolutions declared that the situation constituted a threat to peace and security and that the council was acting under Chapter VII of the UN Charter.

In support of its mission, the Centre for R2P had identified 68 Security Council resolutions between 2006 and January 2018 that use the phrase *responsibility to protect*, although almost all of these references are to the "primary" responsibility of states to protect those within their jurisdiction, not to any responsibility of the United Nations or the international community.[577] The only clear authorization by the UN Security Council for the use of force by individual states to protect civilians (apart from Somalia in 1992) was in Libya in 2011, and this was initially hailed as the high point of the R2P concept. The council authorized "all necessary measures ... to protect civilians and civilian populated areas under threat of attack," based on Muammar Gaddafi's threats against rebels in the city of Benghazi; the resolution was supported by the Arab League.[578] Secretary of State Hillary Clinton was "enthusiastic" about a white paper given to her by Libyan opposition leaders that set out "a spectacular future: Political parties would compete in open elections, a free news media would hold leaders accountable and women's rights would be respected. In retrospect, Mr. Jibril [Mahmoud Jibril, a leader of the opposition] acknowledged in an interview, it was a 'utopian ideal' quite detached from Libyan reality."[579]

The de facto expansion of the Libyan mandate by the US, Qatar, and European countries to justify the overthrow of Gaddafi and their support for the insurgents robbed the resolution of much of its precedential value. For example, one analyst argued that the intervention relied "on two demonstrably false premises: that Qaddafi initiated the violence by targeting peaceful protesters and the NATO intervention aimed primarily to protect civilians."[580] Another observed, "Action taken on the basis of altruistic individual impulses cannot reasonably be cited as constituting a precedent or new norm. Rather, it is more accurately described as aberrant behavior impelled by a unique constellation of necessarily temporal factors."[581]

The subsequent civil war, deterioration of security, and resulting anarchy in Libya tarnished the concept of R2P further. A February 2018 report on the situation to the Security Council opens optimistically, stating that the period under review "was marked by a renewed dynamism and engagement by all Libyan actors to conclude the transitional process, following the launch on 20 September 2017 ... of the United Nations action plan to resume an inclusive political process in Libya."[582] Other sections are probably more realistic:

Armed groups engaged in ongoing fighting committed violations of international human rights and humanitarian law. The weakness of judicial institutions and the general climate of lawlessness and insecurity hampered victims' ability to seek protection, justice and redress ...

The humanitarian situation in Libya deteriorated during the reporting period. Refugees and migrants continued to be subjected to violence, forced labour and other grave violations and abuses. Reports of migrants allegedly being sold into the slave trade in Libya shed light on the appalling conditions the majority endure in a climate of impunity ...

[The Secretary-General is] deeply disturbed by the continuing reports of human trafficking in Libya.[583]

If there is a lesson to be drawn from Libya, it is perhaps as a warning about the unintended – perhaps even inevitable – consequences of using force, even if begun with the laudable intent of saving lives.

The reluctance of Russia, China, and others to authorize "humanitarian" force post-Libya in Syria or elsewhere stems in large part from the reasonable fear that humanitarian goals would quickly turn to the political goal of regime change.[584] Ironically, Russia itself implicitly utilized R2P when it intervened in Georgia to defend its allies in South Ossetia in 2008, an action condemned as an example of "vigilante justice across borders" by the International Crisis Group, a strong supporter of R2P.[585] However, at least some justification for the Russian intervention is provided by an EU fact-finding report, which concluded that the large-scale bombardment of Tskhinvali by Georgia – the alleged trigger for the Russian intervention – was illegal and did not satisfy the requirements of necessity and proportionality required by international humanitarian law; the report also declared illegal the use of force by Georgia against Russian peacekeepers in South Ossetia.[586] The report found that the initial Russian defense of its peacekeepers was legal but that the subsequent expansion of military activities was illegal.[587] It explicitly rejected any argument that the invasion could be justified on the grounds of humanitarian intervention.[588] Russia's 2014 annexation of Crimea followed a similar pattern, as Russia initially asserted (among other arguments) that it was acting to protect Russian citizens, as well as responding to a request from the legitimate president of Ukraine, the ousted Viktor Yanukovych.[589]

It is not viewed as coincidental by most of the world that those countries that promote coercive intervention are, by and large, the same countries that are in the forefront of promoting human rights (Russia being a prominent exception). Combined with the disastrous example of the 2003 invasion of Iraq and the militarism of the Bush Administration, the responsibility to protect is interpreted by some countries (and not only the most repressive) as merely the most extreme example of the West's mission to impose its version of human rights on the rest of the world, recalling the "white man's burden" and *la mission civilatrice* of colonialism. This may be an unfair juxtaposition of different concepts, but it is nonetheless a real concern.

There is no agreement among states or international organizations that the concept of the responsibility to protect legalizes the use of force by any state or group of states for humanitarian or human rights purposes. There is ample evidence that so-called humanitarian interventions occur for many reasons, not the least of which are geopolitical or related to far-fetched notions of national security. Often, such interventions lead to greater suffering, not less; *intervention* and *protection* are euphemisms for bombs and bullets and killing some in order to save others. In every case, states will be constrained by their own capacity and their populations' willingness to provide assistance to ... everyone? those who have a domestic constituency? only those whose plights are headlined by journalists, bloggers, self-proclaimed activists, or Twitter? or only those whom we deem can be saved at the least cost, in lives and treasure, to ourselves?

Even if we trust the wisdom of the UN Security Council or NATO (perhaps unfortunately, the two most obvious multilateral options in many cases) to wage war to end war, do we know how to do it? Rwanda will remain a stark reminder of the cost of nonintervention, but most other situations in which populations are dying are cesspools of conflicting geopolitics, battles over resources, or ethnic or religious rivalries. "Doing something" without understanding the likely outcome of using force is immoral, and killing cannot be justified by anything less than preventing more deaths, not to safeguard fair trials or gender equality or free expression or the right to education without discrimination. Whatever the motives, the consequences of military intervention in Bosnia and Herzegovina, Kosovo, Afghanistan, Iraq, and Libya should give pause to human rights hawks everywhere.

FIGHTING THE WAR: *JUS IN BELLO*

It is clear that human rights law applies in time of armed conflict, alongside international humanitarian law, a position upheld by the International Court of Justice in several advisory opinions and judgments.[590]

> [T]he Court considers that the protection offered by human rights conventions does not cease in case of armed conflict, save through the effect of provisions for derogation of the kind to be found in Article 4 of the [CP Covenant]. As regards the relationship between international humanitarian law and human rights law, there are thus three possible situations: some rights may be exclusively matters of international humanitarian law; others may be exclusively matters of human rights law; yet others may be matters of both these branches of international law ... [T]he Court will have to take into consideration both these branches of international law, namely human rights law and, as lex specialis, international humanitarian law."[591]

These interpretations have been reinforced by the European Court of Human Rights, which has slowly expanded its extraterritorial jurisdiction over a country's actions outside its own territory.[592] The 2014 case of *Hassan v. U.K.* alleged violations of the applicant's right to life, the prohibition against torture, and the legality of his detention by British forces in Iraq in 2003.⁵⁹³ The court first followed its own precedents in finding that, during his detention, Hassan was within the jurisdiction of the U.K. for the purposes of the European Convention on Human Rights (ECHR). It then rejected the British argument that only IHL, and not the human rights norms of the ECHR, applied "in the active hostilities phase of an international armed conflict, where the agents of the Contracting State are operating in territory of which they are not the occupying power".⁵⁹⁴

Consistent with the opinions of the International Court of Justice referenced above, the European Court concluded that, given "the co-existence of the safeguards provided by international humanitarian law and by the Convention in time of armed conflict, the grounds of permitted deprivation of liberty . . . [in the ECHR] should be accommodated, as far as possible, with the taking of prisoners of war and the detention of civilians who pose a risk to security under the Third and Fourth Geneva Conventions."⁵⁹⁵ Finding that, on the facts, the detention was not arbitrary and was consistent with IHL, the court found no violation of the ECHR.⁵⁹⁶ However, a dissenting opinion by four judges argued that the norms of the ECHR could not be displaced by IHL without a formal derogation from Convention norms, as permitted by Article 15. The court must "give priority to the [European] Convention . . . By attempting to *reconcile the irreconcilable*, the majority's finding today does not, with respect, reflect an accurate understanding of the scope and substance of the fundamental right to liberty under the Convention, as reflected in its purpose and its historical origins in the atrocities of the international armed conflicts of the Second World War."⁵⁹⁷

A related issue is how the broader goals of humanitarian or human rights intervention (as opposed to a "normal" armed conflict where military victory is the primary goal) may complicate existing norms of both international human rights law and international humanitarian law. In a recent article, Harvard professor of human rights and humanitarian law Gabriella Blum identifies the crux of the problem:

> With wars becoming about long-term change, requiring a mix of benevolence and aggression that is carefully tailored to individual targets, the political and civilian dimensions of victory have outgrown the military one. As the attempts to define what success looks like in Afghanistan or Iraq show, the formulation of victory now requires more long-term, abstract, and complex, less tangible and immediate terms. War, in other words, can no longer be reduced into a military campaign . . .
>
> With the demise of the practice of formal surrender and greater debates over the classification of outcomes of war, victory has become more difficult to identify and to evaluate . . .
>
> Somewhat paradoxically, by making human rights violations within any single country a matter of international interest – and by deeming gross human rights violations a grave offence that implicate a duty to intervene on the part of the

international community – human rights came to operate as both a limitation on war and a cause for war. They limited the targets and scope of deliberate harm in war, but also revived an earlier interest in the plight of individuals as a just cause for waging wars of "humanitarian intervention" ...

Ultimately, the only uniform restraint upon present-day occupations seems to be the ban on annexation; transformative occupation that brings about reconstruction, democracy, the rule of law, and protection of human rights is now the evolving norm, at least when it comes to war fought by the US ...

[With respect to the requirement of necessity,] [t]he American neo-conservatives' approach [during the George W. Bush administration] was one of exporting liberal-democratic values by hook or by crook; where such export was viewed as especially urgent to combat a threat of terrorism, using force in its support was legitimate. On the eastern side of the Atlantic, Europeans shared the goal of spreading democracy and human rights, but only through a process of dialogue and positive inducements ...

[In the context of proportionality,] [a]s the shadow of victory lengthens to include a democratic government, human rights, and economic reconstruction – all under violent opposition from sections of the local population and armed groups – some degree of constant, trickling force is required throughout the effort ...[598]

Thus, in *human rights wars*, to use John Shattuck's phrase, structural changes, both political and economic, have become "necessary components of victory, not merely post-war missions."[599]

Structural changes mean not only stopping mass killing or creating more honest and functional government institutions; they also implicate "regular" human rights. One instructive example is the situation of women in Afghanistan, both under the Taliban pre-2001 and subsequently. One of the leading advocates on this issue in the United States during the early years of the war in Afghanistan was Mavis Leno, wife of well-known comedian and former talk show host, Jay Leno. "Mavis Leno and her fellow activists have waged an ongoing effort to make sure that the status of Afghan women figures into America's policy calculations ... [They] have been making a special effort to ensure that the rights of women are considered alongside Washington's strategic considerations."[600] The website of the Feminist Majority Foundation, on whose board of directors Leno has served since 1997, describes her as "a leader in the effort to make the restoration of women's rights a non-negotiable element of a post-Taliban Afghanistan ... and ... at the forefront of insuring that the plight of Afghan women is included in the world's reporting of the war in Afghanistan and that the women and girls of Afghanistan are not forgotten."[601]

No one would argue against protecting women and promoting women's equality in Afghanistan, but what impact should or does this goal – like other human rights goals of ensuring physical security, accountability, and socio-economic rights – have on the legitimacy of the use of armed force itself and its modalities? Blum queries whether even such hallowed IHL principles as those of necessity and proportionality can be applied under such circumstances.

... [C]onfiscation [of property] is allowed [under IHL] only for "military necessity." And yet, once gender equality, aid, and reconstruction are made part of the goals of the war [in Afghanistan], no less so than chasing after Al Qaida operatives, it is unclear why confiscation of property for ... [military necessity] should be allowed, while for ... [the construction of a school for girls] it should not. Nor, for that matter, is it clear why that same goal of gender equality would not justify the use of armed force against those who are fighting against it ...

[W]ith the extension of the war into the political and civilian realm, the principle of proportionality – if weighed against those interests – risks becoming meaningless. After all, how can one weigh how many lives the rights of women in Afghanistan are worth?[602]

A similar concern regarding the lack of clarity in human rights norms is expressed by two IHL experts:

As for human rights, the answers are frequently based on general treaties without universal ratification or on regional treaties – while the exact substance of customary human rights is at least as controversial as that of customary humanitarian law. Often those answers are also based on the practice of bodies which cannot take binding decisions and sometimes on soft-law instruments whose binding character is controversial. In addition, human rights limitations are often very flexible, inter alia because of vague limitation clauses which allow them to take the specific nature of each case into account.[603]

We also need to consider what the consequences of broadening the purpose of war to include protecting human rights and establishing democracy might be; how do we know when we have won?

Ending a war is a difficult and delicate business ... In the Hundred Years' War that dragged France and England through the fourteenth century, both sides would have liked to quit but could not, for fear of losing power and status; hate and mistrust fed by the war prevented them from talking. In the ghastly toll and futility of 1914–18, no end could be negotiated short of victory for one side or the other, because each felt it must bring home to its people some compensating gain in the form of territory or a seaport or industrial resource to justify the terrible cost ... For rulers to stop short of the declared war aim, thus acknowledging their own as well as their party's and their nation's incapacity, is as problematic as the camel's passage through the needle's eye.[604]

The United States has now had military forces in Afghanistan since 2001 and in Iraq since 2003. These are the two longest wars in the country's history.

CONCLUDING REMARKS

Beyond the obvious concern of both human rights law and IHL to protect the rights of individuals, their purposes are quite different. While derogation or temporary suspension of rights may be justified in states of emergency, human rights law generally assumes that states operate in conditions of relative peace and that governments are capable of acting effectively (if not perfectly) to ensure rights. IHL, on the other hand, is predicated on the existence of an armed conflict, and its major concern is regulating how that conflict should be conducted. Blum's not-so-rhetorical question is incapable of being answered by human rights law, and IHL is better at quantitative comparisons than qualitative moral judgments. We are left either with no law or the need to develop new law; the former situation would be disastrous, while the human rights hawks too often ignore the latter in favor of rhetoric, tweets, and YouTube video appeals.

As the final quotation from Blum suggests, it is difficult, perhaps impossible, to balance the value of one life against another. It is just as difficult to predict whether a particular use of force will be "successful" or not, and at what cost. Not only political but technological considerations determine which countries will be targeted for armed intervention; millions have died in the Democratic Republic of Congo and Sudan, for example, while interveners tried to save thousands in Kosovo and Libya. Even if an international consensus could be reached over the criteria for intervention, any decision to intervene will reflect national priorities, politics, and capabilities, not only the extent of suffering of the victims.

Advocates of the responsibility to protect pretend that its adoption is an innovative limitation on national sovereignty, the sovereignty that permits atrocity crimes such as genocide and mass murder to be committed without consequence. However, this simplistic equation ignores another basic principle of international law that is held dear not only by war criminals but also by former colonies and less powerful states whose history has been one of too much intervention rather than too little: the prohibition against the use of force that is one of the cornerstones of the United Nations. The history of the past several decades provides little support for the claim that loosening or legalizing the norms against armed force will mitigate disaster, but it is almost certain that government intervention based on "humanitarian" or "R2P" justifications will be used to hide much less laudable goals on the part of the interveners.

Sovereignty has been limited by international human rights law for decades, and there is nothing new about R2P's first principle, that the primary responsibility to protect lies with the state. The obligations accepted by states under human rights treaties are legally binding, not just political statements mouthed by the UN General Assembly. That human rights do not include provisions that would authorize invasion or bombings is not a weakness but a recognition of the fact that implementation of human rights norms is a complex, often long-term, process that cannot be fulfilled exclusively or even primarily by outsiders. Even where violations within a state are serious – e.g., widespread discrimination, regular use of torture, widespread arbitrary detention, fraudulent elections, elite enrichment rather than fulfillment of socio-economic rights – they can only very rarely be redressed at the point of a gun.

The responsibility to protect is an expression of humanitarianism, not the protection of human rights. It should be as concerned with loss of life by inaction or incapacity – failure to respond adequately to a natural disaster or a public health crisis, for example – as by the commission of international crimes. Of course, humanitarianism does not encompass the vast scope of R2P as originally envisaged, particularly not the obligation to rebuild societies or establish the rule of law. This is one of humanitarianism's strengths, in that it seeks to do what is possible to relieve human suffering, without burdening that task with broader political issues.[605]

Human rights law commits states to ensure rights to life, physical safety, food, shelter, health, and more. It is not designed to provide easy solutions to the situations of armed conflict referenced in this chapter. It also is important to remember that human rights law commits governments to ensure rights to all those within their jurisdiction, territory, or control, not to everyone in the world. Human rights advocates need to make it clearer that they do not favor human rights wars and that force should only be used as a last resort in extreme situations, to prevent widespread loss of life that is, indeed, preventable.

At its core, the notion that every individual state and the international community have a shared responsibility to ensure that individuals are protected from atrocity crimes and life-threatening situations no matter where they live is a moral, even noble, goal. It reflects the increasing humanization of international relations and is consistent with the ever-increasing commitment by states to human rights.

However, using the protection of human rights as an excuse for bombs and forced regime change is almost never a good idea. Neither the international community nor "coalitions of the willing" have been particularly successful in (re)constructing states in accordance with human rights principles. Perhaps unfortunately, a saying in Washington after the disastrous Libyan intervention may be worth remembering, and not only by Americans:

> In Iraq, the United States had intervened and occupied – and things had gone to hell. In Libya, the United States had intervened but not occupied – and things had gone to hell. And in Syria, the United States had neither intervened nor occupied – and things had still gone to hell.[606]

A properly defined international responsibility to protect – directed towards preventing widespread loss of life, whatever the cause – could be a meaningful advance in the humanization of international law and the protection of individuals under imminent threat. However, calls for the use of force in order to "do something" in the face of widespread human rights abuses raise unrealistic expectations and may deter adoption of less drastic actions that will be slow and frustrating but that may, in time, be more fruitful and sustainable.

9

The Indispensable State? The United States and Human Rights

In the beginning, there were Eleanor Roosevelt and the Universal Declaration of Human Rights. While, of course, there were many antecedents to the drafting of the UDHR between 1945 and 1948, and many other influences then and later,[607] it is not an overstatement to claim that international human rights law and institutions would not have developed as they did in the twentieth century without the active support of the government of the United States. Whether indispensable or only highly significant, US leadership in promoting human rights norms and international mechanisms has been key to achieving the level of international agreement necessary to move human rights beyond the merely rhetorical to the politically relevant.

The problem with such straightforward statements, however, is that there is not one "United States" or even a consistent US policy on human rights. Most US presidents have resisted Congressional initiatives that sought to mandate attention to human rights as part of US foreign policy, on the ground that such requirements inappropriately interfered with executive prerogatives to conduct foreign affairs. Unsurprisingly, presidential attitudes also have shifted with electoral results.

In addition, the US commitment to certain aspects of human rights has often not been matched with action. While the United States has ratified a number of important multilateral treaties, its record pales beside those of many other countries. It is the only country in the world not to have ratified the UN Convention on the Rights of the Child, and it has consistently refused to ratify any human rights treaty or optional protocol that permitted a court or other treaty body to receive complaints from individuals concerning alleged violations by the United States. Politicians from both major US political parties and many academics and pundits continue to reject the very concept of economic, social, and cultural rights, viewing them instead as mere nonjusticiable entitlements that the government is free to provide or not.

Human rights in US foreign policy cannot be separated from broader US foreign policy goals, an observation that is true for every country. Despite clamor from activists for every foreign policy decision to be based primarily on human rights considerations, legitimate concerns with security, trade, domestic politics, and political ideology are also drivers of foreign policy, and they may outweigh concerns about human rights violations in other countries. Even in this nuanced context, however, matching US actions with US rhetoric on human rights is not always easy.

One of the core arguments of the present book is that human rights are best understood as international human rights law, but this is a problematic correlation with respect to the United States. Outside of the areas of trade and investment, the US attitude to the authority of international courts is generally negative, as exemplified by its self-judging original acceptance of the optional jurisdiction of the International Court of Justice (ICJ);[608] its attempt to exclude disputes concerning Central America from that original acceptance, just prior to Nicaragua's submission of an application against the US to the ICJ;[609] and its total withdrawal of its acceptance of the ICJ's optional jurisdiction in 1985,[610] prior to the ICJ's 1986 judgment against the United States in the *Nicaragua* case.[611] The United States also has refused to ratify the Statute of the International Criminal Court (ICC), although it has been willing to cooperate with the ICC on an ad-hoc basis. This approach is consistent with the US position of not permitting individuals to submit complaints against the United States to human rights bodies, and it hardly signals a deep commitment to the rule of international law.

It would be mistaken to conclude that the United States gives no consideration whatsoever to legal norms, but US compliance with norms of general international law has been hypocritical, at best. According to a respected periodical on foreign affairs, since 1945 the US Central Intelligence Agency has assisted in overthrowing governments in Iran (1953), Guatemala (1954), Congo (1960), Dominican Republic (1961), South Vietnam (1963), Brazil (1964), and Chile (1973).[612] To this list could be added Grenada (1983), Panama (1989), Afghanistan (2001), Iraq (2003), and Libya (2011), although the use of force in some of these latter instances did have colorable claims of legality. Some of these situations are considered more fully in Chapter 8's discussion of the "responsibility to protect."

Returning to the role of human rights in US foreign policy, a very brief summary of shifts in US policy since the 1970s may offer an insight into the basic commitment to human rights that has, in practice, influenced US foreign policy for decades, despite the simultaneous inconsistencies that have undermined US influence in the human rights arena.[613]

Attempts to link human rights with US foreign policy began in earnest with the convening of a series of human rights-related hearings by a number of US Congressmen (notably Donald Fraser and Thomas Harkin), beginning in 1973,[614] and the election of US President Jimmy Carter in 1976. Congress adopted several laws mandating that the executive branch restrict military and economic assistance to any country in which there was "a consistent pattern of gross violations of human rights."[615] Congress also required that the US Department of State prepare annual reports on human rights, initially on countries receiving US assistance and subsequently on all countries.[616]

President Jimmy Carter embraced human rights, and his Secretary of State Cyrus Vance articulated the meaning of human rights for the Carter administration in an early address, which remains perhaps the most robust expression of human rights policy by any US administration:

> ... Our human rights policy must be understood in order to be effective. So today I want to set forth the substance of that policy and the results we hope to achieve.
>
> Our concern for human rights is built upon ancient values. It looks with hope to a world in which liberty is not just a great cause but the common condition. In the past it may have seemed sufficient to put our name in international documents that spoke loftily of human rights. That is not enough. We will go to work, alongside other people and governments, to protect and enhance the dignity of the individual.
>
> Let me define what we mean by "human rights."
>
> 1. **First, there is the right to be free from governmental violation of the integrity of the person.** Such violations include torture; cruel, inhuman, or degrading treatment or punishment; and arbitrary arrest or imprisonment. And they include denial of fair public trial, and invasion of the home.
> 2. **Second, there is the right to the fulfillment of such vital needs as food, shelter, health care, and education.** We recognize that the fulfillment of this right will depend, in part, upon the stage of the nation's economic development. But we also know that this right can be violated by a Government's action or inaction – for example, through corrupt official processes which divert resources to an elite at the expense of the needy, or through indifference to the plight of the poor.
> 3. **Third, there is the right to enjoy civil and political liberties**—freedom of thought, of religion, of assembly; freedom of speech; freedom of the press; freedom of movement both within and outside one's own country; freedom to take part in government.
>
> Our policy is to promote all these rights ...
>
> In pursuing a human rights policy, we must always keep in mind the limits of our power and of our wisdom. A sure formula for defeat of our goals would be a rigid, hubristic attempt to impose our values on others. A doctrinaire plan of action would be as damaging as indifference.
>
> We must be realistic. Our country can only achieve our objectives if we shape what we do to the case at hand ...
>
> It is not our purpose to intervene in the internal affairs of other countries, but as the President has emphasized, no member of the United Nations can claim that violation of internationally protected human rights is solely its own affair. It is our purpose to shape our policies in accord with our beliefs and to state them without stridency or apology when we think it is desirable to do so ...

> We recognize that many nations of the world are organized on authoritarian rather than democratic principles – some large and powerful, others struggling to raise the lives of their people above bare subsistence levels. We can nourish no illusions that a call to the banner of human rights will bring sudden transformations in authoritarian societies.
>
> We are embarked on a long journey. But our faith in the dignity of the individual encourages us to believe that people in every society, according to their own traditions, will in time give their own expression to this fundamental aspiration . . .[617]

The fact that we must go back 40 years to find such support for human rights says a great deal about the twists and turns in US policy in subsequent decades. Carter was in office for only four years, and his successor, Ronald Reagan, sought to undo the focus on human rights that Carter and Congress had initiated. He was only partially successful, due to laws enacted even before Carter and the growing popularity of human rights as a cause and a slogan. Reagan politicized human rights, distinguishing between "authoritarian" (i.e., right-wing regimes friendly to the United States) and "totalitarian" (i.e., Communist) governments, and criticism of the Soviet Union and its allies on human rights grounds was a relatively successful (at least from a public relations perspective) staple of the Cold War.

In addition to the authoritarian/totalitarian distinction, Reagan pointedly excluded economic, social, and cultural rights from the US understanding of human rights. His ambassador to the United Nations, Jeanne Kirkpatrick, launched a scathing attack on such rights, patronizingly claiming that "no great reflection produced them" and that they were no more than a "letter to Santa Claus," based upon "a vague sense that Utopia is one's due."[618] Reagan also did his best to ignore Congressional mandates regarding human rights whenever possible, often by utilizing presidential overrides explicitly permitted by these laws.

Most subsequent US administrations have stayed in between these two relative extremes, and all at least gave lip service to the cause of human rights and accepted that human rights concerns were a legitimate component of US foreign policy. However, the content of those rights and the priorities set by various administrations have become increasingly political and responsive to domestic concerns, rather than being based on a sober analysis of how to influence the situation in particular countries. The administration of George H.W. Bush (1989–1993) was little different from that of Reagan.

President Bill Clinton (1993–2001) implicitly expanded the mandate of the State Department's work on human rights by renaming the responsible office from the Bureau of Human Rights and Humanitarian Affairs to the Bureau of Democracy, Human Rights, and Labor. This suggests either that neither democracy nor labor is included in human rights or that democracy and labor are somehow more important than other human rights; both are dangerous positions to maintain. Nonetheless, this semantic shift pleased Clinton's successors, as well, and democracy promotion soon eclipsed the goal of promoting the full panoply of human rights found in the

UDHR and other international instruments. This shift was criticized by many human rights advocates, as demonstrated by the following comment by a long-time observer of US foreign policy, democracy, and human rights:

> For many in the human rights movement there is a very significant difference in formal status between human rights and democracy: human rights are international legal norms whereas democracy is a political ideology. In their view, U.S. government pressure on a foreign government to improve its human rights behavior is a form of entirely legitimate intervention in the internal affairs of that country because human rights norms are binding under international law on all states. By contrast, they consider that U.S. pressure on a foreign government to become democratic is of questionable legitimacy because democracy is just one of a number of competing political ideologies, not a binding obligation. Democracy promotion by the U.S. government, they hold, constantly runs the risk of veering off into neo-imperialism.[619]

Democracy promotion after the dissolution of the Soviet Union and the end of the Cold War also allowed the United States to emphasize its human rights strengths, including free and fair elections (leaving aside the increasingly obscene role of money in these contests), rule of law, and respect for traditional civil and political rights. Economic and social rights remained unrecognized, however, and countries like China received little or no credit from the United States for economic progress and declining poverty rates. Throughout this period, as had been the case since Carter, critics accused US administrations of paying far more attention to increasing economic opportunities for US companies through increased international trade or protecting political or strategic allies than they did to forthrightly and consistently pursuing human rights goals.

The Clinton years overlapped not only with the end of the Cold War but with a burst of anarchy and violence, let loose in part by the unstable vacuum left by the retreat of communism in eastern Europe and central Asia. Secessionist movements wracked Georgia, Azerbaijan, Russia, Yugoslavia, Somalia, and Sri Lanka in the late 1980s and early 1990s; genocide occurred in Rwanda in 1994; what has been termed "Africa's first world war" in and around the Democratic Republic of Congo claimed perhaps five million lives between 1994 and 2003;[620] and the celebration of the victory of liberal democracy and capitalism over communism soon acquired a decidedly less triumphant aspect. "Ethnic cleansing" in the Balkans startled Europeans, and Rwanda rang loudly in the ears of those who had promised "never again." Apart from the premature welcoming of Russia and most of eastern and central Europe into the Council of Europe and the European Convention on Human Rights, concerns over mere human rights largely gave way to attempts to stop wars and war crimes. The creation of the International Criminal Court, discussed further in Chapter 2, was perhaps the most visible reaction to the violent conflicts of the 1990s.

While the attention of the United States turned to conflict resolution, accountability, democracy, and transitional justice in the 1990s, it also supported strengthening the UN's human rights work, including creation of the post of UN High Commissioner for Human Rights in 1994. In addition, the United States ratified its first UN human rights treaties in this period: the International Covenant on Civil and Political Rights (1992), Convention against Torture (1994), and Convention on the Elimination of All Forms of Racial Discrimination (1994).

THE WAR ON TERROR

Terrorism, whether international or domestic, did not begin in the late twentieth century, but the impact of the attacks on the United States on 9 September 2001 on human rights and the politics of human rights cannot be overstated. Most of the world initially sympathized with the victims of 9/11 and supported the US invasion of Afghanistan as a legitimate act of self-defense. However, subsequent events – the indefinite detention of terrorist suspects at the US military base at Guantánamo Bay, the invasion of Iraq in March 2003, and the subsequent abuses of detainees at the Abu Ghraib prison and elsewhere – soon cast a different light on the "war on terror."

Restrictions on human rights for the purpose of protecting national security are permitted under all of the major human rights treaties,[621] and states have persistently justified violations of human rights by invoking national security. Whether the targets are terrorists, subversives, communists, anticommunists, secessionists, or minority ethnic or religious groups, restrictions on rights in order to safeguard national security have often been utilized by authoritarian governments simply to preserve the power of those in power. In both authoritarian and democratic states, targeting suspected terrorists or subversives can be either a legitimate and temporary response to an imminent threat that cannot be dealt with under normal legal rules or a sweeping, indiscriminate attempt to placate a population and demonstrate that the government is "doing something" about the problem; often government actions fall into both categories at the same time.

In his speech to Congress nine days after the September 11 attacks, President George W. Bush (2001–2009) proclaimed:

> On September the 11th, enemies of freedom committed an act of war against our country . . . and night fell on a different world, a world where freedom itself is under attack . . .
>
> Our war on terror begins with al Qaeda, but it does not end there. It will not end until every terrorist group of global reach has been found, stopped and defeated . . .
>
> Every nation, in every region, now has a decision to make. Either you are with us, or you are with the terrorists. From this day forward, any nation that continues to harbor or support terrorism will be regarded by the United States as a hostile regime.
>
> Great harm has been done to us. We have suffered great loss. And in our grief and anger we have found our mission and our moment. Freedom and fear are at war. The advance of human freedom – the great achievement of our time, and the

great hope of every time – now depends on us. Our nation – this generation – will lift a dark threat of violence from our people and our future. We will rally the world to this cause by our efforts, by our courage. We will not tire, we will not falter, and we will not fail.[622]

A debate ensued within the Bush administration over what applicable US or international law governed US treatment of those captured in Afghanistan and elsewhere.[623] In February 2002, Bush decided that none of the 1949 Geneva Conventions applied to Al Qaeda and that, even though these conventions did apply in principle to Taliban forces, neither Taliban nor Al Qaeda detainees were entitled to prisoner of war status. He also determined that common article 3 of the 1949 Geneva Conventions was inapplicable, since the war in Afghanistan was international in character.[624]

The detention and possible trial of Guantánamo detainees has been the subject of almost constant court challenges in the United States since 2001. While the initial goal of the Bush administration was to place detainees beyond the jurisdiction of any court or tribunal, domestic or international, US courts have refused to grant the president such unlimited powers. In 2004, the US Supreme Court held that detainees in Guantánamo did not fall outside the jurisdiction of US courts, although it did not identify precisely what remedies might be available to such persons to challenge their detention.[625] In partial response to that decision, the United States created "combatant status review tribunals" to review detentions; these also were rejected by the Supreme Court in *Hamdan v. Rumsfeld*.[626] A revised military commissions law was enacted under President Obama in 2009.[627] An attempt by Congress to prohibit Guantánamo detainees from invoking habeas corpus to review their detention also was rejected, by a deeply divided court.[628]

Despite promises by candidate Barack Obama during the 2008 presidential campaign to close the detention facility at Guantánamo, Congressional action prevented him from doing so after he assumed office in 2009. Despite repeated unsuccessful attempts in subsequent years to change the mind of the Republican majority in Congress, Obama eventually abandoned his oft-stated goal of closing the facility. From a high of nearly 800 detainees, the number had fallen to 41 by the end of Obama's term in January 2017; the vast majority of detainees were transferred to one of nearly 60 countries that had agreed to accept them. Of those remaining, most will apparently remain detained indefinitely.[629]

President Bush's February 2002 memorandum stated that all detainees were to be treated humanely, but that proved not to be the case. Soon after the invasion of Afghanistan, concerns began to be expressed over the interrogation techniques used by US forces and their allies. On 28 April 2004, the CBS television program 60 *Minutes II* broadcast a series of disturbing photographs taken in the fall of 2003 at Abu Ghraib, a notorious prison under Saddam Hussein before the US invasion. The now infamous photographs included depictions of mock executions, inmates in degrading simulated sex poses, and naked detainees being threatened with barking military dogs. The moral credibility of the United States plummeted around the world. Subsequent investigations of Abu Ghraib resulted in the court martial and conviction of a number of military personnel, although the investigations also concluded that no officer had ordered abuse and that there was no policy of torture.

Abu Ghraib was not unique, and subsequent investigations uncovered numerous examples of ill-treatment and even death in US detention centers in Afghanistan and Iraq.[630] Much of this mistreatment stemmed from interrogators' use of "enhanced interrogation techniques," including wall-standing, hooding, deprivation of sleep, physical ill-treatment, and water-boarding (during which water is poured down a detainee's throat in order to simulate drowning). Many of these same methods (except water-boarding) had been used by British security forces during the conflict in Northern Ireland in the 1970s; they were deemed to constitute "inhuman treatment" by the European Court of Human Rights.[631]

In June 2004, following public outrage over the photos from Abu Ghraib and other disclosures of ill-treatment of detainees, the White House "disavowed" a 2002 memorandum that had advocated an extremely restrictive interpretation of torture and had concluded that enhanced interrogation did not violate either domestic or international law.[632] A subsequent Justice Department ethics investigation concluded that the author of the memorandum (Jay S. Bybee, who was appointed a judge on the Ninth Circuit Court of Appeals by President Bush in 2003) and another former Justice Department attorney (John Yoo, now a law professor at the University of California, Berkeley), had committed "professional misconduct" in connection with this and other advice given to the Bush administration; that finding was rejected by a higher official, who said only that their work had "significant flaws."[633]

An additional blow to US prestige and credibility arose when it became known that the United States was sending suspected terrorists, whether from Guantánamo or elsewhere, to countries with long records of torturing prisoners. Allegations of secret detention centers controlled by the CIA became more frequent. In January 2006, the European Parliament created a committee to investigate these allegations, which noted in its final report that at least 1,245 flights operated by the CIA flew into European airspace or stopped at European airports between the end of 2001 and the end of 2005. In its conclusion, the committee "[c]ondemns extraordinary rendition as an illegal instrument used by the United States in the fight against terrorism; condemns, further, the acceptance and concealing of the practice, on several occasions, by the secret services and governmental authorities of certain European countries; ... [and condemns] any participation in the interrogation of individuals who are victims of extraordinary rendition, because it represents a deplorable legitimisation of that type of illegal procedure, even where those participating in the interrogation do not bear direct responsibility for the kidnapping, detention, torture or ill-treatment of the victims."[634]

Several cases involving rendition and secret detention were brought to the European Court of Human Rights, against Poland, Romania, Italy, Lithuania, and Macedonia, respectively; the court found violations of the prohibition against torture and the right to liberty. The rendition program was described by the court in a case brought against Poland:

> The Court observes that secret detention of terrorist suspects was a fundamental feature of the CIA rendition programme. As can be seen from the CIA declassified documents, the rationale behind the programme was specifically to remove those persons from any legal protection against torture and enforced disappearance and to strip them of any safeguards afforded by both the US Constitution and international law against arbitrary detention, to mention only the right to be brought before a judge and be tried within a reasonable time or the habeas corpus guarantees. To this end, the whole scheme had to operate outside the jurisdiction of the US courts and in conditions securing its absolute secrecy, which required setting up, in cooperation with the host countries, overseas detention facilities.[635]

On his second day in office, President Obama ordered an end to water-boarding and other enhanced interrogation techniques, which had already been discontinued for some time.[636] A few weeks later, however, the Obama administration announced that it would not prosecute any of the Bush administration officials who had authorized torture.[637] The explanation for that decision may be found in a statement that accompanied the release of additional internal memoranda related to interrogation a few days earlier: "This is a time for reflection, not retribution ... We have been through a dark and painful chapter in our history. But at a time of great challenges and disturbing disunity, nothing will be gained by spending our time and energy laying blame for the past ... ."[638]

This statement is reminiscent of those made by many other leaders who chose reconciliation or stability over accountability. However, human rights advocates were quick to note that, under article 7 of the Convention against Torture, ratified by the United States in 1994, allegations of torture are to be investigated and criminal prosecutions brought "in the same manner as in the case of any ordinary offence of a serious nature." One more strike against international law.

Since 2006, interrogation practices have been governed in US law by a revised version of the Army's Field Manual on Human Intelligence Collector Operations, which states that all detainees "shall be treated humanely" and that "no person in the custody or under the control of DOD [the US Department of Defense] ... shall be subject to torture or cruel, inhuman, or degrading treatment or punishment, in accordance with and as defined in US law."[639] The manual explicitly prohibits the enhanced interrogation techniques utilized in the early post-2001 years, including waterboarding.[640] Nonetheless, in 2017 it was reported that the prosecutor for the International Criminal Court had requested authorization to investigate allegations of crimes committed within Afghanistan, including charges of rape and torture by US military and the CIA, crimes against humanity by the Taliban, and war crimes by Afghan security forces.[641]

Both what torture is and whether it should ever be used continue to be debated. A March 2016 online poll asked US respondents if torture can be justified "against suspected terrorists to obtain information about terrorism." Approximately 25% said that it is "often" justified while another 38% said that it is "sometimes" justified; only 15% said that torture should never be used.[642] During the election campaign in 2016, now President Donald Trump said that he would seek to roll back Obama's ban on waterboarding and vowed to "bring back a hell of a lot worse" if elected.[643] Thus far, however, this has not occurred.

US FOREIGN POLICY

As noted above, human rights concerns have formally been a part of US foreign policy since the early 1970s. In his farewell address at the end of his presidency, Ronald Reagan extolled the fact that "[c]ountries across the globe are turning to free markets and free speech and turning away from the ideologies of the past. For them, the great rediscovery of the 1980s has been that, lo and behold, the moral way of government is the practical way of government: Democracy, the profoundly good, is also the profoundly productive."[644] Reagan mentioned human rights only once in this speech, when contrasting the US with the Soviet Union, but the model of the United States as "the shining city upon a hill" he referenced reflects the often self-serving view of many Americans that it is enough for the United States to lead by example, rather than being an integral partner in the shared values of universal human rights law. "With a mission driven by Providence, we have sought to extend the blessings of freedom and democracy to the far corners of the earth."[645] For better or worse, this justification is hardly unique to the United States, and countries react to their own "exceptionalism" not only through interventionist exploits but also through isolationism and nationalism.

No foreign policy, at least in a relatively democratic country, can be sustained unless it enjoys a degree of popular support. Of course, the role of human rights in US foreign policy depends on ideology – liberal Democrats are more publicly supportive of international law, international organizations, and human rights than are conservative Republicans, who are wary of the United Nations, prefer bilateral to multilateral engagements, and view democracy promotion as a geopolitical weapon to be utilized primarily against US adversaries. Many US citizens are fairly isolationist, and domestic support is often weak for initiatives that go beyond the standard "national interests" of security and promoting American economic interests abroad.

Reflecting American interests and pressure groups, the US Congress has responded over the years by highlighting a number of specific issues for attention, in addition to retaining the place of human rights in US foreign policy. It has directed the government to withhold loans from states with a known history of female genital mutilation, unless they are attempting to eradicate it;[646] created an Ambassador at Large and a US Commission, as well as mandated an annual report by the State Department, on religious persecution;[647] and required a separate annual report on advancing freedom and democracy promotion worldwide.[648]

Continuing the chronological summary begun earlier in this chapter, similar ideological differences distinguished the George W. Bush administration from both its predecessor, Bill Clinton, and its successor, Barack Obama. Clinton was criticized not only for introducing democracy into the human rights equation, as noted above, but also for seeming to be more concerned with trade (especially with a modernizing China) than with speaking out forcefully on human rights. In addition to China, Clinton was accused of being too lenient in criticism of two erstwhile allies with bad human rights records, Turkey and Indonesia.[649] Nonetheless, Clinton appointed State Department officials who were knowledgeable about and sincerely committed to promoting human rights; recognized that economic, social, and cultural rights were a legitimate part of the human rights pantheon (although he did little to establish these "rights" in domestic law or politics); and was more supportive of and cooperative with the United Nations in its human rights and humanitarian work.

While Barack Obama's opposition to the 2003 invasion of Iraq was a major issue in both his Democratic primary campaign against Hilary Clinton and the general election against Senator John McCain, human rights per se and their role in US foreign policy have not played a significant role in the past three presidential campaigns, not surprising in light of the 2008 global financial crisis and its impact on the US economy. As noted above, Obama rolled back some of Bush's "war on terror" policies, and he actively sought to reengage the United States with the United Nations and its new Human Rights Council. The United States successfully stood for election to the Council in 2009 and, like most candidate states, made a number of formal commitments as part of its campaign for a seat.

Commitment to Advancing Human Rights, Fundamental Freedoms and Human Dignity and Prosperity Internationally

1. The United States commits to continue supporting states in their implementation of human rights obligations, as appropriate, through human rights dialogue, exchange of experts, technical and inter-regional cooperation, and programmatic support of the work of non-governmental organization.
2. The United States commits to continue its efforts to strengthen mechanisms in the international system to advance the rights, protection, and empowerment of women . . .

[The remaining international commitments concerned workers rights, human trafficking, freedom of religion, fighting HIV/AIDS and other global health challenges, "promoting voluntary corporate social responsibility," freedom of expression and the media, and racial discrimination.]

Commitment to Advancing Human Rights and Fundamental Freedoms in the United States

1. The United States executive branch is committed to working with its legislative branch to consider the possible ratification of human rights treaties, including but not limited to the Convention on the Elimination of

Discrimination against Women and ILO Convention 111 Concerning Discrimination in Respect of Employment and Occupation.

2. The United States is committed to meeting its UN treaty obligations and participating in a meaningful dialogue with treaty body members.

3. The United States is committed to cooperating with the UN's human rights mechanisms, as well as the Inter-American Commission on Human Rights and other regional human rights bodies, by responding to inquiries, engaging in dialogues, and hosting visits . . .[650]

Despite these promises, a generally liberal pro–human rights perspective. and the successive appointments of well-known US human rights activists from Human Rights First and Human Rights Watch, respectively, as assistant secretaries of state for human rights, Obama, too, was criticized for not doing enough to criticize countries that were persistent human rights violators, such as China, Iran, Sudan, and Burma.[651] On her first trip to China as Obama's Secretary of State, Hillary Clinton was accused of downplaying human rights issues in favor of economic and strategic considerations. In late 2009, however, Clinton gave a major speech at George Washington University, in which she set forth the administration's human rights agenda:

Our human rights agenda for the twenty-first century is to make human rights a human reality, and the first step is to see human rights in a broad context. Of course, people must be free from the oppression of tyranny, from torture, from discrimination, from the fear of leaders who will imprison or "disappear" them. But they also must be free from the oppression of want – want of food, want of health, want of education, and want of equality in law and in fact.

To fulfill their potential, people must be free to choose laws and leaders; to share and access information, to speak, criticize, and debate. They must be free to worship, associate, and to love in the way that they choose. And they must be free to pursue the dignity that comes with self-improvement and self-reliance, to build their minds and their skills, to bring their goods to the marketplace, and participate in the process of innovation. Human rights have both negative and positive requirements. People should be free from tyranny in whatever form, and they should also be free to seize the opportunities of a full life. That is why supporting democracy and fostering development are cornerstones of our twenty-first century human rights agenda.

This Administration, like others before us, will promote, support, and defend democracy. We will relinquish neither the word nor the idea to those who have used it too narrowly, or to justify unwise policies. We stand for democracy not because we want other countries to be like us, but because we want all people to enjoy the consistent protection of the rights that are naturally theirs, whether they were born in Tallahassee or Tehran. Democracy has proven the best political system for making human rights a human reality over the long term.

But it is crucial that we clarify what we mean when we talk about democracy, because democracy means not only elections to choose leaders, but also active citizens and a free press and an independent judiciary and transparent and responsive institutions that are accountable to all citizens and protect their rights equally and fairly. In democracies, respecting rights isn't a choice leaders make day by day; it is the reason they govern ...

At the same time, human development must also be part of our human rights agenda. Because basic levels of well-being—food, shelter, health, and education—and of public common goods like environmental sustainability, protection against pandemic disease, provisions for refugees—are necessary for people to exercise their rights, and because human development and democracy are mutually reinforcing. Democratic governments are not likely to survive long if their citizens do not have the basic necessities of life. The desperation caused by poverty and disease often leads to violence that further imperils the rights of people and threatens the stability of governments ...

So human rights, democracy, and development are not three separate goals with three separate agendas ... [W]e have to tackle all three simultaneously with a commitment that is smart, strategic, determined, and long-term. We should measure our success by asking this question: Are more people in more places better able to exercise their universal rights and live up to their potential because of our actions?

... [T]here is not one approach or formula, doctrine or theory that can be easily applied to every situation. But I want to outline four elements of the Obama Administration's approach to putting our principles into action, and share with you some of the challenges we face in doing so. [Clinton goes on to discuss the commitment to universal standards for human rights; being "pragmatic and agile" in pursuit of the US human rights agenda; supporting change driven by civil society; and widening the US focus to reinforce positive change "where hope is on the rise" and not to ignore "places of seemingly intractable tragedy and despair."][652]

These prescriptions are nuanced and reasonable, but they also leave a great deal of discretion to "pragmatic and agile" policy makers. The impact of these principles was tested little more than a year later, in the context of the so-called Arab spring uprisings in Tunisia, Egypt, Syria, and Libya. Obama addressed the uprisings just a few weeks after they began, in a tone that emphasized the US interest in human rights both for their own sake and in pursuit of the more traditional national interest in peace and security.

... For six months, we have witnessed an extraordinary change taking place in the Middle East and North Africa. Square by square, town by town, country by country, the people have risen up to demand their basic human rights. Two leaders have stepped aside. More may follow. And though these countries may be a great distance from our shores, we know that our own future is bound to this region by the forces of economics and security, by history and by faith ...

The question before us is what role America will play as this story unfolds. For decades, the United States has pursued a set of core interests in the region: countering terrorism and stopping the spread of nuclear weapons; securing the free flow of commerce and safe-guarding the security of the region; standing up for Israel's security and pursuing Arab-Israeli peace.

We will continue to do these things, with the firm belief that America's interests are not hostile to people's hopes; they're essential to them . . .

Yet we must acknowledge that a strategy based solely upon the narrow pursuit of these interests will not fill an empty stomach or allow someone to speak their mind. Moreover, failure to speak to the broader aspirations of ordinary people will only feed the suspicion that has festered for years that the United States pursues our interests at their expense . . .

So we face a historic opportunity . . . [A]fter decades of accepting the world as it is in the region, we have a chance to pursue the world as it should be.

Of course, as we do, we must proceed with a sense of humility. It's not America that put people into the streets of Tunis or Cairo – it was the people themselves who launched these movements, and it's the people themselves that must ultimately determine their outcome . . .

[Obama then outlined a set of "core principles" to guide the US response, including opposition to violence and repression, supporting universal rights, and political and economic reform.]

Our support for these principles is not a secondary interest. Today I want to make it clear that it is a top priority that must be translated into concrete actions, and supported by all of the diplomatic, economic and strategic tools at our disposal.

Let me be specific. First, it will be the policy of the United States to promote reform across the region, and to support transitions to democracy . . .

Now, even as we promote political reform, even as we promote human rights in the region, our efforts can't stop there. So the second way that we must support positive change in the region is through our efforts to advance economic development for nations that are transitioning to democracy . . .

For the American people, the scenes of upheaval in the region may be unsettling, but the forces driving it are not unfamiliar. Our own nation was founded through a rebellion against an empire. Our people fought a painful Civil War that extended freedom and dignity to those who were enslaved . . .

It will not be easy. There's no straight line to progress, and hardship always accompanies a season of hope. But the United States of America was founded on the belief that people should govern themselves. And now we cannot hesitate to stand squarely on the side of those who are reaching for their rights, knowing that their success will bring about a world that is more peaceful, more stable, and more just.[653]

Unfortunately, only Tunisia might be said to have become "more peaceful, more stable, and more just," as violent reactions against the protests in Egypt, Syria, and Libya descended into repression, death, and chaos. The situations in Syria and Libya are discussed in Chapter 8, while Egypt serves as an unfortunate example of the "humility" that Obama warned must accompany US advocacy of human rights and democracy.

In Egypt, former president Hosni Mubarak was imprisoned, and a reasonably free and fair election soon thereafter led to a government dominated by the conservative Muslim Brotherhood. Many of the mostly young 2011 protesters were disillusioned, and in 2013, a military coup overthrew the elected government and replaced it with martial law – a result that even many "democracy" advocates welcomed. The US response was ... to cancel a biannual joint military exercise with the Egyptian military and to recognize reality:

America cannot determine the future of Egypt. That's a task for the Egyptian people. We don't take sides with any particular party or political figure ...

From Asia to the Americas, we know that democratic transitions are measured not in months or even years, but sometimes in generations. So in the spirit of mutual interest and mutual respect, I want to be clear that America wants to be a partner in the Egyptian people's pursuit of a better future, and we are guided by our national interest in this longstanding relationship. But our partnership must also advance the principles that we believe in and that so many Egyptians have sacrificed for these last several years – no matter what party or faction they belong to.

So America will work with all those in Egypt and around the world who support a future of stability that rests on a foundation of justice and peace and dignity.[654]

The leader of the 2013 coup, General Abdel Fatah al-Sisi, was subsequently elected president of Egypt. Amnesty International's 2016/2017 Annual Report introduced the situation in Egypt as follows:

The authorities used mass arbitrary arrests to suppress demonstrations and dissent, detaining journalists, human rights defenders and protesters, and restricted the activities of human rights organizations. The National Security Agency (NSA) subjected hundreds of detainees to enforced disappearance; officers of the NSA and other security forces tortured and otherwise ill-treated detainees. Security forces used excessive lethal force during regular policing and in incidents that may have amounted to extrajudicial executions. Mass unfair trials continued before civilian and military courts. The authorities failed to adequately investigate human rights violations and bring perpetrators to justice ...[655]

The annual US Country Reports on Human Rights, released in 2017, painted an equally bleak picture:

The most significant human rights problems were excessive use of force by security forces, deficiencies in due process, and the suppression of civil liberties. Excessive use of force included unlawful killings and torture. Due process problems included the excessive use of preventative custody and pretrial detention, the use of military courts to try civilians, trials involving hundreds of defendants in which authorities did not present evidence on an individual basis, and arrests conducted without warrants or judicial orders ...

Other human rights problems included disappearances; harsh prison conditions; arbitrary arrests; a judiciary that in some cases appeared to arrive at outcomes not supported by publicly available evidence or that appeared to reflect political motivations; reports of political prisoners and detainees; restrictions on academic freedom; impunity for security forces; harassment of some civil society organizations; limits on religious freedom; official corruption; limits on civil society organizations; violence, harassment, and societal discrimination against women and girls, including female genital mutilation/cutting (FGM/C); child abuse; discrimination against persons with disabilities; trafficking in persons; societal discrimination against religious minorities; discrimination and arrests based on sexual orientation; discrimination against HIV-positive persons; and worker abuse, including child labor.[656]

There are several lessons for US foreign policy to be drawn from Egypt. First, as is true with respect to the other Arab Spring countries, the ability of the United States to guide revolutionary changes within other countries is extremely limited. Moral support and promises of economic assistance may be worthwhile, but entrenched dictatorships will fall only when there is sufficiently widespread opposition within the country itself. Still unknown is whether change in these three countries will be profound or will be, like Egypt, little more than the exchange of one authoritarian leader for another. A related lesson is that humility isn't necessarily a bad thing.

Second, US support for human rights and democratic transition is unlikely to be harmful to US interests, even if the transition fails. It is true that Egypt is no longer as reliable a strategic partner as it was under Mubarak, but the strains are manageable. If it costs the United States little to maintain its official stance that international human rights norms do matter, even at the expense of angering a past or future dictator, isn't it worth a try? And when change eventually does arrive, would the United States prefer to be seen as a defender of dictatorship (as in the Shah's Iran, Marcos's Philippines, Sukarno's Indonesia, and much of Central and South America in the 1970s and 1980s) or as a friend of the new, more democratic regimes (as in eastern and central Europe and post-dictatorship Latin America)?

In a long interview on foreign policy in 2016, in which human rights were mentioned only twice, Obama justified promotion of human rights by both US self-interest but also because it "makes the world a better place." At the same time, he said, "there are going to be times where the best that we can do is to shine a spotlight on something that's terrible, but not believe that we can automatically solve it. There are going to be times where our security interests conflict with our concerns about human rights. There are going to be times where we can do something about innocent people being killed, but there are going to be times where we can't."[657]

The frequent references in Obama's speeches to American values and history underscore the importance of domestic support for at least the rhetoric of human rights, and this is true for thematic as well as country-specific foreign policy initiatives. Priorities under Obama included, in particular, support for freedom of expression, freedom of religion, equality for women, and LGBT rights. The first two are guaranteed in the US constitution and widely supported, at least in theory, by the US population. While Hillary Clinton may not have invented the phrase "women's rights are human rights" that she intoned at the UN's Fourth World Conference on Women in Beijing in 1995, equality for women is clearly one of the major goals of human rights activists in the United States and western Europe – and, indeed, much of the rest of the world. While the rights and social acceptance of sexual minorities continues to be divisive, even within the United States, liberals in the Obama administration and the Democratic Party have been among their most staunch and consistent supporters. (This issue is discussed further in Chapter 6.) Obama also created an Interagency Atrocities Prevention Board in 2011, declaring that "[p]reventing mass atrocities and genocide is a core national security interest and a core moral responsibility of the United States."[658]

Perhaps chastened by the aftermath of the Arab Spring and the debacle in Libya, Obama devoted only one minute out of his short 20-minute second inauguration speech in January 2013 to foreign policy.[659] The administration continued to promote human rights, but wars in Syria, Iraq, Yemen, and Afghanistan held the administration's attention. Liberal democracy was in retreat in Hungary, Poland, the Philippines, and Kenya; many African states enacted anti-gay legislation in reaction to others' promotion of LGBT rights; opposition to the surge of Middle Eastern refugees and migrants grew in Europe; and "ordinary" human rights, while not forgotten, dropped from the headlines.

THE NEW NORMAL?

And then came Donald Trump. Once again, human rights were absent from the presidential campaign in 2016. According to several opinion polls, Donald Trump and Hillary Clinton were the most disliked presidential candidates in 40 years, and the election was dominated by character, not issues. Trump's "America First" campaign rhetoric, misogyny, vocal support for torture, and attacks on immigrants led human rights advocates to expect the worst. Their expectations were met.

This is not the time to undertake an evaluation of the lies, missteps, and ignorance of the Trump administration, but his disdain for human rights as a component of US foreign policy goes beyond anything seen from a US president since the 1970s. It may be unfair to indulge in a detailed analysis of the extent of this policy shift less than two years into the Trump presidency, but quotes from a few headlines will give a taste of the commentary in the first few months: "President Trump is responding to terrorism the way demagogues and dictators do";[660] "Rex Tillerson [Trump's secretary of state until March 2018] skips State Department's annual announcement on human rights, alarming advocates";[661] "Tillerson says goodbye to human rights diplomacy";[662] "Endangered America's global influence has dwindled under Donald Trump";[663] "Donald Trump's speech could have been written by Poland's populists – In Warsaw, America's president barely mentions democracy";[664] "Trump's approach to human rights? It's personal, critics say."[665] Nearly two years to the day after Trump's election, a Boston Globe story on Trump's influence abroad was entitled, "Exporting Fury".[666]

Particularly troubling is what appears to be Trump's embrace of authoritarian leaders in all regions of the world, including Rodrigo Duterte in the Philippines, Crown Prince Salman in Saudi Arabia, Vladimir Putin in Russia, Abdel Fattah al-Sisi in Egypt, and Recep Erdogan of Turkey; within the administration's first year, authoritarian leaders of Egypt, Turkey, Vietnam, and Thailand were invited to the White House.[667] The summit meeting with North Korea's Kim Jong-Un in June 2018 is but another example, although we are forced to hope that this might be the first step toward a more peaceful Korean peninsula, as unlikely as that outcome may be. Trump said that it was his "honour" to be meeting with Kim and that "he [Kim] is very talented. Anybody who takes over a situation like he did at 26 years of age and is able to run it and run it tough. I don't say it was nice, I don't say anything about it, he ran it. Very few people at that age – you can take one of 10,000 probably couldn't do it."[668] Trump also commented, "His country does love him ... His people, you see the fervor."[669]

Of course, the Trump administration has singled out some countries for criticism on human rights grounds, including US adversaries such as North Korea (before the meeting with Kim), Iran, Cuba, and Venezuela.[670] On a brief visit to Myanmar, Secretary of State Tillerson called for an investigation of "credible reports of widespread atrocities" committed by Myanmar armed forces against the Rohingya minority; while he initially declined to describe the situation as one of ethnic cleansing, that changed a week later, when the possibility of unilateral US sanctions against Myanmar was raised by Tillerson.[671]

Human rights advocacy continued at the lower levels of government, however, as evidenced by the objection of the Hungarian government to the offer of funding by the US State Department for projects aimed at increasing access to objective media information in Hungary.[672] While President Trump is unlikely to criticize US allies (except Europeans and Canadians, apparently), the annual State Department Country Report released in March 2018 introduces the entry on Saudi Arabia, for example, in fairly direct terms, with no significant changes from the comparable language in the 2017 report, which was prepared primarily by the Obama State Department. The report notes, among other issues, unlawful killings, including execution without requisite due process; torture; arbitrary arrest and detention of lawyers, human rights activists, and antigovernment reformists; and restrictions on freedoms of expression, peaceful assembly, association, movement, and religion; citizens' lack of means to choose their government through free and fair elections; and official discrimination against women.[673]

While the US bureaucracy thus continues to comply with the tasks assigned to it by Congress, it is the attitude at the top that counts. Over a year into his presidency, Trump had given no indication that he would soon appoint anyone to the highest-ranking human rights position in the State Department, and the secretary of state broke precedent by not personally appearing at the release of the department's country reports on human rights in March 2017. Further, the constant refrain of

"America First," the withdrawal from the Paris Agreement on climate change, and the widespread downgrading of US diplomatic engagement with the rest of world has had an obvious knock-on effect in diminishing the importance of anything that the United States says about human rights. In June 2018, the United States withdrew from the UN Human Rights Council, citing the council's "unending hostility toward Israel" as "clear proof that the council is motivated by political bias, not by human rights."[674] The US Ambassador to the United Nations subsequently blamed human rights NGOs and other countries for the withdrawal, because they opposed the US attempts to "reform" the council.[675]

President Trump's September 2017 address to the UN General Assembly essentially rejected multilateralism, consistent with his campaign promise to put "America first."

> Our success [in overcoming threats and achieving the promises of the future] depends on a coalition of strong and independent nations that embrace their sovereignty to promote security, prosperity, and peace for themselves and for the world.
>
> We do not expect diverse countries to share the same cultures, traditions, or even systems of government. But we do expect all nations to uphold these two core sovereign duties: to respect the interests of their own people and the rights of every other sovereign nation ...
>
> If we desire to lift up our citizens, if we aspire to the approval of history, then we must fulfill our sovereign duties to the people we faithfully represent. We must protect our nations, their interests, and their futures. We must reject threats to sovereignty, from the Ukraine to the South China Sea. We must uphold respect for law, respect for borders, and respect for culture, and the peaceful engagement these allow ...[676]

The president also stated that "America stands with every person living under a brutal regime ... All people deserve a government that cares for their safety, their interests, and their wellbeing, including their prosperity."[677] However, praise for foreign leaders such as Putin, Duterte, and other autocrats suggests that Trump's America is standing very far behind, indeed.

THE MYTH OF CONSISTENCY

Any worthwhile lobbyist will demand that her or his cause should receive priority attention, and human rights advocates are not exceptions. At the same time, recalling Ralph Waldo Emerson's warning that "a foolish consistency is the hobgoblin of little minds," an unrealistic expectation that the foreign policy of any country will always put the situation of human rights in other countries first is not helpful. The following observations, made by a senior State Department official over 30 years ago, still ring true:

> The key issue of implementation for U.S. policymakers is not direction, but degree. How much, realistically, can be done? The United States cannot take on the

promotion of all human rights all at once in all countries, given the awesome
political and economic constraints on its resources. Nor should it . . .

The task before the United States is to differentiate among the categories of the
ideal, the desirable, and the possible . . .

Concentration on consistency . . . misses the point. There can and should be
consistent determination to take human rights into serious account for U.S. foreign
policy. Yet stress on human rights must at all times be weighed against other factors.
A rigid rubric for human rights can obscure the importance of other goals, some of
which may have overarching global significance.[678]

There have been many instances in which US foreign policy has worked against
human rights, has selectively advocated only those rights with which it is comfort-
able, or has chosen to be silent about human rights violations even when there
would be little or no cost to speaking out. However, what is perhaps most surprising
is that international human rights norms continue to influence US foreign policy,
even if the result, particularly since 2017, may be little more than rhetoric.

CONCLUDING REMARKS

In the last quarter of the twentieth century, when human rights acquired a prominent position in the foreign policies of a great number of countries, the United States
was *the* superpower, economically, politically, militarily, and (at least in its own
mind) morally. Most Americans, even in the time of Trump, still cannot resist the
temptation to use this power to change the world, and like most interventionists,
they believe that their own country "knows more and sees further than other
countries."[679] The United States has long advocated its particular form of civil
and political rights and democracy; the "will of the people" remains the theoretical
basis of government, no matter how warped it has become by money, power, and
prejudice. As Chapter 8 argues, military force has long been felt by US administrations to be a useful, and often used, alternative to diplomacy, and it is said that
more personnel serve in just one aircraft carrier task force than the total number of
US foreign service officers.[680]

Nonetheless, "if the place of the United States in the making of a global human
rights order was always less central than Americans often acknowledged . . . it has
further diminished in the early twenty-first century."[681] The United States has
asserted consistently that its view of human rights is unique, an argument made by
many other countries, both supporters and opponents of the concept of universal
human rights. Most non-Americans view this attitude of exceptionalism as one of
hubris and arrogance, even if they might support the freedom, equality, and self-
governance that the United States espouses.

The US desire to lead is perhaps no more arrogant than the propagation of
communism by the former Soviet Union or contemporary China's belief in its
own infallibility, based on its long history and recent rise to near parity with the

United States. However, the preeminent position of the United States in the world for more than half a century is the context in which any evaluation of the role of human rights in its foreign policy must occur. Sweden and The Netherlands may feel and act in an even more consistent fashion, including exhibiting their own moral arrogance on occasion, but they simply don't matter as much and cannot push other states around (excuse me, "encourage" other states) in the same manner as the United States.

The brief summary of US policies in this chapter draws distinctions among different administrations, and the attitudes of the president and Congress are significant shapers of those policies. However, the appeal of human rights has resisted attacks from left and right for nearly five decades and eight presidents. Although written prior to the election of Donald Trump, the following statement still reflects the attitudes of a large proportion of the American population:

> The liberal-conservative consensus that shapes ... [the US] approach to the world embraces both major political parties, most of the press, and the multinational economy. It leads to foreign policy that is not simply interventionist, but utopian, visionary, millennarian. Setting out to remake nations and entire regions, seeking to implant our version of democracy in distant lands, deposing governments and imposing others in their place, springing to the rescue of people we consider oppressed – these are breathtakingly radical projects.[682]

This description is not necessarily positive, but it also should be noted that US interventionism is often welcomed by human rights advocates around the world, who constantly press the United States to "do something" about discrimination and despotism.

The real danger of Trump's retrenchment on human rights is not just that it seeks to downplay the "liberal" preoccupation with people in other countries, for that is likely to change with the next election or the one after that. It is rather the broad disengagement of the United States from the world – on trade, the environment, human rights, immigration, the role of multilateralism and international organizations, and many other subjects – that may be difficult to overcome simply by electing a different president. As many pundits have observed, "American first" is increasingly equivalent to "America alone."

Nature is said to abhor a vacuum, and the space left by US withdrawal is already being filled by those who are more concerned with sovereignty and nationalism than human rights and more equitable benefits from globalization. Europe has been weakened by the 2008 financial crisis, the anticipated departure of the United Kingdom from the European Union, and its own internal divisions brought about by populist national rhetoric, rising racism, fear of immigration, and a widespread feeling of insecurity. China is increasingly assertive politically and economically, and it formally rejects the notion of international human rights, asserting that "[p]romoting 'universal values' ... [is] an attempt to weaken the theoretical foundations of the Party's leadership."[683] Putin's Russia is working diligently to disrupt the Western alliance and ensure that it can continue its authoritarianism at home and adventures abroad unhindered by serious criticism.

For all of its flaws – and there are many – the United States at least retains the strength to say what it wants, where it wants, and to whom it wants. Rhetorical support by the United States for human rights, if matched with greater respect for rights at home as well as a concern for the rights of others, is essential if the ideological struggle between proponents and opponents of universal rights is not to cede ground irretrievably to the opponents.

However articulated or imagined, the appeal of human rights to oppressed individuals and communities around the world remains strong. The United States is not indispensable to ensure that human rights become a reality everywhere, for that will always result primarily from conditions and struggles within countries, not from pressure from outside.[684] However, without US support for this universalist project, the path to achieving human rights will be longer and considerably more difficult, and it may permanently expose Ronald Reagan's "shining city upon a hill" as a hypocritical mirage. The United States need not prance through the halls of the United Nations or the battlefields of the Middle East as a savior on a white steed, but someone needs to provide the rhetorical and political horses to support the millions of foot soldiers scattered across the globe who are struggling for human rights. If not the United States, then who?

10

The Way Forward: Less Is More

Calls for restraint and moderation rarely inspire the emotional commitment that flows from appeals to absolute truth and fundamentalist conviction. There is a fine line between admirable dedication to a cause and inflexible zealotry, however, whether the cause is human rights or saving the whales.

This book is an appeal for radical moderation, which values and promotes human rights norms without distorting or deifying them. It criticizes starry-eyed human rights lawyers who aspire to be social reformers. It rejects narrow libertarians and positivists who believe that states and law are nuisances to be tolerated only so long as they do not interfere with individual greed and intolerance. Underlying many of the book's arguments is the belief that human rights cannot provide dispositive answers to all of the world's problems, although they may be a necessary precondition for resolving many of them. Addressing disparities in political and economic power, promoting inclusion and tolerance, and supporting meaningful participation of all individuals within a society require not only law but also ethical standards, honesty, open-mindedness, and a recognition that many answers are better found in compromise and respect for the views of others, rather than in the often zero-sum-game of competing rights.

This limited view of human rights is consistent with three principles. First, international law does matter. Second, the universality of human rights, properly understood, is not only possible but essential to ensuring a modicum of global fairness. Third, maintaining the distinctions between law and morality or law and politics is important. Recognizing that these concepts are created and enforced differently does not diminish any of them; if anything, it should reinforce the idea that social progress can only be achieved by appealing to law, politics, *and* morality.

WHY THE CRITICS ARE WRONG

One problem with many of those who criticize the relevance and efficacy of human rights is that they conflate human rights law too closely with other concerns, particularly humanitarianism and international crimes, which are addressed in Chapters 2 and 8. For example, much of the commentary by Emilie Hafner-Burton,[685] Hopgood, Moyn, and others immediately and consistently conflates the success or failure of human rights with the record of the International Criminal Court.[686] Stephen Hopgood, for example, sees no hope for the "overambitious, unaccountable, alienated and largely ineffectual" international human rights project, which he consistently confuses with humanitarian and other internationalist goals and condemns as a US-led construct, although he professes admiration for local and transnational activists who use human rights as a means, not an end in themselves.[687] With all due respect to the ICC, it is a relatively easy target, due to its limited track record, its cost, and the overwhelming task that it faces, i.e., prosecuting those responsible for the most serious international crimes. As demonstrated in Chapter 2, however, both the means and the ends of international human rights law and international criminal law are very different, as the latter has a more difficult standard of proof to meet, while the former deals with a much broader range of rights that implicates far more than mere individual criminal responsibility. Similarly, faulting human rights for failing to stop war mistakes the target, which should be the UN Security Council and/or regional political institutions, not human rights mechanisms that were never intended to prevent war.

Eric Posner favors abandoning the concept of human rights altogether in favor of a micro-development approach that "consider[s] each country on its own terms," because human rights rules "do not necessarily advance the well-being of the citizens in the target country." Therefore, wealthy countries should provide assistance, using "tools of coercion if necessary," if they believe that such aid "will enhance the well-being of the population," irrespective of whether the country complies with human rights treaties.[688] Samuel Moyn also promotes humanitarianism over human rights when he calls for "America's human rights policy . . . [to] be reframed to focus on helping the poorest around the world."[689]

Most such criticism evidences dissatisfaction with human rights as the critics wish to interpret them, not with human rights as they are. As discussed in Chapter 3, in the context of development, the commitment of states under the ESC Covenant is primarily to the people living under their jurisdiction, not to all of the world's poor. Human rights give no guidance as to how countries should go about "helping the poorest around the world," and billions more dollars and euros are already spent annually on attempts to do just that than will ever be spent on guaranteeing the international human rights of everyone, not just the poor. Expanding the formal scope of human rights is likely only to distract from the woefully unfinished task of protecting existing rights, including economic, social, and cultural rights.

Another major source of frustration for many critics is the inability of international institutions to impose norms or coerce behavior when countries do not abide by their international legal obligations. For example, Posner is oblivious to the domestic focus of human rights when he states that behind human rights is "the moral obligation not to harm strangers, and possibly ... to help them if they are in need."[690] A similar focus on what "others" can do leads some critics to seek alternative sources of power and authority in the much-maligned international community, powerful governments, or Hafner-Burton's self-appointed stewards who will ensure compliance through both carrots and sticks, when necessary.

This problem is not unique to human rights but inheres in almost every aspect of international law. International law is not hierarchical; as noted in Chapter 1, it still rests on the consent of sovereign states. Some international regimes do provide mechanisms of self-help, as when the World Trade Organization permits countries to impose unilateral counter-measures if a trading partner has acted unfairly and violated WTO rules. Members of the United Nations agree when they join the organization that the Security Council has the power to impose economic sanctions and authorize the use of force, when international peace and security are threatened. From a human rights perspective, broad economic sanctions that affect an entire country are also problematic, and so-called smart or targeted sanctions seem to have only marginal impact.

This lack of hierarchy should be welcome in the field of human rights, for it is all too easy to imagine the potential disasters that might arise if the United Nations (or the Council of Europe, African Union, or other regional organizations) tried to force countries to abide by ... all? the most important? the most popular? provisions of the human rights treaties to which they are parties. As noted in the discussion of the "responsibility to protect" in Chapter 8, the experiences of attempted military coercion in Afghanistan, Iraq, Kosovo, and Libya should serve as sufficient cautionary examples.

Given the principles of universality and flexibility referred to throughout this book, it simply is impossible for outsiders to undertake the reforms, including significant restructuring of institutions, that would be necessary to bring almost any country into full compliance with even basic norms. There is no alternative to the primary responsibility of states to protect human rights, even if the path to creating or supporting rights-protecting governments is slow and uneven.

International pressure legitimized by human rights norms has surely influenced the behavior of states, and hundreds of millions of people have benefited from such pressure.[691] However, international human rights law per se has had very little impact on the conduct of war, the conclusion of peace agreements, the reconstruction of post-conflict societies, the redistribution of wealth and resources, economic theories of development, or restructuring power relationships within families or geopolitically. The solutions to most conflicts or malfunctioning societies are too complex to be aided in a significant way by simplistic appeals to human rights law, given the latter's properly narrow focus on the relationship between individuals and their governments. Human rights do not provide a blueprint for the (re)construction of society itself, and wishing won't make it so.

At the margins, human rights provide a foundation for a more responsive and equitable system of government; they promote transparency and accountability and undermine assumed entitlements to privilege and impunity; they facilitate wider participation for more people and minimize at least de jure discrimination. Respect for human rights also may have a preventative impact that renders the outbreak of violent conflict or the disintegration of a society less likely.

Criticisms of human rights as overly conservative or detracting from broader revolutionary goals are accurate, but they miss the point. At least the following statement by the little-known US Human Rights Network is honest about its own perspective on what is necessary to bring about fundamental change.

> The feature that distinguishes the people-centered framework from all of the prevailing schools of human rights theory and practice is that it is based on an explicit understanding that to realize the full range of the still developing human rights idea requires: (1) an epistemological break with a human rights orthodoxy grounded in Euro-centric liberalism, (2) a reconceptualization of human rights from the standpoint of oppressed groups, (3) a restructuring of prevailing social relationships that perpetuate oppression and (4) the acquiring of power on the part of the oppressed to bring about that restructuring. As opposed to the fraudulent claims of being "non-political" and value neutral made by mainstream human rights practitioners and organizations, PCHRs [people-centered human rights] is a political project that has identified all forms of oppressive relations, including capitalism, neoliberalism, white supremacy, patriarchy, colonialism and imperialism, as structural and ideological constraints on the ability to realize the full range of human rights.[692]

Only the final phrase of this call to battle is inaccurate, in that "the full range of human rights" deliberately excludes many (but not all) of the identified wrongs. Such struggles for revolutionary change may well be necessary in many situations, but they should not cloak themselves in the language of human rights, while at the same time rejecting the essential characteristics of those rights.

ARE SOME RIGHTS MORE EQUAL THAN OTHERS?

Human rights advocates and most governments rhetorically insist that "[a]ll human rights are universal, indivisible and interdependent and interrelated,"[693] but this is unrealistic in either theory or practice. People demand rights that are most immediately necessary or that in some manner facilitate enjoying additional rights. For example, while education is not a formal prerequisite for participating in political decision-making or ensuring an adequate standard of living for one's family, it will probably increase the likelihood that the two latter goals can be achieved. Protecting women from endemic violence and minorities from discrimination are de facto prerequisites if individuals in these categories are to enjoy other rights.

It is tempting to believe that a focus on the most fundamental and achievable human rights is more likely to lead to progress than is a diffuse approach that plays on momentary outrage or reflects a social agenda designed to pander to (or, perhaps more kindly, reflect) the preferences of Western donors and politicians. Just as in medical triage, such a focus does not imply a rejection or diminution of the entire gamut of internationally recognized rights, any more than treating the most urgent cases first undermines the physician's Hippocratic Oath. Human rights triage may even have an advantage over medical triage, since effective protection of rights such as free expression, the prohibition against torture, due process, nondiscrimination, and the rights to food and health care is likely to have a snowball effect that will make it easier in the future to enjoy all rights.

The notion of rights triage is practiced by every human rights NGO, although it is rarely discussed publicly. Obviously, some NGOs are limited by their own mandates, which may be restricted to, for example, preventing torture or protecting minority rights, or by their focus on a particular country or region. Human and financial resources are limited, and selection is often based on matters unrelated to the type of violation: Is this an issue in which our NGO has expertise? Is the situation one in which our intervention might make a difference? Is the situation likely to become worse if we do not respond? Is this a serious violation that evidences a broader pattern of abuse or an individual harm that is unlikely to be repeated or that is of little importance to society as a whole?

The grandiose proposal for a World Court of Human Rights discussed briefly in Chapter 7 observes, "While all human rights find their moral and philosophical rationale in human dignity, not every violation or denial of human rights also constitutes an attack on human dignity. The [proposal for a world court] ... aims primarily at addressing those core human rights issues directly linked to human dignity, which is characterized by powerlessness, humiliation and dehumanization. This core is composed of fundamental civil, political, social, economic and cultural rights." Unfortunately, like most others, the proposal does not identify with greater specificity which core rights are *fundamental*.[694]

Hafner-Burton devotes an entire chapter to the triage that she recommends be exercised by human rights steward states, so that they might be able to exercise their influence and power more effectively. Disappointingly, however, she notes only that "the issues and victims that should get attention ... require a major investment in human rights policy specialists, rooted in fact-based analysis and projections and a practical assessment of leverage."[695] She goes on to describe a complex process that would include high-level human rights administrators, systematic research on human rights policy evaluation, translation of research into practical policy, and opening formal channels with like-minded states to coordinate and exchange information.[696] Although Hafner-Burton refers earlier in her book to the need to act "in everyday circumstances where people suffer violations of their rights,"[697] the lack of any substantive guidance as to which rights these are undermines the entire project of engaging the assistance of state stewards to ensure human rights in the world.

A few brave individuals have actually identified rights that they think are core or basic.

The early work by Cornell philosopher and professor of ethics and policy Henry Shue remains influential, although it is not strictly grounded in principles of international human rights law. His essential argument is that subsistence rights are as important as security rights, and that both should be prioritized.

> Basic rights are a shield for the defenseless against at least some of the more devastating and more common of life's threats, which include ... loss of security and loss of subsistence ...
>
> By minimal economic security, or subsistence, I mean unpolluted air, unpolluted water, adequate food, adequate clothing, adequate shelter, and minimal preventive public health care ....
>
> No one can fully, if at all, enjoy any right that is supposedly protected by society if he or she lacks the essentials for a reasonably healthy and active life. Deficiencies in the means of subsistence can be just as fatal, incapacitating, or painful as violations of physical security.[698]

Shue subsequently adds social/political participation, freedom of physical movement, and due process to his non-exhaustive list of basic rights.

Michigan law professor Stephen Ratner grounds his thoughtful proposal for an international legal regime based on global justice on two pillars, peace and "basic human rights." He advocates only a "thin" morality for international legal norms (a much broader category than human rights) that is "a 'moral minimum' – universal in scope, reflecting values shared across cultures that are a baseline from which thicker, community-based morality may be developed."[699] These values encompass "the fundamental freedom of the individual vis-à-vis the states and other powerful actors that threaten him or her, coupled with the basic material goods and conditions necessary to a minimally flourishing life."[700] They include nondiscrimination based on certain traits, freedom to form a family, freedom of religion and culture, "some" freedom of political expression, freedom from alien rule, "some type of" representative government, primary education, and a safe workplace.

While it seems logical to begin any list of basic or priority rights with a right to subsistence or the right to life, this is a woeful understatement of the human rights obligations imposed on states by international law. There are billions of people in the world who survive by subsistence farming or other precarious activities, and few would accept that a guarantee of mere subsistence is an acceptable interpretation of the rights set forth in the ESC Covenant. Although the concept of a minimum core obligation is not found in the covenant itself, the approach adopted by the ESC

Committee at an early session is useful and appears to have been largely accepted by states. The committee calls for countries "to ensure the satisfaction of, at the very least, minimum essential levels of each of the rights" in the covenant. "Thus, for example, a State party in which any significant number of individuals is deprived of essential foodstuffs, of essential primary health care, of basic shelter and housing, or of the most basic forms of education is, prima facie, failing to discharge its obligations under the Covenant."[701] Indeed, it is difficult to imagine that any government that is consistently unable to provide this minimum core of rights is worthy of the name.

Unlike the ESC Committee, the Human Rights Committee has not identified any core rights or obligations, although it notes that the general obligation to respect and ensure rights has "immediate effect" and that a state's obligations are both "negative and positive in nature."[702] It has been frequently suggested by advocates and academics that rights from which there can be no derogation or suspension in an emergency (article 4) are somehow more fundamental than the rights that can be suspended. The nonderogable rights are the prohibition against discrimination based solely on race, color, sex, language, religion, or social origin; the prohibition against the arbitrary deprivation of life; the prohibition against torture or cruel, inhuman or degrading treatment or punishment or of nonconsensual medical or scientific experimentation; the prohibition against slavery; the prohibition against imprisonment for failure to fulfill a contractual obligation; the right not to be punished for an act that was not a crime at the time that it was committed; the right to recognition as a person before the law; and the right to freedom of thought, conscience, and religion. These rights are surely important, although it is difficult to distinguish them from rights such as the right not to be arbitrarily arrested or detained (article 9.1), the right of detainees to be treated with humanity (article 10.1), or the right to hold opinions (article 19.1).

Approaching the issue from the opposite perspective, some human rights in the ESC and CP Covenants might appear to be marginal, such as the right to periodic paid holidays (ESC article 7.d) or to be protected from attacks on one's honor and reputation (CP article 17.1). However, every country limits working hours to ensure workers' health and safety, and laws against libel and slander are found around the world. Would you rather be slandered than tortured? Of course you would, so perhaps the severity of the impact of a violation of rights might be a sensible beginning to identifying a set of core or fundamental rights. However, much would still depend on the specific circumstances, and it would be an extremely minimal definition of human rights if we limited priority rights to physical integrity, even if they are broadened to include Shue's concept of subsistence security.

One of the fundamental principles of international human rights is the principle of nondiscrimination. Article 2 in both UN covenants, which sets forth the basic obligations of countries that become a party to each treaty, include the requirement that rights be guaranteed to all "without distinction of any kind." This is followed in both treaties by a somewhat repetitive, but important, article that proclaims the equal rights of men and women, and the CP Covenant includes a third reference to nondiscrimination in article 26, which concerns everyone's right to equal protection before the law.

As discussed in Chapter 7, "without distinction of any kind" is something of an overstatement, since laws do frequently distinguish between different categories of persons and treat them differently. The issue is whether such distinctions – such as tax rates that vary depending on one's income or residency requirements for eligibility to vote – are closely related to and necessary to achieve a legitimate and pressing need. Distinctions based purely on identity, such as race, color, sex, religion, birth, or national origin, are more suspect than those based on changeable attributes, such as wealth, residence, language, age, or occupation.

Unfortunately, such textual analyses ultimately get us no further than do the musings of philosophers about subsistence. After all, the basic principle of human rights is that they are *all* fundamental, which is what justifies their universal applicability. Since rights are themselves flexible, however, as discussed in Chapter 7, this does not mean that we cannot prioritize among rights, depending on the context and circumstances.

How to balance a particular person's right against the rights of others or the general welfare, which are permissible grounds for limiting rights under the CP and ESC Covenants, can only be determined in specific contexts. For example, a "core health services package" might be identified, in order to concretize a minimum component of the right to health.[703] Similarly, two international trade experts identify democratic governance; the rights of women, workers, and indigenous peoples; and the rights to health and a healthy environment as the most important and relevant rights in the area of trade and the WTO.[704] This kind of prioritization is not legally or philosophically tidy, but it reflects the fact that context does matter and that rights are not just abstract constructs to be admired in theory but rather are concrete guides to the messy relationships between humans and governments.

In essence, the task of deciding which rights are more or less important is a matter of common sense and circumstance: what may be important and worth fighting for vigorously in one society may be less important or an exercise in futility in another. One of the advantages of the relatively restrained interpretation of rights advocated in the present book is that it permits us to take all human rights seriously. At least for those countries that have ratified them, "fundamental" rights would have to include all of the civil, cultural, economic, political, and social rights contained in the two covenants. While the Universal Declaration on Human Rights is more general in many of its formulations of rights, its use as a backup to treaty obligations is justified by its acceptance by states (rhetorically, at least) and the fact that all states have agreed to use it as a source of rights during the HR Council's Universal Periodic Review process (discussed in Chapter 5).

States also must be held accountable for all of the obligations that they have accepted by ratifying more specialized or regional treaties. At the same time, the institutions that oversee these treaties should be careful not to mistake difference for violation. Individual members of such bodies must honestly address the issues before them while bearing in mind that their task is not to promote their own views as to what is the best or broadest interpretation of a treaty might be. If recommendations, quasi-judicial views, and even binding judgments are ignored because the opinions are overly ambitious, neither law nor justice is likely to be well served, and the very legitimacy of human rights may suffer.

NEW RIGHTS AND SEEKING CONSENSUS

As a lawyer, I am obligated to represent the interests of my client to the best of my ability, and pushing the envelope of human rights norms may sometimes be a legitimate tactic. At the same time, claiming that a desired outcome is already included in the universe of rights protected by international law requires some intellectual honesty, at least outside the courtroom. Is the "human right" being advocated one that can reasonably be expected to be recognized in diverse countries around the world, as opposed to reflecting only a particular society at a particular time? In other words, can it be plausibly argued that the right is universal, even in the somewhat relativist way in which that term has been presented in this book?

This limit on human rights may be thought of as internal, reflecting the nature of existing rights and how far it is appropriate to stretch their interpretation. A different, but perhaps even more important, question (posed particularly in Chapters 3, 5, and 5) is whether other interests not explicitly found in current international human rights law – protection of the environment, obligations on business and other non-state actors, eradication of poverty, ending corruption, promoting inclusion, social equity – should be brought under the human rights umbrella.

The admittedly minority position taken in this book is that, in most cases, the answer is no. As discussed in Chapters 3 and 4, ensuring free-standing human rights such as nondiscrimination, the right to participate in public affairs, and freedom of expression and association makes it more likely that non–rights issues will be considered domestically in an atmosphere that ensures that the needs and preferences of all relevant parts of society are taken into consideration. Such deliberation permits the informed decision-making that is essential to responding adequately and fairly to major issues such as those just mentioned. Whether a society develops new law or simply applies existing principles of equity and fairness to arrive at domestic decisions doesn't really matter; the fact is that human rights law is incapable by itself of providing the solutions.

Suggesting limits such as these on human rights is the antithesis of a revolutionary approach, and "[a] vision of a society compatible with the articles of the international covenants on human rights is in and of itself nobody's rallying cry,

I think."[705] The restrained approach advocated here also may be interpreted, incorrectly, to support an overly conservative approach that discourages the formulation of new rights that are required to respond to social, political, and technological change. As correctly understood, however, it will not ask law to do more than it can possibly accomplish, while at the same time it will ensure that human rights are not lost or misused in the midst of passionate disagreements that are better resolved by appeals to science, logic, morals, economic considerations, and, yes, even politics. Resolution of these disagreements must be sought in the shadow of human rights, which constrain options that might violate rights even if they cannot often provide a clear guide to substantive solutions.

"Perhaps instead of focusing exclusively on the flaws of the modern human rights enterprise, including the deficiencies of its legal core, those who are committed to human rights should question their confidence that the system is stable and that the only change to be anticipated in the future is further progress."[706] It would be inexcusable hubris to expect that human rights will look exactly the same 50 years from now as they do today, and it is overly optimistic to assume that future changes will necessarily broaden the list of what we today consider to be rights worth protecting. Creating new rights or significantly widening the scope of existing rights is not only difficult but may not measurably increase protection, if such creation or expansion is not widely supported.

Despite the difficulties in dealing with the frontiers of human rights law or setting priorities, we should not ignore the consensus that exists in all regions of the world over the core content and legitimacy of most human rights. Fair trials, equality before the law, prohibitions against arbitrary killings and systematic racial discrimination, obligations on the state to recognize basic socio-economic rights – all of these norms are widely accepted in principle, even if practice leaves much to be desired. If this seems doubtful, just imagine the likelihood of any government arguing publicly that it does *not* accept such norms, that its goals are to decrease standards of living, increase unemployment, conduct unfair trials, torture anyone who criticizes the country's leaders, and let the homeless starve in the streets. Possible, yes, but unlikely. Where a government (likely to be a dictatorship) does espouse such views, appeals to protect human rights are likely to be ignored, and revolution then may be the only sensible recourse.

This consensus comes with conditions, however, and most countries reserve to themselves the final authority to interpret human rights norms in a way that is most appropriate for their own societies, as argued in Chapter 7. This caveat does not apply where a country has accepted the authority of an international court to make binding judgments in human rights cases, but international courts have no direct coercive power.

Economic, social, and cultural rights are the most obvious examples of the understanding that countries have about interpreting rights, because these rights not only are to be achieved progressively but also must be tailored to domestic economic conditions and operate within the constraints of available financial, natural, and human resources. The fact that the United States is a notorious outlier and has often publicly rejected the idea that these are "rights" should not obscure the widespread expectations of everyone else in the world regarding the role that government must play in order to fulfill ESC rights.[707]

Civil and political rights are no less context-dependent than ESC rights, despite the implicit mandate of the CP Covenant that they be ensured immediately and fully in every country. Is there not always room for improvement in "fair" trial procedures, the degree to which electoral systems accurately reflect the will of the people, decreasing abuses by law enforcement personnel, and fine-tuning the balance between free expression and protecting the rights of others? No review of any state's report on human rights conditions within its jurisdiction has ever received the full blessing of any of the UN's treaty bodies; no committee has ever concluded that even a single right has been fully, completely, and irrevocably guaranteed. The enjoyment of CP rights can be improved in every country, if only to respond to changing social, economic, and political conditions.

One of the most valuable weapons in the human rights quiver is the ability to expose the hypocrisy of governments that refuse to comply with norms that they themselves have formally accepted. Emphasizing the legal consensus that is reflected in the widespread ratification of human rights treaties supports domestic human rights advocates and counters insincere attempts to paint human rights as Western or neocolonial.

HUMAN RIGHTS AND POLITICS

The long-time president of Human Rights Watch, Kenneth Roth, summarized the political situation in the world in early 2018 as follows:

> Real issues lie behind the surge of populism in many parts of the world. Globalization, automation, and technological change have caused economic dislocation and inequality. Fear of cultural change has swept segments of the population in Western nations as the ease of transportation and communication fuels migration from war, repression, poverty, and climate change. Societal divisions have emerged between cosmopolitan elites who welcome and benefit from many of these changes and those who feel their lives have become more precarious. Demagogues have exploited the traumatic drumbeat of terrorist attacks to fuel nativism and Islamophobia. Addressing these issues is not simple, but populists tend to respond less by proposing genuine solutions than by scapegoating vulnerable minorities and disfavored segments of society . . .
>
> Invoking their self-serving interpretation of the majority's desires, populists seek to replace democratic rule – elected government limited by rights and the rule of law – with unfettered majoritarianism.[708]

Unfortunately, Roth falls back into politically correct sound bites when he states in the same article that "inclusivity, tolerance, and respect . . . lie at the heart of the human rights movement."[709] These are very important social values, and they certainly have influenced the content and direction of human rights. However, for the national populist and his or her supporters, this requires too much: inclusivity implies opening the country's borders to immigrants; tolerance means succumbing to foreign cultural influences that undermine the country's own history and values; and respect implies an acceptance of difference that flies in the face of the nationalist underpinning of most populist rhetoric. In fact, human rights law directly requires little of this social tolerance from individuals, even though it certainly requires that people not be discriminated against for being different or thinking differently from the majority, that minorities be protected from violence and threats, and that everyone's right to advocate change be protected legally and in reality.

UN High Commissioner for Human Rights Zeid offered this comment in an impassioned speech directed against the rise of populist demagogues:

> Populists use half-truths and oversimplification – the two scalpels of the arch propagandist, and here the internet and social media are a perfect rail for them, by reducing thought into the smallest packages: sound-bites; tweets. Paint half a picture in the mind of an anxious individual, exposed as they may be to economic hardship and through the media to the horrors of terrorism. Prop this picture up by some half-truth here and there and allow the natural prejudice of people to fill in the rest. Add drama, emphasizing it's all the fault of a clear-cut group, so the speakers lobbing this verbal artillery, and their followers, can feel somehow blameless . . .
>
> Ultimately, it is the law that will safeguard our societies – human rights law, binding law which is the distillation of human experience, of generations of human suffering, the screams of the victims of past crimes and hate. We must guard this law passionately, and be guided by it.[710]

Guarding the law in a time of anti-international, anti-immigrant, anti-minority, and anti-elite politics is one means of countering the contemporary rightward swing toward exalting majoritarian pseudo-democracy and authoritarianism. If law and politics cannot be distinguished, observations such as the following (written with reference to the United States in the time of Trump) will be applied with even greater frequency to many Western and other human rights advocates:

> Many liberal elites, who see right-leaning voters as blindly following the edicts of an unbending dogma on many issues, have little to no awareness of their own blind allegiance to an unbending dogma on many issues . . . [T]he left's lack of awareness of the excesses of their own evolving dogma makes it increasingly easy for [right-wing news outlets, such as] Breitbart, Fox News, and similar-minded others to portray liberals as hypocritical and out of touch with the day-to-day lives of many Americans.[711]

Similar are the following comments from the conservative British magazine, *The Spectator,* made in the context of contemporary central Europe:

> The umbrella explanation of central Europe is that populists are undermining the EU, and putting democracy there into crisis – that the so-called Visegrad Four – the Czech Republic, Hungary, Poland and Slovakia – are descending into authoritarianism. Look closer, however, and you can see something else. In their first 20 years these young democracies found that too many levers of power – the courts, the media – were in post-communist hands under rules, constitutions and bureaucracies shaped by the communists. They're doing what democracies are supposed to do: reforming institutions to channel into government policy what their voters chose through elected politicians.
>
> But whether you seek to co-opt or resist populism, the issue is the same: unless the elites are willing to treat other people and social groups as equals in a democratic system, there will be intractable clashes. The philosopher Pierre Manent has argued that European politics will end up a competition between an unrespectable national-populism and an arrogant cosmopolitan centrism. Or, in his words, between populist demagogy and the fanaticism of the centre.
>
> In the old left versus right world, both sides essentially accepted that the other would win power occasionally. But now we have a centrist establishment in Europe that does not really accept the right of its challengers to come to power. And when they do, it casts them as being illegitimate, or extremists, and seeks to use supranational legal and political powers [such as human rights?] to constrain or oust them. But this has not so far worked, given how few voters in the offending nations wish to back down. Brexit Britain may end up watching from the sidelines, but a new battle for Europe has begun.[712]

Attacks such as these on the so-called liberal elites are usually made by those who wish to undermine the entire concept of universal human rights, and they are prime examples of the half-truths condemned above by High Commissioner Zeid. They seek to explain the rejection of international law and rights as merely an understandable response to liberalism by conservative nationalists who see themselves as legitimate (at least in some cases), based on their electoral successes. Unfortunately, there may be more than a shred of truth to such opinions.

Human rights NGOs and advocates must look more seriously at diversity among their supporters. If the overwhelming proportion of donors and activists could be fairly described as Western, well-educated, and liberal, then universality will never be achieved. If the primary means of pressuring countries to comply with their human rights obligations is to seek assistance from the United States or EU, this is unlikely to quiet allegations of neocolonialism from those who are targeted. Indeed, one of the most worrying aspects of the current status of human rights is the lack of many champions among developing countries (although there are a few exceptions, and the pro-human rights rhetoric of most Latin American countries, in particular, is a welcome change from the former dictatorships).

Fortunately, the major international NGOs and the national NGOs with whom they collaborate do not operate in a vacuum. Most of their activities are aimed at responding to clear violations of easily identified rights, and it is not elitist to try to end torture, discrimination, or homelessness. Indeed, if human rights are now considered to fall within the "arrogant cosmopolitan center," then perhaps calibrated "fanaticism" is just what we need – although I would probably want to call it "moderate fanaticism."

Human rights are inherently political, insofar as they require changes in government behavior. However, human rights should not be used to achieve purely political or partisan goals, lest rights be seen as relevant only to the opposition. Of course, supporting a party that proclaims its support for human rights norms is a political act that serves human rights, but NGOs should tread carefully when they publicly advocate one party over another. To offer a positive (if somewhat dated) example, the Washington-based International Human Rights Law Group had actively supported South Korean dissident and former political prisoner Kim Dae Jung in the 1980s, and it sent observers to monitor what was South Korea's first democratic election in 1987. Roh Tae Woo, the designated successor to the incumbent authoritarian, won the election, narrowly defeating two democratic candidates, Kim Dae Jung and Kim Young Sam. The Law Group and other human rights advocates were bitterly disappointed, but they did not attack the results of an election that they considered had been reasonably free and fair. The legitimacy of this election, despite its result, became an essential element in South Korea's transformation from an authoritarian state to a democracy, and both Kim Dae Jung and Kim Young Sam were subsequently elected to the presidency.

Human rights have often been politicized, during the Cold War, in disputes over global economic equity between developing and developed countries, and today by populist and nationalist attacks on the so-called liberal elites. Human rights advocates and their supporters should not compound the problem by succumbing to the illusion that progress on human rights is co-extensive with progressive politics. This is indeed often the case, but disagreement over a country's shifts to the left or right should not be confused with the apolitical preservation of the human rights that are essential to ensure that disagreement remains possible. It is important to struggle for both human rights and political objectives, but one must also respect the fine line that lies between them.

CONCLUDING REMARKS

Words are power, and those who would be masters of the words (as suggested by the epigraph at the beginning of this book) must be aware of the consequences of their misuse. Good intentions do not excuse bad policies; dedication to an ideal does not excuse acts that render that ideal less realizable. As Bob Dylan observes at the end of his classic saga about a young man's journey to understanding the world, "I'll know my song well before I start singin'."[713]

Responsible and effective human rights advocacy, whether by governments or NGOs, requires reinforcing consensus, recognizing limits, and remembering that the goal is to enable individuals and societies to determine their own future in dignity and independence. Such an approach does not exclude vigorous advocacy by lawyers and others seeking to achieve particular social and political goals, and it does not require setting human rights in the concrete of the 1940s or 1970s. What it does require is a recognition and constant awareness of the true universality of human rights, so that rights will remain meaningful and enjoy popular support from people in China and Cameroon, Thailand and Turkey, Germany and Guatemala.

There can be no doubt that the human rights, as well as economic well-being, of billions of people around the world have improved in recent decades, not only since 1945 but even since modern human rights influence began to surge in the 1970s.[714] Latin American military dictatorships prevalent in the 1970s and 1980s have disappeared. Apartheid in South Africa ended in the early 1990s, after decades of struggle and international condemnation, much of it couched in the language of human rights. South Korea has moved from dictatorship to democracy and is today a stalwart supporter of human rights internationally. While eastern and central Europe are hardly bastions of tolerance, they are light-years away from the repressive regimes kept in place by the Soviet Union and the secret police. Hundreds of millions of people in China are no longer at risk of starvation. Gay rights are much more widely recognized now than in the 1970s, despite the continuing challenges discussed in Chapter 6. While populism is the bogeyman of Europe and North America, repressive leaders have been removed in South Africa, Zimbabwe, and Angola. Jordan, Morocco, and Tunisia have repealed laws that permitted rapists to escape punishment by marrying their victims, and Saudi Arabia has taken a few minor steps towards greater freedom for women. Human rights law cannot claim sole credit for all of these changes, but many of these improvements can be traced to assertions of rights by domestic and international groups, coupled with political isolation or public disapproval of repressive governments.

Microsoft founder and philanthropist Bill Gates has said, "The only reason things have improved is because people get upset about things and decide to do something about it."[715] This book is not meant to encourage retrenchment or a return to the "good old days" of human rights norms, institutions, and lawyers. However, whether building a foundation for a house or for an ethical and legal guide for governments, expansion without consolidation along the way will result in a shaky edifice. Medieval European cathedrals required flying buttresses on the outside to support the vast vaulted ceilings inside, and solid support is essential to the success of human rights, as well.

In a review of two recent books that analyze current social and political trends in the United States, the reviewer concludes, "The American experiment is not just worth the fight – it *is* the fight. With passion always strained, the pursuit of prosperity, freedom and belonging is an endless battle, an enterprise in equal measures exhausting and exhilarating."[716] Perhaps the same can be said about the human rights experiment, which was never likely to lead to a quick and satisfying conclusion but rather to remain an "endless battle" waged by those who share the belief that individuals in all societies have enough in common that they should enjoy similar rights to freedom, prosperity, and equality.

The role of a human rights advocate demands perseverance and patience, and solutions to complex problems will not come merely from quoting international treaties and declarations. Appreciating both the limits and the potential of international human rights law, however, may make the task of establishing and maintaining peace and social justice easier than it was just a few short decades ago. This would not be a meaningless advance. Without sacrificing the goal of universal compliance with universal standards, a moderate – but persistent – approach to promoting and ensuring human rights will prevent the erosion of one of the twentieth century's greatest legacies: the recognition of rights that we all should enjoy, simply because we are human.

Notes

1 A now somewhat dated analysis of these mechanisms may be found in Hurst Hannum ed., *Guide to International Human Rights Practice* (Brill/ Nijhoff 4th ed. 2004); also see id., "Reforming the Special Procedures and Mechanisms of the Commission on Human Rights," 7 *Hum. Rts. L. Rev.* 73 (2007).

2 Geoff Dancy and Christopher J. Fariss, "Rescuing Human Rights Law from International Legalism and Its Critics," 39 *Hum. Rts. Q.* 1 (2017) at 36.

1 INTRODUCTION: ASSUMPTIONS AND PRINCIPLES

3 Slavery Convention, adopted 25 Sept. 1926, entered into force 9 Mar. 1927. Art. 2 of the convention obligated countries to "prevent and suppress the slave trade" and "[t]o bring about, progressively and as soon as possible, the complete abolition of slavery in all its forms."

4 Cf., e.g., Elizabeth Borgwardt, *A New Deal for the World: America's Vision for Human Rights* (Belknap Press/Harvard University Press 2005); Mary Ann Glendon, *A World Made New: Eleanor Roosevelt and the Universal Declaration of Human Rights* (Random House 2001); Mark Goodale ed., *Letters to the Contrary: A Curated History of the UNESCO Human Rights Survey* (Stanford University Press 2018); Lynn Hunt, *Inventing Human Rights: A History* (Norton 2007); Micheline R. Ishay, *The History of Human Rights: From Ancient Times to the Globalization Era* (University of California Press 2008); Johannes Morsink, *The Universal Declaration of Human Rights: Origins, Drafting, and Intent* (University of Pennsylvania Press 1999); Samuel Moyn, *The Last Utopia: Human Rights in History* (Belknap Press/Harvard University Press 2010), including the useful Bibliographical Essay at 311–321; Aryeh Neier, *The International Human Rights Movement: A History* (Princeton University Press 2012).

5 UN Charter, art. 1.3.

6 See, e.g., the comments of the government of Sri Lanka regarding a commission of inquiry created by the UN Human Rights Council to examine alleged human rights violations and

international crimes committed during the Sri Lankan civil war: The resolution of the Council "challenges the sovereignty and independence of a member state of the UN [and] violates principles of international law ..." Statement by H.E. Mr. Ravinatha P. Aryasinha, Permanent Representative of Sri Lanka to the UN Human Rights Council, Geneva, 10 June 2014, para. 22, quoted in "Sri Lanka reiterates rejection of UN rights investigation," *Business Standard* (India), 10 June 2014.

7 This figure includes the Cook Islands, Holy See, Niue, and Palestine, none of which is a member of the United Nations. The United States is the only one of the 193 UN member states not to have ratified the convention.

8 Wiktor Osiatynski, *Human Rights and Their Limits* (Cambridge University Press 2009).

9 Eric A. Posner, *The Twilight of Human Rights Law* (Oxford University Press 2014).

10 Stephen Hopgood, *The Endtimes of Human Rights* (Cornell University Press 2013).

11 Samuel Moyn, supra note 4.

12 Conor Gearty, *Can Human Rights Survive?* (Cambridge University Press 2006).

13 Mark Goodale ed., *Human Rights at the Crossroads* (Oxford University Press 2013).

14 Two books even share the same title: Alice Bullard ed., *Human Rights in Crisis* (Ashgate 2008), and Genevieve Souillac, *Human Rights in Crisis* (Lexington 2005).

15 Cindy Holder and David Reidy eds., *Human Rights: The Hard Questions* (Cambridge University Press 2013).

16 Rob Dickinson, Elena Katselli, Colin Murray, and Ole W. Pedersen eds., *Examining Critical Perspectives on Human Rights* (Cambridge University Press 2012).

17 Stephen Hopgood, Jack Snyder, and Leslie Vinjamuri eds., *Human Rights Futures* (Cambridge University Press 2017).

18 Hopgood, supra note 10 at 171.

19 Id. at 103.

20 See Francis Fukuyama, *The End of History and the Last Man* (Free Press 1992).

21 See generally Andrew Clapham, *Human Rights Obligations of Non-State Actors* (Oxford University Press 2006).

22 Victor Abramovich, "State regulatory powers and global legal pluralism," 12 *Sur J.*, [International Journal on Human Rights] 1 (Aug. 2015) at 2, http://sur.conectas.org/en/state-regulatory-powers-global-legal-pluralism/.

23 See Amnesty International, Global Arms Trade Treaty – a beginners' guide: 50th ratification update, 25 Sept. 2014, www.amnesty.org/en/latest/news/2014/09/global-arms-trade-treaty-beginners-guide-th-ratification-update/.

24 See Amnesty International, Global movement votes to adopt policy to protect human rights of sex workers, 11 Aug. 2015, www.amnesty.org/en/latest/news/2015/08/global-movement-votes-to-adopt-policy-to-protect-human-rights-of-sex-workers/.

25 Report of the Committee on the Elimination of Discrimination against Women, UN Doc. A/35/38 (2000), para. 361.

26 A list of all of the Council's thematic "special procedures" may be found at www2.ohchr.org/english/bodies/chr/special/themes.htm. They are discussed more fully in Chapter 5.

27 347 US 483 (1954).

28 Mae Sot, "South-East Asia's future looks prosperous but illiberal," *Economist*, 18 July 2017.

29 "Cambodia calls US democracy 'bloody and brutal' as charity row escalates," *Guardian*, 24 Aug. 2017; "The demise of the opposition sounds the death knell for democracy in Cambodia," *Guardian*, 17 Nov. 2017.

30 François Godement and Abigaël Vasselier, *China at the Gates: A New Power Audit of EU-China Relations* (European Council on Foreign Relations, Dec. 2017) at 14.

31 Patrick Wintour, "Western Balkans backsliding on democracy, says Lords committee," *Guardian*, 9 Jan. 2018.

32 Rowena Mason and Vikram Dodd, "May: I'll rip up human rights laws that impede new terror legislation," *Guardian*, 6 June 2017.

33 Kareem Shaheen, "Erdoğan clinches victory in Turkish constitutional referendum," *Guardian*, 16 Apr. 2017.

34 "Turkey is sliding into dictatorship," *Economist*, 15 Apr. 2017.

35 See "Africa's political leaders some of the world's longest serving," ABC News (Australia), 20 Nov. 2017, www.abc.net.au/news/2017-11-20/africas-longest-serving-political-leaders/9168874; Linsey Chutel, "2017 Has Been a Tough Year for Africa's Strongmen," *Quartz*, 21 Nov. 2017, https://qz.com/1135317/africas-longest-serving-leaders-list-is-shrinking-after-mugabe-dos-santos-and-yahya-jammeh/.

36 N.Y. *Times*, 11 Aug. 2017.

37 "List: The world's longest-serving leaders," *Daily Monitor* (Uganda), 12 Mar. 2018, www.monitor.co.ug/News/National/list-world-longest-serving-leaders/688334-4337826-wcsxuh/index.html.

38 Opening speech to the High Level Segment of the Human Rights Council, 2 Mar. 2015, www.ohchr.org/EN/NewsEvents/Pages/media.aspx?IsMediaPage=true.

39 Allen Buchanan, *The Heart of Human Rights* (Oxford University Press 2013) at vii. Emphasis deleted.

40 Mark Lattimer, "Two Concepts of Human Rights," 40 *Hum. Rts. Q.* 406 (2018) at 418.

41 Id. at 408. For a similar view, see, e.g., Alison Brysk and Michael Stohl eds., *Expanding Human Rights: 21st Century Norms and Governance* (Elgar 2018).

42 See, e.g., Ryan Goodman and Derek Jinks, *Socializing States: Promoting Human Rights through International Law* (Oxford University Press 2013); Thomas Risse, Stephen C. Ropp, and Kathryn Sikkink eds., *The Persistent Power of Human Rights: From Commitment to Compliance* (Cambridge University Press 2013); Kathryn Sikkink, *Evidence for Hope: Making Human Rights Work in the 21st Century* (Princeton University Press 2017); Beth A. Simmons, *Mobilizing for Human Rights: International Law in Domestic Politics* (Cambridge University Press 2009).

2 CRIME AND (OCCASIONAL) PUNISHMENT

43 Hopgood, supra note 10 at 123, 165.

44 For a recent article that assumes that "human rights accountability" means criminal prosecution, see Leigh A. Payne, Francesca Lessa, and Gabriel Pereira, "Overcoming Barriers to Justice in the Age of Human Rights Accountability," 37 *Hum. Rts. Q.* 728 (2015).

45 Rome Statute of the International Criminal Court, adopted 17 July 1998, entered into force 1 July 2002.

46 For a current list of ICC cases and activities, see the court's website, www.icc-cpi.int.

47 See Report of the Board of Directors of the Trust Fund for Victims to the 16th Session of the Assembly of States Parties 4 Dec. 2017, available via www.trustfundforvictims.org/en/reports. See generally Trust Fund for Victims, www.trustfundforvictims.org/.

48 Jon Silverman, "Ten years, $900m, one verdict: Does the ICC cost too much?" BBC News, 12 Mar. 2012, www.bbc.com/news/magazine-17351946.

49 ICC Assembly of State Parties, Res. ICC-ASP/15/Res.1 (Nov. 24, 2016).

50 Silverman, supra note 48.

51 See Stuart Ford, "How Leadership in International Criminal Law Is Shifting from the U.S. to Europe and Asia: An Analysis of Spending on and Contributions to International Criminal Courts, 55 *Saint Louis U. Law J.* 953 (2011).

52 Office of the High Commissioner for Human Rights, OHCHR's Funding and Budget, www.ohchr.org/EN/AboutUs/Pages/FundingBudget.aspx. OHCHR received $143 million in voluntary contributions in 2017. The top 13 contributors were Western states (including the European Commission and UNDP), with the top 3 contributors (United States, Sweden, and Norway) totaling over $50 million; Saudi Arabia, Qatar, and Russia were the only non-western states in the top 20. Id., "Voluntary contributions to OHCHR in 2017."

53 While the comparison may be between apples and some as yet undiscovered fruit, the cost of a single cruise missile is approximately $700,000, Peter Jackson, "Libya: Is cost of military mission sustainable?" BBC News, 22 Mar. 2011, www.bbc.com/news/uk-12806709, and the cost of the Reaper armed drone is a staggering $28 million, Christopher Drew, "Costly Drone Is Poised to Replace U-2 Spy Plane," *N.Y. Times*, 2 Aug. 2011.

54 UN Wire, 28 Jan. 2015, www2.smartbrief.com/servlet/encodeServlet?issueid=D6C33A3E-C55D-40EA-886E-C9BC4##027AD&sid=04791a24-2b21-460b-b93e-a329a0224878.

55 Reuters, 27 Jan. 2015, http://in.reuters.com/article/2015/01/26/ukraine-crisis-un-idNKBN0KZ26J20150126.

56 Report of the commission of inquiry on human rights in the Democratic People's Republic of Korea, UN Doc. A/HRC/25/63 (2014).

57 BBC News, www.bbc.com/news/world-asia-26220304.

58 Craig Brown, "North Korea branded 21st-century Nazis by UN dossier on atrocities," *The Scotsman*, 18 Feb. 2014, at 6.

59 Stephanie Thurrott, "Justice to the World," *Tufts Magazine* (Summer 2015), at 18.

60 See American Society of International Law Events Calendar, 12 June 2013, www.asil.org/activities_calendar.cfm?action=detail*rec=290.

61 American Society of International Law, http://asil.org/annualmeeting.

62 See, e.g., Jan Arno Hessbruegge, "Justice Delayed, Not Denied: Statutory Limitations and Human Rights Crimes," 43 *Georgetown J. Int'l L.* 335 (2012); Diane Orentlicher, "Owning Justice and Reckoning with Its Complexity," 11 *J. Intl. Criminal Justice* 517 (2013), at 523, 524.

63 Louise Arbour (2004–2008) served as chief prosecutor for the International Criminal Tribunals for Rwanda and the former Yugoslavia; Navi Pillay (2008–2014) was a judge on both the International Criminal Tribunal for Rwanda and the International Criminal Court; and Zeid Ra'ad Al Hussein (2014–2018) played a central role in the establishment of the ICC and served as its first President of the Assembly of States Parties.

64 Michelle Nichols, U.N. Rights Chief Rebukes Security Council for Failures to Act," Reuters, 21 Aug. 2014, www.reuters.com/article/2014/08/21/us-rights-un-idUSKBN0GL1TN20140821.

65 OHCHR, Opening Statement by Zeid Ra'ad Al Hussein, 8 Sept. 2014, www.ohchr.org/EN/NewsEvents/Pages/Media.aspx?IsMediaPage=true&LangID=E.

66 BBC News, "UN agrees to delay Sri Lanka UN war crimes report," 17 Feb. 2015, www.bbc.com/news/world-asia-31497983?utm_source=Sailthru&utm_medium=email&utm_term=*Morning%20Brief&utm_campaign=2015_MorningBrief_New_America_PROMO.

67 OHCHR, International Commissions of Inquiry, Commissions on Human Rights, Fact-Finding missions and other investigations, www.ohchr.org/EN/HRBodies/HRC/Pages/COIs.aspx.

68 OHCHR, List of HRC-mandated Commissions of Inquiries / Fact-Finding Missions & Other Bodies (As of November 2017), www.ohchr.org/EN/HRBodies/HRC/Pages/ListHRCMandat.aspx.

69 HR CouncilRes. S-17–1 (2011), para. 13.

70 HR Council Res. S-19–1 (2012), para. 8.

71 HR Council Res. 21–26 (2012), para. 10.

72 HR Council Res. S-21/1 (2014), para. 13.

73 HR Council Res. 25/1 (2014), para. 10(b).

74 OHCHR Press Release, "Yemen: Zeid appoints group of eminent international and regional experts," 4 Dec. 2017, www.ohchr.org/EN/HRBodies/HRC/Pages/NewsDetail.aspx?NewsID=22483&LangID=E.

75 OHCHR Press Release, "ISIL may have committed war crimes, crimes against humanity and genocide: UN report," 19 Mar. 2015, www.ohchr.org/EN/NewsEvents/Pages/DisplayNews.aspx?NewsID=15720&LangID=E.#sthash.ySLpAFFm.dpuf. See HRC Res. RES/S-22/1 (2014).

76 OHCHR, Violations and abuses committed by Boko Haram and the impact on human rights in the countries affected, UN Doc. A/HRC/30/67 (2015). See OHCHR, "Human Rights Council concludes special session on atrocities committed by the terrorist group Boko Haram," press release of 1 Apr. 2015, www.ohchr.org/EN/NewsEvents/Pages/DisplayNews.aspx?NewsID=15790&LangID=E.

77 Overview, The Human Rights Violators & War Crimes Unit, www.ice.gov/human-rights-violators/.

78 See, e.g., IACtHR, Aguirre and others v. Peru, Series C, no. 75, 14 Mar. 2001. For a contrasting view, which rejected a challenge to the conditional amnesty provisions of South Africa's Truth and Reconciliation Commission, see Azanian Peoples Organisation (AZAPO) and others v. President of the Republic of South Africa, Const. Ct. South Africa (1996), 4 South Af. Rpts. 671. Contrast Miguel de Serpa Soares, "An Age of Accountability" (Special Editorial), 13 *J. Int'l Crim. Justice* 669 (2015) at 673 (asserting "that it is clearly established that there is a direct connection between accountability and achieving sustainable peace").

79 For the early history of these movements, see Naomi Roht-Arriaza, *Impunity and Human Rights Violations in International Law and Practice* (Oxford University Press 1995). For a comprehensive survey of more recent practice that concludes that granting amnesties per se does not violate customary international law, see Louise Mallinder, *Amnesty, Human Rights and Political Transitions* (Hart 2009).

80 See Regina v. Bow St. Metro, Stipendiary Magistrate, ex parte Pinochet Ugarte (No. 3), [2000] 1 A.C. 147 (H.L. 24 March 1999).

81 A brief summary of the activities of Spanish Judge Baltazar Garzon, perhaps the most celebrated jurist to attempt to address international crimes committed in Latin American under the military regimes, may be found at http://baltasargarzon.org/jurisdiccion-univer sal/universal-jurisdiction/. Judge Garzon's work included investigating crimes against Spanish citizens, as well as invoking the principle of universal jurisdiction over genocide and crimes against humanity.

82 Juan Mendez (with Marjory Wentworth), *Taking a Stand: The Evolution of Human Rights* (Palgrave Macmillan 2011) at 137, 154–155, 157.

83 Karen Engle, Zinaida Miller, and D. M. Davis, "Introduction," in id., eds., *Anti-Impunity and the Human Rights Agenda* (Cambridge University Press 2016) at 1–2, 3.

84 Principle 6(e). The Guidelines are available at www.ulster.ac.uk/__data/assets/pdf_file/ 0005/57839/TheBelfastGuidelinesFINAL_000.pdf. For a general discussion of the approach taken by the Principles, see, e.g., Malinder, supra note 79; Tom Hadden, "Transitional Justice and Amnesties," in Cheryl Lawther, Luke Moffett, and Dov Jacobs eds., *Research Handbook on Transitional Justice* 358–376 (Edward Elgar 2017). It should be noted that I was a member of the group and also that the three Latin American members of the group ultimately decided not to join in signing the final document, primarily because of their belief that impunity is, indeed, prohibited by customary international law.

85 Id., Principle 1(a), n.3.

86 Eur. Ct. H.R., Zdanoka v. Latvia, App. No. 58278/00, Judgment of 16 Mar. 2006.

87 Sejdic and Finci v. Bosnia and Herzegovina, Apps. nos. 27996/06 and 34836/06, Judgment (GC) of 22 Dec. 2009. Nearly a decade later, Bosnia had not yet amended its constitution to comply with the judgment.

88 The impact of human rights law on transitional justice is discussed in Frederic Megret and Raphael Vagliano, "Transitional Justice and Human Rights," in Lawther, Moffett, and Jacobs, supra note 84. 95–116. A longer unedited version of the chapter is available at https://ssrn.com/abstract=2753191 or http://dx.doi.org/10.2139/ssrn.2753191. Also see Eva Brems, 'Transitional Justice in the Case Law of the European Court of Human Rights' 5 *Int'l J. Transitional Justice* 282, 286 (2011).

89 IACtHR, Chumbipuma Aguirre et al. v. Peru (Barrios Altos Case), Judgment of 14 Mar. 2001, at 41. Also see also IACommHR, The Right to Truth in the Americas, OAS Doc. OEA/Ser.L/V/II.152 Doc. 2 (2014).

90 See, e.g., Cecilia M. Bailliet, "Measuring Compliance with the Inter-American Court of Human Rights: The Ongoing Challenge of Judicial Independence in Latin America," 31 *Nordic J. Hum. Rts.* 477 (2013); Alexandra Huneeus, "Courts Resisting Courts: Lessons from the Inter-American Court's Struggle to Enforce Human Rights," 44 *Cornell Int'l L. J.* 493 (2011). One analyst concluded that only one of 54 court judgments that had demanded investigation and prosecution could be deemed fulfilled. Thomas M. Antkowiak, "An Emerging Mandate for International Courts: Victim-Centered Remedies and Restorative Justice," 47 *Stanford J. Int'l L.* 279, 303 (2011), cited in Bailliet at 483 n.17.

91 IACtHR, Gomes Lund et al. ("Guerrilha do Arguaia") v. Brazil, judgment of 24 Nov.2010., para. 325.***

92 OAS AG/Res. 2406 (XXXVIII-O/08), Right to the Truth (2008), para. 1.

93 Report of the independent expert to update the set of principles to combat impunity, Diane Orentlicher, UN Doc. E/CN.4/2005/102/Add.1 (2005).

94 International Convention on the Suppression and Punishment of the Crime of Apartheid, 1015 U.N.T.S. 243, opened for signature 30 Nov. 1973, entered into force 18 July 1976.

95 Helen Jarvis, "Trials and Tribulations: The Long Quest for Justice for the Cambodian Genocide," in S.M. Meisenberg and I. Stegmiller eds., *The Extraordinary Chambers in the Courts of Cambodia* 13–44 (Springer 2016) at 14.

96 See GA Res. 52/135 (1998).

97 See, e.g., Charlie Campbell, "Cambodia's Khmer Rouge Trials Are a Shocking Failure," *Time Magazine*, 13 Feb. 2014; Seth Mydans, "11 Years, $300 Million and 3 Convictions. Was the Khmer Rouge Tribunal Worth It?" *N.Y. Times*, 10 Apr. 2017.

98 Mydans, supra note 97.

99 Id.

100 See OHCHR in Cambodia, www.ohchr.org/EN/Countries/AsiaRegion/Pages/KHSummary.aspx.

101 See www.ohchr.org/EN/HRBodies/SP/CountriesMandates/KH/Pages/SRCambodia.aspx.

102 Chansy Chhorn, "Cambodia's Hun Sen vows to stay in power for at least another 10 years," Reuters, 10 Feb. 2018, www.reuters.com/article/us-cambodia-politics/cambodias-hun-sen-vows-to-stay-in-power-for-at-least-another-10-years-idUSKBN1EL090.

103 UN Doc. A/HRC/36/61 (2017), para. 67.

104 www.hrw.org/world-report/2018/country-chapters/cambodia.

105 www.amnesty.org/en/countries/asia-and-the-pacific/cambodia/report-cambodia/.

106 www.state.gov/j/drl/rls/hrrpt/humanrightsreport/index.htm#wrapper.

107 "45 countries urge Cambodia to conduct free election, release opposition leader Kem Sokha," *South China Morning Post*, 22 Mar. 2018.

108 This was the original articulation of ICTJ's mission, as quoted in the History portion of Wikipedia's entry on the organization, http://en.wikipedia.org/wiki/International_Center_for_Transitional_Justice.

109 See http://www.ictj.org/about/vision-and-mission. An intermediate formulation of mission and vision retained the goals "to promote accountability, pursue truth, provide reparations, and build trustworthy institutions ..." Id.

110 Mahmood Mamdani, "Beyond Nuremberg: The Historical Significance of the Post-apartheid Transition in South Africa," 43(1) *Politics & Society* 61(2015) at 80–82.

111 Rome Statute, art. 5(1).

112 HR Council Res. 22/13 (2013).

113 HR Council Res. 26/24 (2014).

114 For an account of civilians killed by US coalition forces in airstrikes against ISIS, see Azmat Khan and Anand Gopal, "The Uncounted," *N.Y. Times Magazine*, 16 Nov. 2017.

115 See Madeleine A. Albright and Ibrahim A. Gambari, "World losing battle against terror, climate change & cyberattacks: Albright," *USA Today*, 16 June 2015.

116 See Commission on Global Security, Justice & Governance; The Hague Institute for Global Justice; and the Stimson Center, *Confronting the Crisis of Global Governance* (June 2015), www.globalsecurityjusticegovernance.org/wp-content/uploads/2015/06/Commission-on-Global-Security-Justice-Governance-Letter.pdf.

117 Id., sec. 7.3.4.3, at 90.

3 THE IMPORTANCE OF GOVERNMENT, FOR BETTER OR WORSE

118 United Nations, *The Report on the Millennium Development Goals 2015* (UN 2015), Foreword. For another positive analysis of progress over the past several decades, see Hans Rosling, *Factfulness: Ten Reasons We're Wrong about the World-and Why Things Are Better Than You Think* (Flatiron 2018).

119 Report of the Special Representative of the Secretary-General on the issue of human rights and transnational corporations and other business enterprises, John Ruggie, Protect, Respect and Remedy: A Framework for Business and Human Rights, UN Doc. A/HRC/8/5 (2008), para. 3. The website of the Business and Human Rights Resource Centre, www.business-humanrights.org/en, is an excellent source for information on contemporary developments in this area and allegations of corporate misconduct.

120 See, e.g., Report of the Special Representative of the Secretary-General on the issue of human rights and transnational corporations and other business enterprises, corporations and human rights: A Survey of the Scope and Patterns of Alleged Corporate-Related Human Rights Abuse, UN Doc. A/HRC/8/5/Add.2 (2008).

121 Declaration on the Establishment of a New International Economic Order, UN G.A. Res. 3201 (S-VI) (1974).

122 For a brief summary, see generally Sean D. Murphy, "Taking Multinational Corporate Codes of Conduct to the Next Level," 43 *Colum. J. Transnat'l L.* 389 (2005).

123 The UN website is www.unglobalcompact.org/.

124 UN Doc. E/CN.4/Sub.2/2003/12/Rev.2 (2003).

125 UN Doc. E/CN.4/Sub.2/2002/13 (2002) at 6. See David Weissbrodt and Muria Kruger, "Norms on the Responsibilities of Transnational Corporations and Other Business Enterprises with Regard to Human Rights," 97 *Am. J. Int'l L.* 901 (2003); David Kinley, Justine Nolan, and Natalie Zeria, "The Politics of Corporate Social Responsibility: Reflections on the United Nations Human Rights Norms for Corporations," 25 *Co. & Securities L.J.* 30 (2007).

126 UN Comm'n HR, Decision 2004/116, para. c (2004).

127 HR Council Res. 17/4 (2011).

128 Report of the Special Representative of the Secretary-General on the issue of human rights and transnational corporations and other business enterprises, John Ruggie, UN Doc. A/HRC/14/27 (2010).

129 Id., UN Doc. A/HRC/17/31 (2011), para. 14.

130 2010 Ruggie Report, supra note 128, para. 1; emphasis added.

131 Id., para. 55; emphasis added.

132 ESC Committee, General Comment No. 24 on State obligations under the International Covenant on Economic, Social and Cultural Rights in the context of business activities (2017), para. 11.

133 Interim Report of the Special Representative of the Secretary-General on the issue of human rights and transnational corporations and other business enterprises, John Ruggie, U.N. Doc. E/CN.4/2006/97 (2006), para. 66.

134 See Guiding Principles, Principle 12 and commentary.

135 Id., Principle 14.

136 Id., Principle 17(a).

137 Id., Principle 17, commentary.

138 See HR Council Res. 17/4 (2011).

139 Communications to all of the UN special procedures may be found at https://spcommre ports.ohchr.org/Tmsearch/TMDocuments and may be searched by mandate, country concerned, and other criteria.

140 See Communications reports of special procedures, www.ohchr.org/EN/HRBodies/SP/Pages/CommunicationsreportsSP.aspx.

141 These descriptions are taken from the program of the 2017 Forum; it and programs from other sessions are available at www.ohchr.org/EN/Issues/Business/Pages/WGHRandtrans nationalcorporationsandotherbusiness.aspx.

142 James Harrison, "Human Rights and Business: Is the United Nations Helping?" *Lacuna*, 20 Nov. 2016, https://lacuna.org.uk/economy/human-rights-business-united-nations-helping/.

143 HR Council Res. 26/9 (2014), para. 1.

144 See id., footnote 1, which states that the phrase "other business enterprises ... does not apply to local businesses registered in terms of relevant domestic law."

145 See, e.g., Rana Plaza Arrangement Coordination Committee, https://ranaplaza-arrange ment.org/.

146 See, e.g., Sarah Landers, "Chinese companies are making toxic rice out of plastic," *Natural News*, 5 Feb. 2016, www.naturalnews.com/052868_Chinese_companies_toxic_rice_plastic.html; Yanzhong Huang, "2008 Milk Scandal Revisited," *Forbes Asia*, 16 July 2014, www.forbes.com/sites/yanzhonghuang/2014/07/16/the-2008-milk-scandal-revisited/#18eb6374105b.

147 See Elements for the Draft Legally Binding Instrument of Transnational Corporations and other Business Enterprises with Respect to Human Rights, 29 Sept. 2017, available through www.ohchr.org/EN/HRBodies/HRC/WGTransCorp/Session3/Pages/Session3 .aspx.

148 Report on the third session of the open-ended intergovernmental working group on transnational corporations and other business enterprises with respect to human rights, UN Doc. A/HRC/37/67 (2018) at 22. The first two sessions also reflect the wide range of viewpoints on the merits and scope of the proposed treaty; see UN Docs. A/HRC/31/50 (2016) and A/HRC/34/47 (2017).

149 See, e.g., Cees van Dam, "Tort Law and Human Rights: Brothers in Arms: On the Role of Tort Law in the Area of Business and Human Rights," 22 *J. Eur. Tort L.* 221 (No. 3 2011).

150 See Guiding Principles 25–31.

151 Piercing the corporate veil means holding the parent company liable for the torts committed by the subsidiary. The phrase also is used to describe holding individual shareholders liable for the actions of a company, as well as for holding parent companies responsible for the actions of their subsidiaries.

152 The Guiding Principles use the word *violations* only once, in the commentary to Principle 28, in reference to violations considered by regional and international human rights bodies.

153 Filartiga v. Peña-Irala, 630 F.2d 876 (2d Cir. 1980). *Filartiga* also was ground-breaking in that it held that the prohibition of torture was a norm of customary international law.

154 US Supreme Court, Sosa v. Alvarez-Machain, 124 S.Ct. 2739 (2004).

155 Kiobel et al. v. Royal Dutch Petroleum, 133 S.Ct. 1659 (2013).

156 Id., p. 12.

157 Id., concurring opinion of Justice Breyer, with whom Justices Ginsburg, Sotomayor, and Kagan join, p. 2. Numerous articles have traced the history and impact of ATCA cases. For post-Kiobel analyses, see, e.g., Earth Rights International, *Out of Bounds: Accountability for Corporate Human Rights Abuse After Kiobel* (ERI 2013); Ralph G. Steinhardt, "Kiobel and the Weakening of Precedent: A Long Walk for a Short Drink," 107 *Am. J. Int'l L.* 845 (2013); Ernest A. Young, "Universal Jurisdiction, the Alien Tort Statute, and Transnational Public-law Litigation after Kiobel," 64 *Duke L. J.* 1023 (2015).

158 See Roel Nieuwenkamp, "CSR is dead! What's next?" OECD Insights (22 Jan. 2016), http://oecdinsights.org/2016/01/22/2016-csr-is-dead-whats-next/.

159 For a less than flattering view of the new "philanthrocapitaism," see Carl Rhodes and Peter Bloom, "The trouble with charitable billionaires," *Guardian*, 24 May 2018. The article is based on the authors' recent book, *CEO Society: The Corporate Takeover of Everyday Life* (Zed Books 2018).

160 UK Companies Act 2006, sec. 172.

161 Directive 2014/95/EU of 22 Oct. 2014, adding new article 19(1) to Directive 2013/34/EU. The requested information may be based on national, EU, or international frameworks, including, inter alia, the Guiding Principles. Preamble, para. 9.

162 See Sandra Cossart, Jerome Chaplier, and Tiphaine Beau de Lomenie, "The French Law on Duty of Care: A Historic Step towards Making Globalization Work for All," 2 *Business and Hum. Rts. J.* 317 (2017) at 318-319.

163 OECD, Codes of Corporate Conduct: Expanded Review of their Contents, Working Papers on International Investment No. 2001 (6 May 2001),

164 Australian Competition and Consumer Commission (2011), www.accc.gov.au/publica tions/guidelines-for-developing-effective-voluntary-industry-codes-of-conduct.

165 David Kinley, *Necessary Evil: How to Fix Finance by Saving Human Rights* (Oxford University Press 2018) at 201.

166 Human Rights Watch is a member of the Sport and Rights Alliance, founded in early 2015 "to address the decision-makers of international sports mega-events to introduce measures to ensure these events are always organized in a way that respects human rights (including labour rights), the environment and anti-corruption requirements at all stages of the process – from bidding, through to the development and delivery phase to final reporting." Other partners in SRA are Amnesty International Netherlands, Transparency International Germany, the International Trades Union Confederation, Football Supporters Europe, UNI World Athletes, and Terre des Hommes. See www.sportandhu manrights.org/wordpress/index.php/2015/07/06/sport-and-rights-alliance/.

167 International Olympic Committee, "IOC strengthens its stance in favour of human rights and against corruption in new Host City Contract," 28 Feb. 2017, www .olympic.org/news/ioc-strengthens-its-stance-in-favour-of-human-rights-and-against-cor ruption-in-new-host-city-contract.

168 Interim Report of the Special Representative of the Secretary-General on human rights and transnational corporations and other business enterprises, UN Doc. A/EN.4/2006/97 (2006), para. 68.

169 See, e.g., NYU Stern Center for Human Rights, *Harmful Content: The Role of Internet Platform Companies in Fighting Terrorist Incitement and Politically Motivated Disinformation* (2017); Charles Duhigg, "The Case Against Google," *N.Y. Times Magazine*, 20 Feb. 2018. For a dystopian fictional view of the internet giants, see Dave Eggers, *The Circle* (Knopf 2013).

170 John Chipman, "Why Your Company Needs a Foreign Policy," *Harvard Business Review*, Sept. 2016.

171 Interim report of the Special Representative, supra note 168, para. 11.

172 With respect to individual government, police, or military officials, a comprehensive study published by the International Committee of the Red Cross in 2005 observed that "it is the majority view that international human rights law only binds governments and not armed opposition groups." This does not detract from the idea that individuals may commit and be held responsible for international crimes, as discussed in Chapter 2, but it is far from clear what expanding human rights obligations to individuals is designed to achieve. Jean-Marie Henckaerts and Louise Doswald-Beck, *Customary International Humanitarian Law, Vol. 1: Rules* (Cambridge University Press 2005) at 209.

173 Clapham, supra note 21.

174 See, e.g., Hurst Hannum, Book Review, "Human Rights Obligations of Non-State Actors," 101 *Am. J. Int'l L.* 514 (2007).

175 For an overview of "soft law," see, e.g., Stephanie Lagoutte, Thomas Gammeltoft-Hansen, and John Cerone eds., *Tracing the Roles of Soft Law in Human Rights* (Oxford University Press 2017).

176 OHCHR's relatively broad definition of "human rights defender" may be found at www .ohchr.org/EN/Issues/SRHRDefenders/Pages/Defender.aspx.

177 Cf. the work of NGOs such as the International Service for Human Rights (Geneva), Front Line Defenders (Dublin), Fédération Internationale des Droits de l'Homme (Paris), and Amnesty International (London, whose "prisoners of conscience" have long included those imprisoned for seeking to ensure human rights). See generally OHCHR, Fact Sheet No. 29, Human Rights Defenders: Protecting the Right to Defend Human Rights (2004), www.ohchr.org/Documents/Publications/FactSheet29en.pdf.

178 Res. 53/144 (1999).

179 Available at http://eeas.europa.eu/human_rights/guidelines/defenders/docs/16332-re02_ 08_en.pdf.

180 See, e.g., Sabrina Tavernise, "MacArthur Foundation to Close Offices in Russia," *N.Y. Times*, 22 July 2015; Edward Wong, "China Approves Sweeping Security Law, Bolstering Communist Rule," *N.Y. Times*, 1 July 2015; Human Rights Watch, News Release, "Egypt: Renewed Crackdown on Independent Groups," 15 June 2015; Nida Najarapril, "Ford Foundation," *N.Y. Times*, 23 April 2015. For an argument that such restrictions violate international human rights law, see Elizabeth A. Wilson, "Restrictive National Laws Affecting Human Rights Civil Society Organizations: A Legal Analysis," 8 *J. Hum. Rts. Practice* 329 (2016).

181 Steven A. Cook, "The Real Reason the Middle East Hates NGOs," *Economist*, 7 June 2018.

182 Cf. China's 475 "Confucius Institutes" for studying Chinese language, which have been established in 120 countries in the past decade. "Confucius says, Xi does," *Economist*,

25 July 2015. Also see Central Committee of the Communist Party of China's General Office, Communiqué [No. 9] on the Current State of the Ideological Sphere (22 Apr. 2013), available at China File, www.chinafile.com/document-9-chinafile-translation. For comparison, George Soros has contributed $8 billion to the global network of Open Society Foundations. George Soros, "My Philanthropy," *N.Y. Rev. of Books*, 22 June 2011. In 2010, Soros contributed $100 million as a "challenge grant" to Human Rights Watch; for their 2016 fiscal year, the organization's net assets were over $200 million and its annual budget approximately $75 million. www.charitynavigator.org/index.cfm?bay=search.summary&orgid=3845.

183 Kenneth Roth, "Defining Economic, Social and Cultural Rights: Practical Issues Faced by an International Human Rights Organization," 26 *Hum. Rts. Q.* 63, 67 (2004).

184 Tom Farer, "The Rise of the Inter-American Human Rights Regime: No Longer a Unicorn, Not Yet an Ox," 19 *Hum. Rts. Q.* 510 (1997) at 517. For a constructive critique of the "naming and shaming" approach, see Stephen Sonnenberg and James L. Cavallaro, "Name, Shame, and Then Build Consensus? Bringing Conflict Resolution Skills to Human Rights," 39 *Washington U.J.L. & Policy* 257 (2012). Cf. Hurst Hannum, Ellen Lutz, and Eileen Babbitt, "Human Rights and Conflict Resolution from the Practitioners' Perspective," 27 *Fletcher Forum of World Affairs* 173 (Winter/Spring 2003).

185 Cook, supra note 181.

186 At the end of 2016, OHCHR had 14 stand-alone country offices and 12 regional offices or centers, plus nearly 30 human rights advisers to in-country UN Resident Representatives and human rights components in over a dozen UN peacekeeping operations. See OHCHR in the World: making human rights a reality on the ground, www.ohchr.org/EN/Countries/Pages/WorkInField.aspx.

187 The producer of a 2014 film highly sympathetic to the Tahrir Square movement commented that "he doesn't see direct politics as the protesters' responsibility." Quoted in Max Fisher, "'The Square' is a beautiful documentary. But its politics are dangerous." *Wash. Post*, 17 Jan. 2014.

188 On the difficulties of responding to the erosion of human rights by a democratically elected government, see Renata Uitz, "Can You Tell When an Illiberal Democracy Is in the Making? An Appeal to Comparative Constitutional Scholarship from Hungary," 13 *Int'l J. Constitutional L.* 279 (2015). For the same problem in an almost democratic setting, cf. Johannes Chan, "A Storm of Unprecedented Ferocity: The Shrinking Space of the Right to Political Participation, Peaceful Demonstration, and judicial independence in Hong Kong," 16 *Int'l J. Const. L.* 373 (2018).

4 HUMAN RIGHTS AND...WHATEVER

189 Osiatynski, supra note 8 at 187–188.

190 Economic Justice News Online (April 2000), www.50years.org/cms/ejn/story/176.

191 George F. Russell, Jr., "The Power of Globalization," *NBR Analysis*, vol. 16, no. 2 (Nov. 2005) at. 7.

192 See, e.g., Mazibuko & others v City of Johannesburg & others 2010 (4) SA 1 (CC); Minister of Health & others v Treatment Action Campaign & Others (No 2) 2002 (5) SA 721 (CC); Government of the Republic of South Africa & others v Grootboom & Others

2001 (1) SA 46 (CC); Soobramoney v Minister of Health, KwaZulu-Natal 1997 (12) BCLR 1696 (CC).

193 Robert Howse and Makau Mutua, "Protecting Human Rights in a Global Economy: Challenges for the World Trade Organization," in Hugo Stokke and Anne Tostensen eds. *Human Rights in Development Yearbook 1999/2000*, 51–82 (2001), https://ssrn.com/abstract=1533544. A similar situation exists with respect to human rights and finance; see Kinley, supra note 165.

194 Roger Mark Selya, "A Geography of Human Rights Abuses," 34 *Hum. Rts. Q.* 1045 (2012) at 1067–1068; citations omitted.

195 Richard Conniff, "What the Luddites Really Fought against," *Smithsonian Magazine* (Mar. 2011), www.smithsonianmag.com/history/what-the-luddites-really-fought-against-264412/.

196 UN Doc. A/HRC/22/43 (2013), Summary.

197 African Charter on Human and Peoples' Rights, art. 24.

198 Protocol to the African Charter on Human and Peoples' Rights on the Rights of Women in Africa (2003).

199 ASEAN Human Rights Declaration, art. 28(f); the right to development is found in arts. 35–37.

200 Additional Protocol to the American Convention on Human Rights in the area of Economic, Social and Cultural Rights ("Protocol of San Salvador"), adopted 17 Nov. 1988, entered into force 16 Nov. 1999, art. 11.

201 IACtHR, State Obligations in Relation to the Environment in the Context of the Protection and Guarantee of the Rights to Life and to Personal Integrity – Interpretation and Scope of Articles 4(1) and 5(1) of the American Convention on Human Rights, Advisory Opinion OC-23/18 (15 Nov. 2017). For initial reactions to the opinion, see, e.g., Maria L. Banda, "Inter-American Court of Human Rights' Advisory Opinion on the Environment and Human Rights," 22 *ASIL Insights* (No. 62018), www.asil.org/insights/volume/22/issue/6/inter-american-court-human-rights-advisory-opinion-environment-and-human; Nicolás Carrillo-Santarelli, "The Politics behind the Latest Advisory Opinions of the Inter-American Court of Human Rights," *Int'l J. Const. L. Blog* (24 Feb. 2018), www.iconnectblog.com/2018/02/the-politics-behind-the-latest-advisory-opinions-of-the-inter-american-court-of-human-rights/.

202 Dinah Shelton, "Developing Substantive Environmental Rights," 1 *J. Hum. Rts. & Environment* 89 (No. 1, 2010) at 120.

203 Concept Note for a High Level Expert Meeting on the New Future of Human Rights and Environment, co-organized by OHCHR and the UN Environment Program, www.unep.org/environmentalgovernance/Portals/8/documents/Events/Concept_Note_High_Level_Experts_meeting.pdf.

204 IACommHR, Press Release 140/15, IACHR Expresses Concern Regarding Effects of Climate Change on Human Rights, 2 Dec. 2015, https://us6.campaign-archive.com/?u=afob024f4f6c25b6530ff4c66&id=c1ce5615f5&e=a76337149d.

205 Ad Hoc Working Group for the Durban Platform for Enhanced Action, 13 Feb. 2015, https://carbonmarketwatch.org/wp-content/.../The-Geneva-Pledge-13FEB2015.pdf.

206 References to all of the special rapporteur's reports may be found at www.ohchr.org/EN/Issues/Environment/SREnvironment/Pages/Overview.aspx.

207 See Report of the Special Rapporteur on the issue of human rights obligations relating to the enjoyment of a safe, clean, healthy and sustainable environment, UN Doc. A/HRC/ 37/59 (2018), paras. 14, 15.

208 Id., para. 9.

209 Id., paras. 8, 9, 11, 12.

210 See id., principles 1–5.

211 Id., principles 6–9.

212 Id., principles 14, 15.

213 Cf. a case in Colorado in which the Colorado River was the putative plaintiff. See Lindsay Fendt, "Colorado River 'personhood' case pulled by proponents," *Aspen Journalism,* 5 Dec. 2017, www.aspenjournalism.org/2017/12/05/colorado-river-personhood-case-pulled-by-proponents/.

214 Amnesty International USA, "Shell Oil: Own up, pay up and clean up," email from alerts@takeaction.amnestyusa.org, 10 Nov. 2011 (on file with author).

215 OHCHR, summary of panel discussion, "The Human Rights Case Against Corruption" (27 Mar. 2013), www.ohchr.org/EN/NewsEvents/Pages/HRCaseAgainstCorruption.aspx.

216 For brief arguments on both sides of the issue, compare, e.g., Matthew Murray and Andrew Spalding, "Freedom from Official Corruption as a Human Right," Governance Studies at Brookings, Jan. 2015, www.brookings.edu/~/media/research/files/papers/2015/ 01/27-freedom-corruption-human-right-murray-spalding/murray-and-spalding_v06.pdf, with Anusha Pamula, "The Problem with Framing Freedom from Corruption as a Human Right," GAB/The Global Anticorruption Blog, 29 May 2015, http://globalanticor ruptionblog.com/2015/05/29/the-problem-with-framing-freedom-from-corruption-as-a-human-right/.

217 Final report of the Human Rights Council Advisory Committee on the issue of the negative impact of corruption on the enjoyment of human rights, UN Doc. A/HRC/28/73 (2015), para. 5.

218 Morten Koch Andersen, "Why Corruption Matters in Human Rights," 10 *J. Hum. Rts. Practice* 179 (2018), abstract.

219 UN Convention against Corruption, adopted 31 Oct. 2003, entered into force 14 Dec. 2005.

220 Neither is there any reference to human rights in the Inter-American Convention against Corruption (B-58), adopted 29 Mar. 1996, entered into force 6 Mar. 1997, which has been ratified by 34 states, or the African Union Convention on Preventing and Combating Corruption, adopted 11 July 2003, entered into force 5 Aug. 2006, ratified by 38 of the 55 member states. Two of the four European conventions on corruption contain only a preambular reference to human rights; see GAN Integrity, Anti-Corruption Legislation, www.business-anti-corruption.com/anti-corruption-legislation/european-anti-corruption-conventions.

221 OHCHR, Human Rights and Anti-Corruption, www.ohchr.org/EN/Issues/Development/ GoodGovernance/Pages/AntiCorruption.aspx.

222 Id.

223 IACommHR Res. 1/18, Corruption and Human Rights (2 Mar. 2018), preamble.

224 Id., preamble and paras. 2.i, 3.c, 3.e.iii.

225 Murray and Spalding, supra note 216.

226 See http://rwi.lu.se/2018/02/blockchain-human-rights/, which also includes a transcript of the first episode.

227 Sherif Elsayed-Ali, "Can technology help solve human rights challenges? We believe it can." 19 Dec. 2016, www.amnesty.org/en/latest/research/2016/12/technology-can-help-solve-human-rights-challenges/.

228 Thanassis Cambanis, "Meet the international revolutionary geek squad," *Boston Globe*, 23 June 2013, www.bostonglobe.com/ideas/2013/06/22/meet-international-revolutionary-geek-squad/HP4iljWroxdBods6d9kD5I/story.html.

229 www.hrw.org/news/2018/03/07/want-worry-about-ai-then-worry-about.

230 See, e.g., Jay D. Aronson et al., "Reconstructing Human Rights Violations Using Large Eyewitness Video Collections: The Case of Euromaidan Protester Deaths," 10 *J. Hum. Rts. Practice* 159 (2018).

231 "UN uses social media to mark Human Rights Day on 63rd anniversary of Universal Declaration," *Wash. Post*, 9 Dec. 2011.

232 John Naughton, "The new surveillance capitalism," *Prospect Magazine*, 19 Jan. 2018. For an account of the shift of major tech companies from idealism to commercialism, see Noam Cohen, *The Know-It-Alls: The Rise of Silicon Valley as a Political Powerhouse and Social Wrecking Ball* (New Press 2017).

233 A recent Council of Europe report includes an appendix listing 34 European Fact-checking and Debunking Initiatives; 40% are attached to news organizations, and 60% are NGOs. See Claire Wardle and Hossein Derakhshan, *Information Disorder: Toward an interdisciplinary framework for research and policy making*, Council of Europe Report DGI (2017)09, Appendix.

234 Kate Lamb, "Muslim Cyber Army: a 'fake news' operation designed to derail Indonesia's leader," *Guardian*, 13 Mar 2018.

235 Vidhi Doshi, "India's millions of new Internet users are falling for fake news — sometimes with deadly consequences," *Wash. Post*, 1 Oct. 2017.

236 "How the Cambodian government and Prime Minister Hun Sen are using Facebook to silence dissent before election," *South China Morning Post*, 10 Feb. 2018.

237 Simon Denyer, "The walls are closing in: China finds new ways to tighten Internet controls," *Wash. Post*, 27 Sept. 2017; also see Elizabeth C. Economy, "The great firewall of China: Xi Jinping's internet shutdown," *Guardian*, 29 June 2018.

238 Adam Greenfield, "China's Dystopian Tech Could Be Contagious," *Atlantic*, 14 Feb. 2018.

239 CP Covenant, art. 19.3.

240 ESC Covenant, art. 4.

5 UNDERMINING OLD RIGHTS WITH NEW ONES

241 Posner, supra note 9 at 94.

242 Michael Ignatieff, "Human Rights as Idolatry," in Amy Gutman ed., *Human Rights as Politics and Idolatry* (Princeton University Press 2003) at 90.

243 Buchanan, supra note 39 at 286.

244 See, e.g., Philip Alston, "Conjuring Up New Human Rights: A Proposal for Quality Control," 78 *Am. J. Intl. L.* 607 (1984) and Theodor Meron, *Human Rights Law-Making in the United Nations* (Oxford University Press 1986).

245 GA Res. 41/120 (1986), para. 4.

246 For a convenient short summary of some of the pro- and anti- new rights positions, see the papers, including bibliographies, prepared by professors Rosa Freedman and Malcolm Langford, respectively, for a recent workshop organized by the Subcommittee on Human Rights of the European Parliament, *Expansion of concept of human rights: Impact on rights promotion and protection*, 24 Jan. 2018, available through www.europarl .europa.eu/thinktank/en/document.html?reference=EXPO_STU(2018)603865. Also see the summary of objections to new rights in Shaver, infra note 258 at 43–50.

247 Adopted 23 May 1969, entered into force 27 Jan. 1980.

248 Eur. Ct. Hum. Rts., Demir and Baykara v. Turkey, App. 34503/97, Judgment (GC) of 12 Nov. 2008, paras. 67, 68, 86. For criticism of the court's "dynamic" approach to interpretation, see Marc Bossuyt, *International Human Rights Protection* (Intersentia 2016).

249 IACtHR, Juan Humberto Sanchez case, Interpretation of the Judgment on Preliminary Objections, Merits and Reparations (ser. A), No. 102 (2003), para. 56, citing the Court's Advisory Opinion No. 16, The Right to Information on Consular Assistance in the Framework of the Guarantees of the Due Process of Law (1999).

250 Kerstin Mechlem, "Treaty Bodies and the Interpretation of Human Rights," 42 *Vanderbilt J. Transnat'l L.* 904 (2009) at 945–946.

251 See, e.g., Eur. Ct. Hum. Rts., Dudgeon v. U.K., App. No. 7525/76, Judgment of 28 Oct. 1981; HR Committee., Toonen v. Australia, Comm. No. 488/92, Views of 31 Mar. 1994. For summaries of relevant European cases, see Eur. Ct. Hum. Rts., Factsheet, *Sexual Orientation Issues* (Feb. 2018).

252 For summaries of the relevant European cases, see Eur. Ct. Hum. Rts., Factsheet, *Gender Identity Issues* (Apr. 2017); see also Council of Europe, Sexual orientation and gender identity, www.coe.int/en/web/sogi.

253 See, e.g., IACtHR, Mayagna (Sumo) Awas Tingni Community v. Nicaragua, Judgment of 31 Aug. 2001; AfCommHPR v. Kenya (Ogiek case), App. No. 006/2012, Judgment of 26 May 2017.

254 This issue is discussed further in Chapter 6.

255 See Committee on the Rights of Persons with Disabilities, Nyusti and Takacs v. Hungary, Comm. No. 1/2010, Views of 16 Apr. 2013.

256 For an analysis of whether obesity might be treated as a disability or a prohibited ground of discrimination, see Krista Nadakavukaren Schefer, "The European Court of Justice Rules on Obesity Discrimination," 19 *Am. Soc. Int'l L. Insights*, 24 Apr. 2015, www.asil .org/insights/volume/19/issue/9/european-court-justice-rules-obesity-discrimination.

257 Associated Press, "UN says access to contraception a human right, better family planning would cut health costs," *Wash. Post*, 14 Nov. 2012.

258 Lea Shaver, "The Right to Read," 54 *Columbia J. Transnat'l L.* 1, 49 (2015).

259 The ILC's work on crimes against humanity is summarized and analyzed at http://legal .un.org/ilc/guide/7_7.shtml.

260 GA Res. 41/128 (1986).

261 Arjun Sengupta, "On the Theory and Practice of the Right to Development," 24 *Hum. Rts. Q.* 837 (2002) at 837, 845–846, 848, 851.

262 Jack Donnelly, "In Search of the Unicorn: The Jurisprudence and Politics of the Right to Development," 15 *Cal. West. Intl. L.J.* 473 (1985) at 508.

263 Kinley, supra note 165 at 136; references omitted.

264 Adopted 4 June 2012, OAS Doc. OEA/Ser.P, AG/doc.5242/12 rev. 2 (2012).

265 GA Res. 48/141 (1993), para. 4(c).

266 UN Comm'n HR Res. 1998/72 (1998).

267 HRC Res. 33/14 (1998).

268 Id., para. 14(b).

269 UNDP, *Human Development Report 1990, Concept and Measurement of Human Development* (Oxford University Press 1990).

270 UNDP, HDRO Outreach, What is Human Development? http://hdr.undp.org/en/content/what-human-development.

271 There is a preambular reference to the right to development in the African Charter on Human and Peoples' Rights, which also declares rather vaguely in article 22.2: "States shall have the duty, individually or collectively, to ensure the exercise of the right to development." There also is a preambular reference to "the right of.. [the "peoples" of the Americas] to development, self-determination, and the free disposal of their wealth and natural resources" in the Additional Protocol to the American Convention on Human Rights in the Area of Economic, Social and Cultural Rights (Protocol of San Salvador).

272 UNICEF, Human Rights-based Approach to Programming, www.unicef.org/policyanalysis/rights/index_62012.html. Among many works on this rights-based approach, see, e.g., Andrea Cornwall and Celestine Nyamu-Musembi, "Putting the 'Rights-Based Approach' to Development into Perspective," 25 *Third World Q.* 1415 (2004); Paul Gready and Jonathan Ensor, *Reinventing Development?: Translating Rights-Based Approaches from Theory into Practice* (Zed Books 2005); Sam Hickey and Diana Mitlin eds., *Rights-Based Approaches to Development: Exploring the Potential and Pitfalls* (Kumarian 2009); Shannon Kindornay, James Ron, and Charli Carpenter, "Rights-Based Approaches to Development: Implications for NGOs," 34 *Hum. Rts. Q.* 72 (2012); Oche Onazi, *Human Rights from Community: A Rights-Based Approach to Development* (Edinburgh University Press 2013); Peter Uvin, "From the right to development to the rights-based approach: how 'human rights' entered development," 17 *Development in Practice* 597 (2007).

273 On the subject of human rights and international financial institutions, see generally, e.g., Philip Alston and Mary Robinson eds., *Human Rights and Development: Towards Mutual Reinforcement* (Oxford University Press 2005); Sanae Fujita, *The World Bank, Asian Development Bank and Human Rights: Developing Standards of Transparency, Participation and Accountability* (Edward Elgar 2013); Willem van Genugten, *The World Bank Group, the IMF and Human Rights: A Contextualised Way Forward* (Intersentia 2015); Galit A. Sarfaty, *Values in Translation; Human Rights and the Culture of the World Bank* (Stanford University Press 2012).

274 Report of the Special Rapporteur on extreme poverty and human rights [Philip Alston], UN Doc. A/70/274 (2015), para. 68.

275 Id., paras. 64, 65.

276 Id., para. 66.

277 Id.

278 World Bank, Articles of Agreement, art. IV, sec. 10.

279 World Bank, *Gender Program: Impact Evaluation to Development Impact (i2i)* (2015) at 1.
280 World Bank, *Environmental and Social Framework* (World Bank 2017) at 1–2.
281 Id. at 76.
282 Alston, supra note 274, para. 54.
283 See United Nations, We Can End Poverty, www.un.org/millenniumgoals/.
284 United Nations, 17 Goals to Transform Our World, www.un.org/sustainabledevelop ment/.
285 www.un.org/sustainabledevelopment/sustainable-development-goals/.
286 www.un.org/sustainabledevelopment/peace-justice/.
287 For a quantitative assessment of the MDGs, see John W. McArthur and Krista Rasmus-sen, "Change of Pace: Accelerations and Advances during the Millennium Development Goal Era," 105 *World Development* 132 (2018).
288 Nick Cumming-Bruce, "For U.N. Leader on Human Rights, Finish Line Looks Blurry," *New York Times* (13 Aug. 2014).
289 A complete list may be found at OHCHR, Thematic Mandates, http://spinternet.ohchr .org/_Layouts/SpecialProceduresInternet/ViewAllCountryMandates.aspx?Type=TM.
290 The relatively long titles are either quotes or close paraphrases of the mandates.
291 Rosa Freedman and Jacob Mchangama, "Expanding or Diluting Human Rights?: The Proliferation of United Nations Special Procedures Mandates," 38 *Hum. Rts. Q.* 164 (2016) at 193.
292 See generally OHCHR, Background Information on the Advisory Committee, www .ohchr.org/EN/HRBodies/HRC/AdvisoryCommittee/Pages/AboutAC.aspx.
293 See OHCHR, www.ohchr.org/EN/HRBodies/HRC/AdvisoryCommittee/Pages/Mandates.aspx.
294 See, e.g., Ted Piccone, *The Future of the United Nations Special Procedures* (Brookings 2014); Aoife Nolan, Rosa Freedman, and Therese Murphy eds., *The United Nations Special Procedures System* (Brill/Nijhoff 2017); Humberto Cantu Rivera ed., *The Special Procedures of the Human Rights Council: A brief look from the inside and perspectives from outside* (Intersentia 2015).
295 Report of the Special Rapporteur in the field of cultural rights [Farida Shaheed], UN Doc. A/69/286 (2014).
296 Report of the Special Rapporteur in the field of cultural rights, Farida Shaheed, Addendum, Visit to Viet Nam (18–29 Nov. 2013), UN Doc. A/HRC/28/57/Add.1 (2015), paras. 97, 114. For critical commentary, see Pedro Pizano, "The Human Rights That Dictators Love: Does the concept of 'human rights' still have meaning in a world where everything qualifies?" *Foreign Policy*, 26 Feb. 2014, http://foreignpolicy.com/2014/02/26/ the-human-rights-that-dictators-love/.
297 Report of the Special Rapporteur in the field of cultural rights [Farida Shaheed], UN Doc. A/67/287 (2012), para. 4, quoting Marsha Freeman, n.4.
298 Id., paras. 14, 28, 65, 70, 71, 78; references omitted.
299 Report of the Special Rapporteur on the right of everyone to the enjoyment of the highest attainable standard of physical and mental health, Anand Grover, UN Doc. A/HRC/14/20 (2010), para. 43.
300 Report of the Special Rapporteur on the promotion and protection of the right to freedom of opinion and expression, Frank La Rue, UN Doc. A/HRC/17/27 (2011), para. 60.

301 Randall Lane, "The United Nations says broadband is basic human right," *Forbes*, (15 Nov. 2011), www.forbes.com/sites/randalllane/2011/11/15/the-united-nations-says-broad band-is-basic-human-right/#4a14c57a5daa.

302 Report of the Special Rapporteur on the rights to freedom of peaceful assembly and of association on his follow-up mission to the United States of America [Maina Kiai], UN Doc. A/HRC/35/28/Add.2 (2017), paras. 7, 13–15; references omitted.

303 Id. para. 10.

304 GA Res. 66/281 (2012), preamble. The most recent World Happiness Report may be found at http://worldhappiness.report/ed/2018/; it does not mention "human rights" in its 172 pages.

305 Global Happiness Council, *Global Happiness Policy Report 2018* (2018) at 169, 189; references omitted.

306 HR Council Res. 36/11 (2017), Preamble.

307 See www.ohchr.org/EN/HRBodies/HRC/WGMilitary/Pages/OEIWGMilitaryIndex.aspx.

308 Declaration on the Right to Peace, GA Res. 71/189 (2016).

309 For an overview, see Christophe Golay, *Negotiation of a United Nations Declaration on the Rights of Peasants and Other People Working in Rural Areas* (Geneva Academy of International Humanitarian Law and Human Rights, In-Brief No. 5, 2015); Noha Shawki, "New Rights Advocacy and the Human Rights of Peasants: La Via Campesina and the Evolution of New Human Rights Norms," 6 *J. Hum. Rts. Practice* 306 (2014).

310 See UN Docs. A/HRC/16/63 (2011) and A/HRC/19/75 (2012).

311 The activities of the working group are described at OHCHR, Human Rights Council, www.ohchr.org/EN/HRBodies/HRC/RuralAreas/Pages/WGRuralAreasIndex.aspx.

312 GA Res. 36/55 (1981).

313 GA Res. 47/135 (1992).

314 GA Res. 61/295 (2007).

315 UN Doc. A/HRC/WG.15/5/2 (2018).

316 See Report of the open-ended intergovernmental working group on a United Nations declaration on the rights of peasants and other people working in rural areas, UN Doc. A/HRC/39/67 (2018), paras. 11–44.

317 General Statement of the European Union at the 5th session of the working group, 13–19 Apr. 2018, available via www.ohchr.org/EN/HRBodies/HRC/RuralAreas/Pages/5thSes sion.aspx.

318 Inter-American Convention on Protection of the Human Rights of Older People (A70), adopted 15 June 2015, entered into force 11 Jan. 2017, art. 6.

319 Victor Abramovic, "From Massive Human Rights Problems to Structural Patterns: New Approaches and Classic Tensions in the Inter-American Human Rights System," 7 *SUR Int'l J. Hum. Rts.* 6 (no. 11, 2009) at 17.

320 Abramovich, supra note 22 at 1, 5.

321 ETS 176, adopted 20 Oct. 2000, entered into force 1 Mar. 2004.

322 Council of Europe, Committee of Ministers Recommendation CM/Rec(2017)7.

323 Council of Europe, *European Landscape Convention – Contribution to human rights, democracy and sustainable development* (2017).

324 Quoted in John Roderick, "In 2008, Eyes on Beijing," *Winchester Star*, 28 Feb. 2016, at C1, C4. https://newspaperarchive.com/winchester-star-feb-28-2006-p-16/.

325 James Legge, "Ecuador's foreign minister says UK should allow Julian Assange to exercise his 'fundamental right' to sunbathe," *Independent*, 11 June 2013.

326 Raoul Wallenberg Institute, "Will Human Rights Fade Into Oblivion?" 2 Oct. 2018, http://rwi.lu.se/2018/10/olga-bezbozhna-from-the-fluidity-of-borders-in-the-soviet-union-to-ender-perspective-in-regional-asia/.

327 Amnesty International, Don't Let #toxictwitter Silence Women, www.amnesty.org/en/latest/campaigns/2018/03/violence-against-women-online/.

328 Int'l Service Hum. Rts., "HRC38: Online violence against women activists is a continuum of offline violence," 26 June 2018, www.ishr.ch/news/hrc38-online-violence-against-women-activists-continuum-offline-violence.

329 See emails from Margaret Huang for Amnesty International USA, " SYRIA: The deadliest weeks in 7 years," 14 Mar. 2018; id., "SYRIA: The nightmare continues," 20 Mar. 2018; id., "This must stop: You can demand justice," 22 Mar. 2018 (on file with author).

330 See Human Rights Watch, People, www.hrw.org/about/people.

331 Publisher's description of S. Matthew Liao, *The Right to Be Loved* (Oxford University Press 2015), https://global.oup.com/academic/product/the-right-to-be-loved-9780190234836?lang=en&cc=us#.

332 It is a breath of fresh air that at least one rights NGO does not attempt to skirt the issue of just what is a human right. The Nonhuman Rights Project "is the only civil rights organization in the United States working through litigation, public policy advocacy, and education to secure legally recognized fundamental rights for nonhuman animals." See www.nonhumanrights.org/.

333 CP Covenant, art. 12.2; UDHR, art. 13.2.

334 Convention on the Status of Refugees, adopted 28 July 1951, entered into force 22 Apr. 1954, art. 33.

335 UNHCR, Asylum and Migration, www.unhcr.org/en-us/asylum-and-migration.html.

336 See OAU Convention Governing the Specific Aspects of Refugee Problems in Africa, adopted 10 Sept. 1969, entered into force 20 Jan. 1974; EU Council Directive 2001/55/EC of 20 July 2001 on minimum standards for giving temporary protection in the event of a mass influx of displaced persons and on measures promoting a balance of efforts between Member States in receiving such persons and bearing the consequences thereof.

337 UNHCR, Asylum and Migration, supra note 335.

338 International Convention on the Protection of the Rights of All Migrant Workers and Members of their Families, adopted 18 Dec. 1990, entered into force 1 July 2003.

339 Id., art. 35.

340 Reg. No. 604/2013 of 26 June 2013, commonly known as the Dublin III Regulation.

341 New York Declaration for Refugees and Migrants, GA Res. 71/1 (2016). In December 2018, 164 states meeting in Morocco adopted a non-binding Global Compact for Safe, Orderly and Regular Migration, although a few governments refused to sign the compact.

342 Ron Dudai, "Human Rights in the Populist Era: Mourn then (Re)Organize," 9 *J. Hum. Rts. Practice* 16 (2017) at 19.

343 See Kim Willsher, "French parliament gives citizens the 'right to make mistakes,'" *The Guardian*, 24 Jan. 2018.

344 See Dominic McGoldrick, "Developments in the Right to be Forgotten," 13 *Hum. Rts. L. Rev.* 761 (2013).

345 Roger T. Ames, "Rites as Rights: The Confucian Alternative," in Leroy S. Rouner ed., *Human Rights and the World's Religions* (University of Notre Dame Press 1988) at 213.

6 WOMEN, SEX, AND GENDER

346 Doreen Carvajal, "Amnesty International Votes for Policy Calling for Decriminalization of Prostitution," *N.Y. Times*, 11 Aug. 2015.

347 Jessica Elgot, "Amnesty approves policy to decriminalise sex trade," *Guardian*, 11 Aug. 2015. For an opposing view, which accuses AI of "missing a gender lens," see Jessica Neuwirth, "Amnesty International says prostitution is a human right – but it's wrong," *Guardian*, 28 July 2015.

348 Adopted 31 Mar. 1953, entered into force 7 July 1954.

349 See generally Marsha A. Freeman, Christine Chinkin, and Beate Rudolf, *The UN Convention on the Elimination of All Forms of Discrimination Against Women: A Commentary* (Oxford University Press 2012).

350 Protocol to the African Charter on Human and Peoples' Rights on the Rights of Women in Africa, adopted 1 July 2003, entered into force 25 Nov. 2005.

351 Council of Europe Convention on preventing and combating violence against women and domestic violence, adopted 11 May 2011, entered into force 1 Aug. 2014.

352 CEDAW, art. 1.

353 Id., art. 2.a, 2.e. 2.f.

354 Id., art. 5.

355 See generally Patrick Thornberry, *The International Convention on the Elimination of All Forms of Racial Discrimination: A Commentary* (Oxford University Press 2016).

356 CERD, art. 1.

357 It should be noted that CERD applies to discrimination based on "race, colour, descent, or national or ethnic origin," thus making its scope much broader than traditional concepts of "race."

358 R.K.B. v. Turkey, Comm. No. 28/210, Views of 24 Feb. 2012, paras. 8.5, 8.6.

359 Jessica A. Kennedy, Laura Kray, and Gillian Ku, "A social-cognitive approach to understanding gender differences in negotiator ethics: The role of moral identity," Harvard Kennedy School, Women and Public Policy Program, Gender Action Portal (nd), http://gap.hks.harvard.edu/social-cognitive-approach-understanding-gender-differences-negotiator-ethics-role-moral-identity. But compare "Senior female bankers don't conform to stereotypes and are just as ready to take risks," The Conversation, 29 Jan. 2017, https://theconversation.com/senior-female-bankers-dont-conform-to-stereotypes-and-are-just-as-ready-to-take-risks-71891.

360 Zebib Kavuma & Camilla Schramek, "The time for gender-smart action on disaster risk reduction is now," Thompson Reuters Fdn. News (12 Oct. 2018), http://news.trust.org/item/20181012135436-qfg5m/.

361 Referenced in "Billions of women are denied the same choice of employment as men," *Economist*, 24 May 2018.

362 CEDAW, art. 11.1.d. ESC Covenant art. 7(a)(1) has similar language.

363 Alissa J. Rubin, "Afghan Policewomen Struggle Against Culture," N.Y. Times, 1 Mar. 2015.

364 See, e.g., Eur. Ct. Hum. Rts. (GC), S.A.S. v. France, App. No. 43835/11, 1 July 2014, discussed briefly in Chapter 7.

365 Osmanoglu and Kocabas v. Switzerland, App. No. 29086/12, Judgment of 10 Jan. 2017, para. 96.

366 See Richard Adams, "Islamic school's gender segregation is unlawful, court of appeal rules," Guardian, 13 Oct. 2017.

367 UN Doc. A/68/290 (2013).

368 Id., paras. 23, 26.

369 Id., para. 30.

370 Id., para. 73.

371 GA Res. 47/135, Declaration on the Rights of Persons Belonging to National or Ethnic, Religious and Linguistic Minorities (1992).

372 GA Res. 61/295, Declaration on the Rights of Indigenous Peoples (2007).

373 Opened for signature 1 Feb. 1995, entered into force 1 Feb. 1998.

374 Human rights in culturally diverse societies [Guidelines adopted by the Committee of Ministers and Compilation of Council of Europe standards] (2016), para. 32.

375 Eur. Ct. H.R., Dudgeon v. U.K., App. No. 7525/76, Judgment of 22 Oct. 1981.

376 Id., para. 57. The court decided that it was not necessary to consider the issue of discrimination separately, given their finding of a violation of the right to privacy.

377 For a summary of these cases, see Eur. Ct. Hum. Rts. Press Unit, Factsheet, Homosexuality: Criminal Aspects (June 2014).

378 See Eur. Ct. Hum. Rts. Press Unit, Factsheet, Gender identity issues (Mar. 2018).

379 See IACtHR, Atala Riffo and daughters v. Chile, Judgment of 24 Feb. 2012.

380 See IACommHR, Rapporteurship on the Rights of LGBTI Persons, www.oas.org/en/iachr/lgtbi/.

381 AfCommHPR Res. 275, 55th Ordinary Session (2014), www.achpr.org/sessions/55th/resolutions/275/.

382 Dominic McGoldrick, "The Development and Status of Sexual Orientation Discrimination under International Human Rights Law," 16 Hum. Rts. L. Rev. 613 (2016) at 646; references omitted.

383 Id.

384 HR Committee, Toonen v. Australia, App. No. 488/1992, Views of 31 Mar. 1994, paras. 8.2, 8.6. The Committee confined itself to noting that "in its view the reference to 'sex' in articles 2, paragraph 1, and 26 is to be taken as including sexual orientation" and did not address the broader question of whether homosexuality is an "other status" under article 26 of the CP Covenant. Id., para. 8.7. For a discussion of other HR Committee cases and comments, see McGoldrick, supra note 382 at 627–631.

385 Security Council Press Statement on Terrorist Attack in Orlando, Florida, Press Release SC/12399, 13 June 2016, www.un.org/press/en/2016/sc12399.doc.htm.

386 HR Council Res. 17/19 (2011). For references to LGBT+ rights in the work of the special procedures since 2011, see Int'l Service Hum. Rts., LGBTI Factsheet, www.ishr.ch/news/lgbti-rights-factsheets-un-special-procedures.

387 HR Council Res. 17/19 (2011), Preamble.

388 Id., para. 2.

389 McGoldrick, supra note 382 at 620.

390 For a discussion of the debates in the council, see id., at 619–623. For a description of the politics in the General Assembly, see Arvind Narrain and Kim Vance, "A Success in 2016: The First UN Independent Expert on Sexual Orientation and Gender Identity," ARC International, http://arc-international.net/research-and-publications/new-arc-reports/a-suc cess-in-2016-the-first-un-independent-expert-on-sexual-orientation-and-gender-identity/.

391 See Conrad Hackett and David McClendon, "Christians remain world's largest religious group, but they are declining in Europe," Pew Research Center, 5 Apr. 2017; Cindy Wooden, "Global Catholic population tops 1.28 billion; half are in 10 countries," *National Catholic Reporter*, 8 Apr. 2017.

392 See Tom Kington, "Pope's reported comment to a gay man may indicate a new level of acceptance of homosexuality," *L.A. Times*, 20 May 2018.

393 McGoldrick, supra note 382 at 613, 614, 657.

394 See, e.g., HR Committee, e.g., Joslin v. New Zealand, Comm. No. 902/1999, Views of 17 July 2002; Eur. Ct. Hum. Rts., Chapin and Charpentier v. France, Judgment of 9 Sept. 2016.

395 Eur. Ct. Hum. Rts., Oliari and Others v. Italy, Apps. Nos. 18766/11 and 36030/11, Judgment of 21 July 2015.

396 IACtHR, Gender identity, and equality and non-discrimination with regard to same-sex couples. State obligations in relation to change of name, gender identity, and rights deriving from a relationship between same-sex couples, Advisory Opinion OC-24/17 of 24 Nov. 2017, paras. 219, 220, 223; references omitted.

397 Aengus Carroll and Lucas Ramón Mendos, *State Sponsored Homophobia 2017: A world survey of sexual orientation laws: criminalisation, protection and recognition* (ILGA, May 2017).

398 Wikipedia, LGBT in Islam, https://en.wikipedia.org/wiki/LGBT_in_Islam#Criminalization.

399 See generally Afsaneh Najmabadi, *Professing Selves: Transsexuality and Same-Sex Desire in Contemporary Iran* (Duke University Press 2013).

400 Andrew Sullivan, "The Gay Rights Movement Is Undoing Its Best Work," *N.Y. Magazine*, 26 Jan. 2018.

401 Amnesty International, Sexual and Reproductive Rights (n.d.), www.amnesty.org/en/what-we-do/sexual-and-reproductive-rights/.

402 Moki Kindzeka and Loveday Wright, "Anti-gay sentiment on the rise in Africa," *Deutsche Welle*, 17 June 2016, www.dw.com/en/anti-gay-sentiment-on-the-rise-in-africa/a-19338620.

403 "How a tiny West African tourist trap is turning itself into an Islamic republic," *Economist*, 11 Jan. 2016.

404 Graeme Reid, "After a Grim Year for LGBT Rights, the Way Forward," *Los Angeles Rev. Books*, 16 Apr. 2018; also see, e.g., Rachel Banning-Lover, "Where are the most difficult places in the world to be gay or transgender?" *Guardian*, 1 Mar. 2017.

405 Rob Salerno, "Progress, pain and resistance: a look back at global LGBT rights in 2017," Xtra, 29 Dec. 2017, https://www.dailyxtra.com/progress-pain-and-resistance-a-look-back-at-global-lgbt-rights-in-2017-83031.

406 A.L., "How homosexuality became a crime in the Middle East," *Economist*, 6 June 2018.

407 Oxford Living Dictionaries, Usage of "gender," https://en.oxforddictionaries.com/defin ition/gender.

408 Kate Millet, *Sexual Politics* (Hart-Davis 1970), at 29; emphasis in original.

409 "Making sense of the culture war over transgender identity," *Economist*, 18 Nov. 2017. For an anecdotal discussion of the intersex rights movement, see Nora Caplan-Bricker, "Their Time," *Wash. Post*, 5 Oct. 2017.

410 https://lgbtqia.ucdavis.edu/educated/glossary.html.

411 Yogyakarta Principles on the Application of International Human Rights Law in Relation to Sexual Orientation, at 6, n.1 (2005).

412 Yogyakarta Principles Plus 10: Additional Principles and State Obligations on the Application of International Human Rights Law in Relation to Sexual Orientation, Gender Identity, Gender Expression, and Sex Characteristics to Complement the Yogyakarta Principles (2017).

413 Supra note 396 at 16, n.45.

414 Yogyakarts Principles Plus 10, supra note 412, Introduction at 5; emphasis added.

415 Id., Principle 31. Non-gendered passports are currently provided by Australia, Canada, India, Malaysia and New Zealand, among others, and a suit to require that the state provide so-called "X" passports is currently pending in UK courts. See Owen Bowcott, "UK refusal to issue gender-neutral passports unlawful, high court told," *Guardian*, 18 April 2018.

416 Supra note 412, Principle 34.

417 Id., Principle 17.

418 Council of Europe, Sexual Orientation and Gender Identity Unit, www.coe.int/en/web/ sogi/home.

419 Kay Scott, "These schools want to wipe away gender stereotypes from an early age," CNN, 28 Sept. 2017, http://edition.cnn.com/2017/09/28/health/sweden-gender-neutral-pre school/index.html.

420 See Daniel Boffey, "First conviction under sexism law for Belgian who insulted officer," *Guardian*, 6 Mar. 2018; Alissa J. Rubin, "France's New Law against Sexist Catcalls Gets Its First Conviction," *N.Y. Times*, 27 Sept. 2018.

421 www.achpr.org/instruments/declaration-on-gender-equality-in-africa/.

422 Resolution 275, supra note 381.

7 THE FLEXIBILITY OF HUMAN RIGHTS NORMS: UNIVERSALITY IS NOT UNIFORMITY

423 Jack Donnelly, "The Relative Universality of Human Rights," 29 *Hum. Rts. Q.* 281 (2007) at 299. Donnelly has pursued and parsed the issue of universality versus relativism in a number of writings spanning more than two decades; see id. at 282, n.1, for references to many of his earlier works. For a somewhat long-winded critique, see Reza Afshari, "Relativity in Universality: Jack Donnelly's Grand Theory in Need of Specific Illustrations," 37 *Hum. Rts. Q.* 854 (2015) at 889 ("[T]he scope and application of variations (weak or not-so-weak) can be properly evaluated only in references to the records and analyses of actual human rights violations. Donnelly's discourse lacks such a framework

... A human rights theory can be usefully constructed only in synergy with human rights practices – not with mostly hypothetical or unlikely cases.")

424 Donnelly, supra note 423.

425 Id.

426 UDHR, art. 21.

427 On the ESC Covenant, see generally Ben Saul, David Kinley, and Jaqueline Mowbray, *The International Covenant on Economic, Social and Cultural Right: Commentary, Cases, and Materials* (Oxford University Press 2016).

428 Emphasis added.

429 Art. 8.4.

430 See, e.g., Philip Alston, "U.S. Ratification of the Covenant on Economic, Social and Cultural Rights: The Need for an Entirely New Strategy," 84 *Am. J. Int'l L.* 365 (1990) ("[T]he U.S. Government, for almost a decade, has categorically denied that there is any such thing as an economic, a social or a cultural human right."); Susan L. Kang, "The Unsettled Relationship of Economic and Social Rights and the West: A Response to Whelan and Donnelly," 31 *Hum. Rts. Q.* 1006 (2009) ("recent [U.S.] administrations' rejections of international economic and social rights remain particularly striking"). In 2009, then Secretary of State Hillary Clinton gave a major speech on human rights policy in which she mentioned economic rights only once: when referring to women whom she had met in China, she commented that they were "working not just for legal rights, but for environmental, health, and economic rights as well." The implication that economic rights are not legal rights is clear, an interpretation reinforced by other references in the speech to "economic development ... economic empowerment ... [and] economic opportunity" but not to economic rights. Remarks on the Human Rights Agenda for the 21st Century, infra note 652.

431 ESC Committee, General Comment No. 3, para. 1.

432 Id., para. 2.

433 Id., para. 10.

434 CP Covennt, art. 2.1, 2.3.

435 Id., art. 19.3.

436 An excellent analysis may be found in Dominic McGoldrick, "A Defence of the Margin of Appreciation and an Argument for Its Application by the Human Rights Committee," 65 *Int'l & Comp. L. Q.* 21, 22, 24 (2016).

437 See, e.g., Eur. Ct. Hum. Rts., *Practical Guide on Admissibility Criteria* (4th ed. 2017) at 19–27; Alvaro Paul, "The Inter-American Commission on Human Rights' Initial Review of Petitions, Its Backlog, and the Principle of Subsidiarity," 49 *Geo. Wash. Int'l L. Rev.* 19 (2016); Amos O Enabulele, "Sailing Against the Tide: Exhaustion of Domestic Remedies and the ECOWAS Community Court of Justice," 56 *J. African L.* 268 (2012); Minority Rights Group, Guidance: Exhausting domestic remedies under the African Charter on Human and Peoples' Rights, http://minorityrights.org/publications/guidance-exhausting-domestic-remedies-under-the-african-charter-on-human-and-peoples-rights/.

438 A brief summary may be found in McGoldrick, supra note 436 at 11–14.

439 Eur. Ct. H.R., Handyside v. U.K., 1 EHRR 737 (1976), para. 48.

440 David J. Harris et al., *Law of the European Convention on Human Rights* (Oxford University Press 2d ed. 2009) at 13.

441 As of November 2018, Protocol No. 15 had been ratified by all Council of Europe member states except Bosnia and Herzegovina and Italy; it will not enter into force until all council members have ratified it.

442 For references to varying opinions on the margin of appreciation doctrine, see Alistair Mowbray, *Cases and Materials on the European Convention on Human Rights* (Oxford University Press, 2d ed. 2007) at 629–633.

443 See Human Rights Committee, Faurisson v. France (App. No. 550/1993), UN. Doc. A/52/40 vol. II (1996), at 84. For an analysis of European jurisprudence on this issue, see Paolo Lobba, "Holocaust Denial before the European Court of Human Rights: Evolution of an Exceptional Regime," 26 *Eur. J. Int'l L.* 237 (2015).

444 HR Committee, General Comment No. 34 on Freedom of Opinion and Expression, UN Doc. CCPR/C/GC/34 (2011), para. 49.

445 Eur. Ct. H.R., Sahin v. Turkey, 4th Section, Judgment of 29 June 2004.

446 Id., (GC), Refah Partisi v. Turkey, Judgment of 13 Feb. 2003.

447 Id., (GC) S.A.S. v. France, Judgment of 1 July 2014, para. 154.. Id., para. 154.

448 Id., para. 153.

449 Id., (GC), Lautsi v. Italy, Judgment of 18 Mar. 2011.

450 Id., para. 71.

451 Id., (GC), Folgero v. Norway, Judgment of 29 June 2007.

452 Id., paras. 89, 95.

453 Id., Donaldson v. U.K., admissibility dec. of 25 Jan. 2011, para. 28,

454 Luzius Wildhaber, "The European Court of Human Rights: The Past, the Present, the Future," 22 *Am. U. Int'l L. Rev.* 521 (2007) at 535.

455 European Court of Human Rights, Müller v. Switzerland, Judgment of 24 May 1988, para. 35. This phrase has been repeated verbatim in many subsequent cases.

456 HR Committee General Comment No. 34, supra note 444, para. 48.

457 The debate over cultural relativism versus universality is an old one, and little of substance has changed in the past two decades. Compare, e.g., Josiah A.M. Cobbah, "African Values and the Human Rights Debate: An African Perspective," 9 *Hum. Rts. Q.* 309 (1987); Bilahari Kausikan, "Asia's Different Standard," 92 *Foreign Pol'y* 24 (Fall 1993); and Makau Mutua, "Savages, Victims, and Saviors: The Metaphor of Human Rights," 42 *Harv. Int'l L. J.* 201 (2001); with, e.g., Aryeh Neier, "Asia's Unacceptable Standard," 92 *Foreign Pol'y* 42 (Fall 1993); Rhoda E. Howard, "Cultural Absolutism and the Nostalgia for Community," 15 *Human Rts. Q.* 315–38 (1993); and Amartya Sen, "Human Rights and Asian Values," *The New Republic*, 14–21 July 1997.

458 Study of the Human Rights Council Advisory Committee on promoting human rights and fundamental freedoms through a better understanding of traditional values of humankind, UN Doc. A/HRC/22/71 (2012), para. 78.

459 See, e.g., Eur. Ct. Hum. Rts., A. v. United Kingdom, App. No. 25599/94, Judgment of 23 Sept. 1998 (finding that U.K. law allowing the defense of "reasonable chastisement" insufficiently protected children from physical abuse); Damien Gayle, "Italian politician convicted of child cruelty for pulling his son's hair while eating at Swedish restaurant in 'culture clash'," *Daily Mail*, 14 Sept. 2011.

460 See, e.g., Jenna Krajeski, "Women and Men in Tahrir Square," *New Yorker*, 8 Mar. 2011.

461 Rick Gladstone, "Pussy Riot Members Take Tour to New York," *N.Y. Times*, 5 Feb. 2014.

462 Mark Shanahan and Meredith Goldstein, "Pussy Riot bring message to Harvard," *Boston Globe*, 16 Sept. 2014.

463 Quoted in Palash Ghosh, "Amnesty International: The High Cost of Human Rights Activism and Charity," *Int'l Business Times*, 12 June 2013, www.ibtimes.com/ amnesty-international-high-cost-human-rights-activism-charity-1301765.

464 Cf. the 20 "celebrity upstanders" (down from almost 50 a couple of years earlier) who support the work of Enough, an NGO founded "to counter genocide and crimes against humanity," https://enoughproject.org/upstanders/celebrity.

465 Alexandra Cosima Budabin and Lisa Ann Richey, "Advocacy Narratives and Celebrity Engagement: The Case of Ben Affleck in Congo," 40 *Hum. Rts. Q.* 260 (2018) at 286.

466 The text of the Saudi reservation is found at https://treaties.un.org/pages/ViewDetails .aspx?src=TREATY&mtdsg_no=IV-8&chapter=4&clang=_en#4.

467 Objections to reservations by Saudi Arabia and/or similar reservations by other states have been made by Austria, Belgium, Canada, Czech Republic, Denmark, Estonia, Finland, France, Germany, Greece, Hungary, Ireland, Italy, Latvia, Mexico, Netherlands, Norway, Poland, Portugal, Romania, Slovakia, Spain, Sweden, and United Kingdom. See id.

468 Although it is somewhat dated, see Hurst Hannum, "The Status of the Universal Declaration of Human Rights in National and International Law," 25 *Ga. J. Int'l & Comp. L.* 287 (1995/96).

469 Cf. Man Yee Karen Lee, "Universal Human Dignity: Some Reflections in the Asian Context," 3 *Asian J. Comp. L.* 283 (2008).

470 Eur. Ct. Hum. Rts., 3d Section, Mondragon v. Spain, App. No. 2034/07, Judgment of 15 March 2011.

471 See General Comment No. 34, supra note 444, paras. 38, 48, 49.

472 Eur. Ct. Hum. Rts., Mann Singh v France, App. No. 24479/07, admissibility dec. of 13 Nov. 2008.

473 Ranjit Singh v France, Comm. No. 1876/2000 (2011).

474 McGoldrick, supra note 436 at 22, has called this "one of the great intellectual mysteries in international human rights law."

475 Tanalee Smith, "U.N. conference tries to pacify furor created over Mohammed drawings," *Miami Herald*, 1 Mar. 2006.

476 "Minister threatens jail over Islam slurs," *South China Morning Post*, 22 Mar. 2006, p. A11.

477 On the difference between the right to free expression and the responsibility that accompanies that right, see the well-known creator of the Doonesbury cartoon strip, Garry Trudeau, "The Abuse of Satire," *Atlantic*, 11 Apr. 2015.

478 See, e.g., Angelique Chrisafis, "John Galliano found guilty of racist and antisemitic abuse," *Guardian*, 8 Sept. 2011; Mark John, "French cities ban comedian accused of anti-Semitic jibes," Reuters (7 Jan. 2014), www.reuters.com/article/2014/01/07/ us-france-antisemitism-idUSBREA060ES20140107.

479 Article 20.2 provides that "[a]ny advocacy of national, racial, or religious hatred that constitutes incitement to discrimination, hostility or violence shall be prohibited by law." See Sejal Parmar, "Freedom of Expression Narratives after the *Charlie Hebdo* Attacks," 18 *Hum. Rts. L. Rev.* 267 (2018); for contrasting views on the appropriateness and legality of the Charlie Hebdo cartoons, compare Neville Cox, "The Freedom to Publish

'Irreligious' Cartoons," 16 *Hum. Rts. L. Rev.* 195 (2016), with Koen Lemmens, "'Irreligious' Cartoons and Freedom of Expression: A Critical Reassessment," 18 *Hum. Rts. L. Rev.* 89 (2018).

480 Otto-Preminger-Institut v. Austria, Eur. Ct. Hum.Rts., App. No. 13470/87, Judgment of 20 Sept. 1994.

481 See Miller v. California, 413 US 15 (1973).

482 Among many analyses of regional mechanisms, see Dinah Shelton and Paolo Carozza, *Regional Protection of Human Rights* (Oxford University Press 2nd ed. 2013); Basak Cali, "Explaining Variation in the Intrusiveness of Regional Human Rights Remedies in Domestic Orders," 16 *Int'l J. Const. L.* 214 (2018).

483 Trinidad and Tobago and Venezuela withdrew from the Inter-American Convention on Human Rights (and the court) in 1998 and 2012, respectively.

484 Scores of books and hundreds of articles have been written about the European human rights system. See generally David Harris, Michael O'Boyle, Edward Bates, and Carla Buckley, *Harris, O'Boyle, and Warbrick, Law of the European Convention on Human Rights* (Oxford University Press 4th ed. 2018); William A. Schabas, *The European Convention on Human Rights: A Commentary* (Oxford University Press 2017); Pieter van Dijk, Fried van Hoof, Arjen van Rijn, and Leo Zwaak, *Theory and Practice of the European Convention on Human Rights* (Intersentia 5th ed. 2018); Janneke H. Gerards and Joseph Fleuren eds., *Implementation of the European Convention on Human Rights and of the judgments of the ECtHR in national case law* (Intersentia 2014).

485 For recent criticism of European Court's approach, see the generally anti-rights and pro-democracy arguments in Noel Malcolm, *Human Rights and Political Wrongs: A New Approach to Human Rights Law* (Policy Exchange 2017).

486 See Jeremy McBride, *Human rights and criminal procedure: The case law of the European Court of Human Rights* (Council of Europe 2d ed. 2018).

487 See Eur. Ct. Hum. Rights, Press Unit, Fact Sheet, *Pilot Judgments* (2018).

488 See generally Laurence Burgorgue-Larsen and Amaya Ubeda de Torres, *The Inter-American Court of Human Rights: Case-Law and Commentary* (Oxford University Press 2011); Yves Haeck, Oswaldo Ruiz-Chiriboga, and Clara Burbano-Herrera eds., *The Inter-American Court of Human Rights: Theory and Practice, Present and Future* (Intersentia 2015); Jo M. Pasqualucci, *The Practice and Procedure of the Inter-American Court of Human Rights* (Cambridge University Press, 2d ed. 2014).

489 The 23 states that are parties to the convention are bound by its provisions. The remaining OAS member states, including the United States, Canada, and most Anglo-phone Caribbean countries, fall under the jurisdiction of only the Inter-American Commission and the norms set forth in the 1948 American Declaration of the Rights and Duties of Man. In practice, however, there is little, if any, difference in the commission's or court's interpretation of the convention and declaration, and the court has found violations of both with respect to parties to the convention.

490 IACHR Expresses Concern over Impeachment of President of Brazil, Press Release 126/16, 2 Sept. 2016.

491 IACHR Expresses Deep Concern for the Decision to End the Deferred Action for Childhood Arrivals (DACA) and Other Legal Avenues for Migrants and Refugees in the United States, Press Release 155/17, 11 Oct. 2017.

492 IACHR Regrets Ban on Gender Education in Paraguay, Press Release 208/17, 15 Dec. 2017.

493 IACHR Condemns Mass Shooting in the United States, Press Release 154/17, 6 Oct. 2017.

494 IACHR Expresses Deep Concern over Regression in Human Rights in Brazil, Pres Release 67/16, 18 May 2016.

495 Paolo G. Carozza, "The Anglo-Latin Divide and the Future of the Inter-American System of Human Rights," 5 *Notre Dame J. Int'l Comp. L.* 153 (2015) at 154, 161-163.

496 Gerald L. Neuman, "Import, Export, and Regional Consent in the Inter-American Court of Human Rights," 19 *Eur. J. Int'l L.* 101 (2008) at 102, 104, 123.

497 See Sisay Alemahu Yeshanew, *The Justiciability of Economic, Social and Cultural Rights in the African Regional Human Rights System: Theory, Practice and Prospect* (Intersentia 2013); Alexandra Huneeus, "Reforming the State from Afar: Structural Reform Litigation at the Human Rights Courts," 40 *Yale J. Int'l L.* 1 (2015); Obiora Chinedu Okafor, *The African Human Rights System, Activist Forces and International Institutions* (Cambridge University Press 2010); Manisuli Ssenyonjo ed., *The African Regional Human Rights System: 30 Years after the African Charter on Human and Peoples' Rights* (Brill 2011).

498 AfCommHPR, Social and Economic Rights Action Center and the Center for Economic and Social Rights v. Nigeria, Case 155/96, decision of 27 Oct. 2001, paras. 52, 53.

499 See id., paras. 60–66.

500 AfCommHR v. Kenya, App. No. 006/2012, Judgment of 27 May 2017.

501 Id., para. 112.

502 Id., paras. 123, 125.

503 McGoldrick, supra note 436 at 58.

504 See *Protecting Dignity: An Agenda for Human Rights*, www.geneva-academy.ch/docs/ projets/Panel%20on%20Human%20Dignity/GB-ADH%20Brochure%20Agenda% 20Human%20Rights-17x17.pdf. For the background to the initiative, see www.geneva-a cademy.ch/completed-research/human-dignity-panel. For a brief history of earlier pro-posals for such a court, see Rosa Freedman, *Failing to Protect: The UN and the Politicisation of Human Rights* (Oxford University Press 2015), chap. 13.

505 *Protecting Dignity*, supra note 504, para. 76.

506 Philip Alston, "Against a World Court for Human Rights," 18 *Ethics & Int'l Aff.* 197 (2014, no. 2) at 205.

507 Id. at 208.

508 Duncan Jepson, "Reconciling My Two Cultures," *Int'l Herald Trib.*, 15 April 2011.

509 Michael Kimmelman, "'Cultural Revolt' Over Sarkozy's Museum Plans," *N.Y. Times*, 8 Mar. 2011.

510 Luzius Wildhaber, "The European Court of Human Rights: The Past, the Present, the Future," 22 *Am. U. Int'l L. Rev.* 22 (2007) at 25.

511 Quoted in Thomas Fuller, "Those Who Would Remake Myanmar Find That Words Fail Them," *N.Y. Times* , 19 July 2015.

512 These examples are drawn from Dan Bilefsky, "Muslim Boys at a Swiss School Must Shake Teachers' Hands, Even Female Ones," *N.Y. Times*, 26 May 2016.

513 For summaries of these cases, see Eur. Ct. Hum. Rights Press Unit, Factsheet, *Repro-ductive Rights* (April 2018) at 1–2, 11; Eur. Ct. Hum. Rights, Research Report, *Bioethics and the Case-Law of the Court* (2016) at 8–17.

514 Guttmacher Institute, "Abortion in Latin America and the Caribbean," www.guttmacher .org/fact-sheet/abortion-latin-america-and-caribbean.

515 The only significant exception is an early Commission opinion in the so-called "Baby Boy" case, Case No. 2141 (United States), Opinion of 6 Mar. 1981, in which a majority of the commission found that legalization of abortion did not violate the American Declar-ation of the Rights and Duties of Man. Two commissioners dissented, on the grounds that life begins at conception and that abortion therefore violates the right to life; a third commissioner shared that opinion but did not believe that it was legally possible to apply this conclusion to the United States, because the preparatory work on the Declaration demonstrated that the Declaration "sidesteps the very controversial question of determin-ing at what moment human life begins."

516 IACHR Urges All States to Adopt Comprehensive, Immediate Measures to Respect and Protect Women's Sexual and Reproductive Rights, Press Release 165/17, 23 Oct. 2017.

517 Protocol to the African Charter on Human and People's Rights on the Rights of Women in Africa, adopted 11 July 2003, entered into force 25 Nov. 2005.

518 Af Comm HPR, General Comment No. 2 (2014).

519 Mellet v. Ireland, Comm. No. 2324/2013, Views of 31 Mar. 2016, para. 9.

8 HUMAN RIGHTS HAWKS

520 Ad placed by AVAAZ.org (which describes itself as "the campaigning community bringing people-powered politics to decision-making worldwide"), *N.Y. Times*, 18 June 2015, p. A11. It is difficult to discover actual rates for such ads, but $50,000–$100,000 for nonprofits is probably a reasonable guess.

521 Somini Sengupta, *N.Y. Times*, 18 June 2015, p. A10.

522 Azham Ahmed and Paulina Villegas, id.

523 Somini Sengupta, "60 Million People Fleeing Chaotic Lands, U.N. Says," id., p. A1.

524 The only clear exceptions to the use of force are individual or collective self-defense, as set forth in art. 51 of the Charter, or when force is authorized by a decision taken by the UN Security Council pursuant to art. 25 and Chapter VII of the Charter.

525 John Shattuck, *Freedom on Fire, Human Rights Wars and America's Response* (Harvard University Press, 2005) at 7.

526 Id. at 289.

527 Id. at 297; emphasis added. For criticism of confusing human rights violations with international crimes, see Chapter 2.

528 Ruti G. Teitel, *Humanity's Law* (Oxford University Press 2011) at. 114–15.

529 Michael J. Glennon, *The Fog of Law: Pragmatism, Security, and International Law* (Woodrow Wilson Center Press and Stanford University Press 2010) at 98.

530 Anne-Marie Slaughter, "A Regional Responsibility to Protect," in David Held and Kyle McNally eds., *Lessons from Intervention in the 21st Century: Legality, Legitimacy, and Feasibility,* (Global Policy e-book 2014) www.princeton.edu/~slaughtr/Articles/Regional ResponsibilitytoProtect.pdf.

531 Id.

532 Anne-Marie Slaughter, "Stopping Russia starts in Syria," CNBC, 23 Apr. 2014, www.cnbc .com/id/101605835.

533 Cf., e.g., Margaret M. deGuzman, "When Are International Crimes Just Cause for War?" 55 *Va. J. Int'l L.* 73 (2014).

534 Both situations are examined in depth in the Pulitzer-Prize winning book by Samantha Power (later to become the US Ambassador to the United Nations in the Obama Administration), A *Problem from Hell: America and the Age of Genocide* (Harper Collins 2003). Of course, the 1990s saw many other instances of serious internal conflicts and accompanying deaths, including in Somalia, Haiti, Chechnya, Burundi, Transneister, Abkhazia, South Ossetia, and Nagorno-Karabakh.

535 Independent International Commission on Kosovo, *Kosovo Report* (Oxford University Press 2000) at 186, 159, 136.

536 OSCE, "Kosovo/Kosova, As Seen, As Told" (Dec. 1999) at 69, www.osce.org/odihr/ 17772?download=true.

537 See, e.g., Steven Erlanger and Christopher S. Wren, "Early Count Hints at Fewer Kosovo Deaths," *Wash. Post.*, 11 Nov. 1999, at A6.

538 Human Rights Watch, *Civilian Deaths in the NATO Air Campaign* (HRW, Feb. 2000), https://www.hrw.org/reports/2000/nato/.

539 Report of the Special Rapporteur of the Commission on Human Rights on the Situation of Human Rights in Bosnia and Herzegovina, the Republic of Croatia and the Federal Republic of Yugoslavia, UN Doc. A/55/282 (2000), para. 101.

540 Id., para. 104.

541 "West Should Hit KLA Extremists in Kosovo—UN Sleuth," Reuters, 29 Mar. 2000.

542 Report of the Independent Inquiry into the Actions of the United Nations During the 1994 Genocide in Rwanda, UN Doc. S/1999/1257 (1999) at 1, 2–3.

543 See Alan J. Kuperman, "Rwanda in Retrospect," 79 *For. Affairs* 94 (Jan./Feb. 2000) and *Responses*, id. at 141–44 (May/June 2000) and 81 *For. Affairs* at 206–08 (Nov./Dec. 2002); Alan J. Kuperman, *The Limits of Humanitarian Intervention: Genocide in Rwanda* (Brookings 2001). Also see Alison des Forges, *Leave None to Tell the Story: Genocide in Rwanda* (Human Rights Watch 1999); Power, supra note 534, chap. 10.

544 Told to Samantha Power, then a journalist, and quoted in Mark Landler, "Two Liberal Voices for Intervention, but Not in Syrian War," *N.Y. Times*, 5 June 2013.

545 Ann-Marie Slaughter, speaking of Hillary Clinton and quoted in Jo Becker and Stott Shane, "'Smart Power' and a Dictator's Fall," *N.Y. Times*, 27 Feb. 2016.

546 Jeffrey Goldberg, "The Obama Doctrine," *Atlantic*, April 2016. For Obama's reaction to the "Arab Spring" uprisings in the Middle East in 2011, see Remarks by the President on the Middle East and North Africa, Washington, DC, 19 May 2011, www.whitehouse.gov/ the-press-office/2011/05/19/remarks-president-middle-east-and-north-africa.

547 Quoted in Jeffrey Goldberg, "Hillary Clinton: 'Failure' to Help Syrian Rebels Led to the Rise of ISIS," *Atlantic*, 10 Aug. 2014, www.theatlantic.com/international/archive/2014/08/ hillary-clinton-failure-to-help-syrian-rebels-led-to-the-rise-of-isis/375832/.

548 International Commission on Intervention and State Sovereignty, *The Responsibility to Protect* (Ottawa International Development Research Centre, 2001), App. B, p. 81. The full text of the report and related documents are available at http://responsibilityto

protect.org/ICISS%20Report.pdf. See generally Alex Bellamy and Tim Dunne eds., *The Oxford Handbook of the Responsibility to Protect* (Oxford University Press 2016); Peter Hilpold ed., *The Responsibility to Protect (R2P), A New Paradigm of International Law?* (Brill-Nijhoff 2015).

549 ICCIS, supra note 548, para. 1.1.

550 Id., para. 5.5.

551 Statement to the UN General Assembly, 12 Dec. 2002, http://georgewbush-whitehouse.archives.gov/news/releases/2002/09/20020912-1.html.

552 For a stinging condemnation of the "apocalyptic legacy" of the Iraq war, see Frank Rich, "Iraq Everlasting," *N.Y. Magazine*, 4 June 2014.

553 See Ministerial Declaration, 23rd Annual Meeting of the Ministers for Foreign Affairs of the Group of 77, 24. Sept. 1999, para. 69, www.g77.org/doc/Decl1999.html, and the Declaration of the Group of 77 South Summit, 10–14 April 2000, UN Doc. A/55/74 (2000), para. 54.

554 Report of the Secretary-General's High-Level Panel on Threats, Challenges, and Change, *A More Secure World: Our Shared Responsibility*, originally issued as UN Doc. A/59/565 (2004), para. 199. Also see Report of the Secretary-General, *In Larger Freedom: Towards Development, Security, and Human Rights for All*, originally issued as UN Doc. A/59/2005 (2005).

555 World Summit Outcome, UN Doc. A/60/L.1 (2005), paras. 138, 139.

556 The resolution that resulted from the exchanges only "[t]akes note" of the debate and the related report by the Secretary General, GA Res. 63/308 (2009).

557 Letter dated 31 Aug. 2007 from the Secretary-General addressed to the President of the Security Council, UN Doc. S/2007/721 (2007).

558 See www.un.org/en/genocideprevention/about-responsibility-to-protect.html.

559 Report of the Secretary-General, Implementing the Responsibility to Protect, UN Doc. A/63/677 (2009).

560 The phrase "crimes and violations" is repeated on numerous occasions in the report; see id., paras 10(b), 10(d), 17, 18, 19, 23, 29, 32, 35, 38, 43, 49, 50, 54, 56, 57, 58, 59, 60, 66, and Annex, paras 1, 4, 5, and 7.

561 Id., para. 17.

562 Id., para. 19.

563 Id., para. 21.

564 Id., para. 25.

565 Id., para. 27.

566 Some of these issues are also addressed in Chapter 2.

567 For a fuller critique of R2P, from which parts of this section are drawn, see Hurst Hannum, "The Responsibility to Protect: Paradigm or Pastiche?" 60 *Northern Ireland Legal Q.* 135 (no. 2, 2009).

568 Stephen Kinzer, "Are human rights activists today's warmongers?" *Boston Globe*, 25 May 2014.

569 These include Australia, Belgium, Canada, Denmark, France, Germany, Ireland, Liechtenstein, Luxembourg, Mexico, Monaco, The Netherlands, Norway, Republic of Korea, Rwanda, Slovenia, Sweden, Switzerland, and the United Kingdom. See www.globalr2p.org/about_us#supporters.

570 Geneva and the Human Rights Council, www.globalr2p.org/our_work/geneva_and_the_human_rights_council.

571 Security Council Res. 688 (1991), para. 3.

572 Id., Res. 733 (1992), para. 7.

573 Id., Res. 788 (1992), para. 1.

574 Id., Res. 859 (1993), para. 3.

575 Id., Res. 929 (1994), para. 2.

576 Id., Res. 940 (1994), para. 4.

577 www.globalr2p.org/resources/335.

578 UN SC. Res. 1973 (2011), para. 4.

579 Becker and Shane, supra note 545.

580 Alan J. Kuperman, "A Model Humanitarian Intervention?: Reassessing NATO's Libya Campaign," 38 *Int 'l Security* 105 (no. 1, 2013) at 108.

581 Aidan Hehir, "The Permanence of Inconsistency: Libya, the Security Council, and the Responsibility to Protect," id. at 137, 155–156.

582 Report of the Secretary-General on the United Nations Support Mission in Libya, UN Doc. S/2018/140 (2018), para. 2.

583 Id., paras. 38, 75, 99. An Associated Press account of the report is blunt: "UN experts say political settlement in Libya 'out of reach,'" Gulf News, 14 Feb. 2018, http://gulfnews.com/news/mena/libya/un-experts-say-political-settlement-in-libya-out-of-reach-1.2173438.

584 See, e.g., Louis Charbonneau, "Russia U.N. veto on Syria aimed at crushing West's crusade," Reuters, 2 Aug. 2012, www.reuters.com/article/2012/02/08/us-un-russia-idUS TRE8170BK20120208. As of late 2017, Russia had vetoed a total of ten Security Council resolutions on Syria.

585 International Crisis Group, "Russia vs. Georgia: The Fallout" [originally entitled "The Georgia-Russia Conflict and the responsibility to protect"] at 30, 22 Aug. 2008, www.crisisgroup.org/~/media/Files/europe/195_russia_vs_georgia___the_fallout.pdf.

586 Report of the Independent International Fact-Finding Mission on the Conflict in Georgia, at 22–23, Sept. 2009, http://echr.coe.int/Documents/HUDOC_38263_08_Annexes_ENG.pdf. The report found violations of international humanitarian law on all sides.

587 Id., pp. 22–23.

588 Id., p. 24.

589 See, e.g., Kathy Lally and Will Englund, "Putin says he reserves right to protect Russians in Ukraine," *Wash. Post,* 4 Mar. 2014,.

590 See ICJ, Advisory Opinion on The Legality of the Threat or Use of Nuclear Weapons (8 July 1996), para. 25; id., Advisory Opinion on The Legal Consequences of the Construction of a Wall in the Occupied Palestinian Territory (9 July 2004), para. 106; id., Judgment, Armed Activities on the Territory of the Congo (Democratic Republic of Congo (DRC) v. Uganda) (19 Dec. 2005), paras. 215, 216.

591 Id., Legal Consequences of the Construction of a Wall in the Occupied Palestinian Territory, para. 106.

592 For brief descriptions of these cases, see European Court of Human Rights Press Unit, Fact Sheet, *Extra-territorial jurisdiction of States Parties to the European Convention on Human Rights,* (Sept. 2014) at 4–9.

593 Eur. Ct. Hum. Rts. (GC), App. No. 29750/09, Judgment of 16 Sept. 2014.

594 Id., paras. 76, 77.

595 Id., para. 104.

596 Id., paras. 110, 111.

597 Id., dissenting opinion of Judges Spano, Nicolaou, Bianku, and Kalaydjieva, para. 19; emphasis in original.

598 Gabriella Blum, "The Fog of Victory," 24 *Eur. J. Int'l L.* 391 (2013), at 393, 395, 404, 405, 412, 414; notes omitted.

599 Id., at 408.

600 Tina Daunt, "Jay Leno and Mavis Leno turn serious about the plight of Afghan women," *L.A. Times*, 3 Apr. 2009.

601 Feminist Majority Foundation, FMF Board of Directors, www.feminist.org/welcome/board/Mavis-Leno.htm_.

602 Blum, supra note 598 at 416, 420.

603 Marco Sassoli and Laura M. Olson, "The Relationship between International Humanitarian and Human Rights Law Where It Matters: Admissible Killing and Internment of Fighters in Non International Armed Conflicts," 90 *Int'l Rev. Red Cross* 599 (No. 871, Sept. 2008) at 602.

604 Barbara Tuchman, *The First Salute* (Knopf 1988) at 193.

605 These issues have been the subject of a great deal of debate within the humanitarian community and cannot be adequately represented here. See, e.g., Caroline Abu-Sada, *Dilemmas, Challenges, and Ethics of Humanitarian Action: Reflections on Médecins Sans Frontières' Perception Project* (McGill-Queen's University Press 2012); Volker M. Heins, Kai Koddenbrock, and Christine Unrau eds., *Humanitarianism and Challenges of Cooperation* (Routledge 2018); Randolph Kent, Christina Bennett, Antonio Donini, and Daniel Maxwell, *Planning from the Future: Is the Humanitarian System Fit for Purpose?* (Policy Institute at King's College London, Humanitarian Policy Group at the Overseas Development Institute, and Feinstein International Center at Tufts University, 2016); Thomas G Weiss and Cindy Collins, *Humanitarian Challenges and Intervention: World Politics and the Dilemmas of Help* (Westview 2d ed. 2000).

606 Becker and Shane, supra note 545.

9 THE INDISPENSABLE STATE? THE UNITED STATES AND HUMAN RIGHTS

607 See generally Morsink, supra note 4.

608 US acceptance excluded "[d]isputes with regard to matters which are essentially within the domestic jurisdiction of the United States of America as determined by the United States of America." 1 UNTS 9 (1946).

609 See 1354 UNTS 452 (1984).

610 See 1408 UNTS 270 (1985).

611 ICJ, Case Concerning Military and Paramilitary Activities in and against Nicaragua (Nicaragua v. United States), Judgment of 27 June 1986.

612 J. Dana Stuster, "Mapped: The 7 Governments the U.S. Has Overthrown," *Foreign Policy*, 20 Aug. 2013.

613 For fuller accounts, see, e.g., David P. Forsythe and Patrice C. McMahon, *American Exceptionalism Reconsidered: U.S. Foreign Policy, Human Rights, and World Order* (Routledge 2016); Hurst Hannum, Dinah Shelton, S. James Anaya, and Rosa Celorio, *International Human Rights: Problems of Law, Policy, and Practice* (Aspen 6th ed. 2018), chap. 13; Julie A. Mertus, *Bait and Switch: Human Rights and U.S. Foreign Policy* (Routledge 2d ed. 2008); Kathryn Sikkink, *Mixed Signals: U.S. Human Rights Policy and Latin America* (Century Foundation 2007).

614 See, in particular, Report of the House Subcommittee on International Organizations and Movements of the House Committee on Foreign Affairs, International Protection of Human Rights, 93d Cong., 2d Sess. (Comm. Print 1974).

615 See, e.g., new sections 502B and 116b that were added in 1974 and 1975, respectively, to the 1961 Foreign Assistance Act of 1961. For an argument that such restrictions have made little difference in practice, see Wayne Sandholtz, "United States Military Assistance and Human Rights," 38 *Hum. Rts. Q.* 2070 (2016).

616 Current and many past reports are available on the State Dept's. website, www.state.gov/j/drl/rls/hrrpt/.

617 Cyrus R. Vance, "Human Rights and Foreign Policy," 76 *Dept. State Bull.* 505 (1977) at 505–508; emphasis in original.

618 Jeane J. Kirkpatrick, "Establishing a Viable Human Rights Policy," 143 *World Aff.* 323 (1981) at 332.

619 Thomas Carothers, "Democracy and Human Rights: Policy Allies or Rivals?" 17 *Wash. Q.* 109 (1994) at 111. Carothers is currently vice president of studies at the Carnegie Endowment for International Peace.

620 A very brief summary may be found in BBC News, "Q&A: DR Congo conflict," 22 Nov. 2012, www.bbc.com/news/world-africa-11108589.

621 See, e.g., CP Covenant, arts. 12, 13, 14, 19, 20, 22; ECHR, arts. 6, 8, 10, 11; ACPHR, arts. 11, 12; IACHR, arts. 13, 15, 16, 22.

622 George W. Bush, Address to a Joint Session of Congress and to the American People, 20 Sept. 2001 www.whitehouse.gov/news/releases/2001/09/20010920-8.html.

623 Many of the internal memoranda relevant to this debate are collected in Karen J. Greenberg and Joshua L. Dratel eds., *The Torture Papers: The Road to Abu Ghraib* (Cambridge University Press 2005).

624 See Memorandum from President George W. Bush re: Humane Treatment of Al Qaeda and Taliban Detainees, 7 Feb. 2002, www.thetorturedatabase.org/document/memo-white-house-re-humane-treatment-al-qaeda-and-taliban-detainees-none-provision-geneva-a?pdf_page=1.

625 Hamdi v. Rumsfeld, 542 US 507 (2004).

626 548 US 557 (2006).

627 Military Commissions Act of 2009, 10 U.S.C. secs. 948–950.

628 Boumediene v. Bush, 553 US 723 (2008).

629 For a history of releases, see Close Guantánamo, www.closeguantanamo.org/Prisoners.

630 See Dept. of the Army Inspector General Detainee Operations Inspection (Mikolashek Report) (21 July 2004), in Greenberg and Dratel, supra note 623 at 630.

631 Eur. Ct. Hum. Rts., Ireland v. UK, App. No. 5310/71, Judgment of 18 Jan. 1978. The European Commission of Human Rights, whose opinion was appealed to the court, had found that the impugned interrogation techniques constituted "torture."

632 Memorandum from Assistant Attorney General Jay S. Bybee, 1 Aug, 2002, reprinted in Greenberg and Dratel, supra note 623 at 172.

633 Charlie Savage and Scott Shane,"Bush Aide Calls Some Methods Used by C.I.A. Unauthorized," *N.Y. Times*, 16 July 2010.

634 Report on the Alleged Use of European Countries by the CIA for the Transportation and Illegal Detention of Prisoners, EU Doc. A6–0020/2007, paras. 39, 40, www.europarl .europa.eu/comparl/tempcom/tdip/final_report_en.pdf.

635 Eur. Ct. Hum. Rts., Al Nashiri v. Poland, App. No. 28761/11, Judgment of 24 July 2014, para. 530. For a summary of these cases, see Eur. Ct. Hum. Rts., Press Unit, Factsheet, *Secret Detention Centers* (July 2016).

636 Executive Order 13491 – Ensuring Lawful Interrogations, www.whitehouse.gov/the_ press_office/EnsuringLawfulInterrogations.

637 CBS News, "Aide: Obama Won't Prosecute Bush Officials," 20 Apr. 2009, www.cbsnews .com/news/aide-obama-wont-prosecute-bush-officials/.

638 Statement of President Barack Obama on Release of OLC Memos, 16 Apr. 2009, www .whitehouse.gov/the-press-office/statement-president-barack-obama-release-olc-memos.

639 Army Field Manual 2–22.3 (FM 34–52), sec. 5–74.

640 Id., sec. 5–75.

641 Mike Corder, "Prosecutor seeks probe of US personnel in Afghanistan," AP News, 21 Nov. 2017, https://apnews.com/c518dfa441834b278c25a51edfcb4a47/Prosecutor-seeks-probe-of-US-personnel-in-Afghanistan.

642 Chris Kahn, "Exclusive: Most Americans support torture against terror suspects - Reuters/ Ipsos poll," Reuters, Mar. 30, 2016, www.reuters.com/article/us-usa-election-torture-exclu sive-idUSKCN0WW0Y3.

643 Id.

644 Ronald Reagan, Farewell Address to the Nation, 11 Jan. 1989, reprinted by The American Presidency Project, www.presidency.ucsb.edu/ws/index.php?pid=29650.

645 Lawrence J. Haas, *Sound the Trumpet: The United States and Human Rights Promotion* (Rowman and Littlefield 2012) at 21.

646 1996 Female Genital Mutilation Act.

647 1998 International Religious Freedom Act.

648 2007 Advancing Democratic Values Act.

649 See, e.g., Mary McGrory, "Human Rights Retreat," *Wash. Post*, 7 July 1994.

650 US Department of State, Bureau of Democracy, Human Rights, and Labor, Fact Sheet (16 Apr. 2009), www.state.gov/g/drl/rls/fs/2009/121764.htm.

651 See, e.g., Bret Stephens, "Does Obama Believe in Human Rights?" *Wall Street Journal*, 19 Oct 2009.

652 Hillary Rodham Clinton, The Human Rights Agenda for the 21st Century, delivered at Georgetown University, Washington, DC, 14 Dec. 2009, www.state.gov/secretary/ 20092013clinton/rm/2009a/12/133544.htm.

653 The White House, Office of the Press Secretary, 19 May 2011, www.whitehouse.gov/the-press-office/2011/05/19/remarks-president-middle-east-and-north-africa.

654 Remarks by the President on the Situation in Egypt, 15 Aug. 2013, www.whitehouse.gov/ the-press-office/2013/08/15/remarks-president-situation-egypt.

655 www.amnesty.org/en/countries/middle-east-and-north-africa/egypt/report-egypt/.

656 US Dept. of State, Bureau of Democracy, Human Rights and Labor, Country Reports on Human Rights Practices for 2016, Egypt, www.state.gov/j/drl/rls/hrrpt/humanrightsreport/index.htm#wrapper.

657 Barack Obama, quoted in Goldberg, supra note 547.

658 See https://obamawhitehouse.archives.gov/the-press-office/2011/08/04/presidential-study-directive-mass-atrocities.

659 Frida Ghitis, "World to Obama: You can't ignore us," CNN, 22 Jan. 2013, http://edition.cnn.com/2013/01/22/opinion/ghitis-obama-world/index.html?hpt=hp_t2.

660 Terence Szuplat, *Wash. Post*, 3 Nov. 2017.

661 Carol Morello, *Wash. Post*, 3 Mar. 2017.

662 Ted Piccone, Brookings Institution, 5 May 2017, www.brookings.edu/blog/order-from-chaos/2017/05/05/tillerson-says-goodbye-to-human-rights-diplomacy/.

663 *Economist*, 9 Nov. 2017.

664 Id., 7 July 2017.

665 Howard LaFranchi, *Christian Science Monitor*, 13 Nov. 2017.

666 Liz Goodwin, "Exporting Fury," *Boston Globe*, 11 Nov. 2018.

667 LaFranchi, supra note 665.

668 "In quotes: Donald Trump and Kim Jong Un," *Financial Times*, 12 June 2018.

669 David A. Graham, "Trump's Effusive, Unsettling Flattery of Kim Jong Un," *Atlantic*, 12 June 2018.

670 Cf. Remarks by President Trump to the 72nd Session of the United Nations General Assembly, 19 Sept. 2017, www.whitehouse.gov/the-press-office/2017/09/19/remarks-president-trump-72nd-session-united-nations-general-assembly.

671 "US calls Myanmar treatment of Rohingya 'ethnic cleansing,'" *Guardian*, 23 Nov. 2017.

672 "Ministry summons U.S. chargé d'affaires over media tender," *Budapest Business J.*, 15 Nov. 2017, https://bbj.hu/politics/hungary-summons-us-charge-daffaires-over-media-tender_141601.

673 US Dept. of State, Country Reports on Human Rights Practices for 2017, www.state.gov/j/drl/rls/hrrpt/humanrightsreport/index.htm?year=2017&dlid=277263.

674 Statement by US Ambassador to the UN, Nikki Haley, quoted in Gardiner Harris, "Trump Administration Withdraws U.S. from U.N. Human Rights Council," *N.Y. Times*, 19 June 2018.

675 See Gardiner Harris, "Haley Blames Watchdog Groups for U.S. Withdrawal from U.N. Rights Council," *N.Y. Times*, 20 June 2018. For the exchange of letters between the NGOs and US Ambassador Haley, see International Service for Human Rights, "HRC: US withdrawal from Human Rights Council decision of US administration alone," 22 June 2018, www.ishr.ch/news/hrc-us-withdrawal-human-rights-council-decision-us-administration-alone.

676 Trump, supra note 670.

677 Id.

678 Sandy Vogelgesang, *American Dream, Global Nightmare: The Dilemma of U.S. Human Rights Policy* (New York: W. W. Norton, 1980) at 256–257.

679 Stephen Kinzer, "What truly conservative foreign policy looks like," *Boston Globe*, 13 Dec. 2015.

680 James Carroll, "Our misguided faith in strength," *Boston Globe*, 28 Mar. 2011.

681 Mark Philip Bradley, *The World Reimagined: Americans and Human Rights in the Twentieth Century* (Cambridge University Press 2016) at 228.

682 Kinzer, supra note 679.

683 Communist Party of China, "Document 9," supra note 182.

684 For an analysis of the essential role of domestic civil society in turning international norms into domestic policy, even in a "good" country such as Japan, see Petrice R. Flowers, "International Human Rights Norms in Japan," 38 *Hum. Rts. Q.* 85 (2016).

10 THE WAY FORWARD: LESS IS MORE

685 Emilie Hafner-Burton, *Making Human Rights a Reality* (Princeton University Press 2013).

686 See, e.g., Darcy and Fariss, supra note 2; Hopgood, supra note 10; Moyn, supra note 4.

687 Hopgood, supra note 10 at 182, vii–ix.

688 Posner, supra note 9 at 145, 144, 148.

689 Samuel Moyn, "Economic Rights Are Human Rights," *Foreign Policy* (April 2018).

690 Posner, supra note 9 at 9.

691 See the sources cited in note 42 supra.

692 US Human Rights Network (Building a People-Centered Movement), Advancing Human Rights 2017, A Status Report on Human Rights in the United States (2018) at 2–3.

693 World Conference on Human Rights, Final Declaration and Programme of Action, UN Doc. A/CONF.157/23 (1993), sec. I, para. 5.

694 *Protecting Dignity*, supra note 504 at 82.

695 Hafner-Burton, supra note 585 at 186–187.

696 Id. at 187–188.

697 Id. at 184.

698 Henry Shue, *Basic Rights: Subsistence, Affluence, and U.S. Foreign Policy* (Princeton University Press 1980, 2d ed. 1996) at 18, 23, 24.

699 Stephen R. Ratner, *The Thin Justice of International Law: A Moral Reckoning of the Law of Nations* (Oxford University Press 2015) at 90.

700 Id. at 76–77.

701 ESC Committee, General Comment No. 3, "The Nature of States Parties' Obligations," UN Doc. E/1991/23, annex III at 86 (1990), para. 10.

702 HR Committee, General Comment No. 31, "The Nature of the General Legal Obligation Imposed on States Parties to the Covenant," UN Doc. CCPR/C/21/Rev.1/Add. 13 (2004), paras. 5, 6.

703 See Audrey R. Chapman, Lisa Forman, Everaldo Lamprea, and Kajal Khanna, "Identifying the Components of a Core Health Services Package from a Human Rights Perspective to Inform Progress toward Universal Health Coverage," 40 *Hum. Rts. Q.* 342 (2018).

704 Stephen J. Powell and Trisha Low, "Beyond Labor Rights: Which Core Human Rights Must Regional Trade Agreements Protect?" 12 *Rich. J. Global L. & Bus.* 91 (2012) at 93.

705 Dudai, supra note 342 at 17.

706 Buchanan, supra note 39 at 303.

707 For a highly critical analysis of the situation in the United States by the former Chairman of the ESC Committee, see Report of the Special Rapporteur on extreme poverty and human rights [Philip Alston] on his mission to the United States of America, UN Doc. A/HRC/38/33/Add.1 (2018) (recommending that the US decriminalize being poor, acknowledge the plight of the middle class and the damaging consequences of extreme inequality, recognize a right to health care, and "get real about taxes").

708 Kenneth Roth, "How to Stand Up for Human Rights in the Age of Trump," *Foreign Policy* (Jan. 2018).

709 Id.

710 OHCHR, Zeid warns against populists and demagogues in Europe and US, address delivered at the Peace, Justice and Security Foundation gala, The Hague, 5 Sept. 2016, www.ohchr.org/EN/NewsEvents/Pages/DisplayNews.aspx?NewsID=20452.

711 Arthur Lupia, professor of political science at the University of Michigan, quoted in Thomas B. Edsall, "Democrats Are Playing Checkers While Trump Is Playing Chess," *N.Y. Times*, 12 Oct. 2017.

712 John O'Sullivan, "East vs West: the new battle for Europe," *Spectator*, 27 Jan. 2018.

713 Bob Dylan, A Hard Rain's A-Gonna Fall (The Freewheelin' Bob Dylan, 1963).

714 For evidence that the world is, in fact, making progress toward improving the lives of most people, see, e.g., Steven Pinker, *The Better Angels of Our Nature: Why Violence Has Declined* (Viking 2011); id., *Enlightenment Now: The Case for Reason, Science, Humanism, and Progress* (Viking 2018); Rosling, supra note 118; Sikkink, supra note 42.

715 Quoted in Daniel Finkelstein, "Here's how to make the world a better place," *Times (London)*, 28 Apr. 2018.

716 Carlos Lozada, "Stop saying the Trump era is 'not normal' or 'not who we are.' We've been here before." Review of *The Soul of America*, by Jon Meacham, and *Our Towns: A 100,000-Mile Journey Into the Heart of America*, by James Fallows and Deborah Fallows, *N.Y. Times*, 10 May 2018; emphasis in original.

Index

abolitionist campaigns, human rights and, 1
abortion rights, 117–118
Abramovich, Victor, 74
Abu Ghraib prison, 141–142
accountability
  Belfast Guidelines on Amnesties and
    Accountability, 18
  human rights and, 16–22
  in right to development, 63
Affleck, Ben, 104–105
Afghanistan, 136
  Al Qaeda in, 141
  US invasion of, 140
  women's rights in, 85, 103, 131–132
Africa. *See also specific countries*
  abortion rights in, 117–118
  authoritarianism in, 6–7
  democratic movements in, 6–7
  ECOWAS, 126–127
  sexual orientation in, 87
African Charter on Human and Peoples' Rights, 2,
    47, 113, 189
African Commission on Human and Peoples'
    Rights, 87, 112
African Court on Human and Peoples' Rights, 2,
    112–113
African Women's Convention, 47
Alien Tort Claims Act (1789) (ATCA) (U. S.),
    33–34
Alston, Philip, 64–66, 114
American Convention on Human Rights, 2, 47, 87,
    110–111, 117
American Declaration of the Rights and Duties of
    Man, 202
American Society of International Law, 14

amnesty
  Belfast Guidelines on Amnesties and
    Accountability, 18
  under Brazilian Amnesty Law, 19
  human rights and, 16–22
  transitional justice and, 18
Amnesty International, 5, 22, 74–75
  decentralization of organization,
    104–105
  on decriminalization of sex trade, 80
  on technology, 53
Amnesty Law (1979) (Brazil), 19
Annan, Kofi, 27, 124
anti-impunity advocates, 17–18, 178
apartheid, 19–20, 23
Apartheid Convention, 19–20
Arab Spring, 53, 147
Arbour, Louise, 176
ASEAN Human Rights Declaration, 87
Asia
  ASEAN Human Rights Declaration, 87
  sexual orientation in, 87
asylum, for migrants, 76–77
ATCA. *See* Alien Tort Claims Act
authoritarianism
  in Africa, 6–7
  international rise of, 6

Ban Ki-Moon, 26–27
basic human rights, 70, 147, 162
Belfast Guidelines on Amnesties and
    Accountability, 18
B&HR. *See* business and human rights
Bielefeldt, Heiner, 85–86
bilateral investment treaties (BITs), 45

bisexuality. *See* Lesbian, Gay, Bisexual, Transgender community
BITs. *See* bilateral investment treaties
Boko Haram, 16
Bosnia and Herzegovina, 18. *See also* International Criminal Tribunal for the former Yugoslavia
Brazil, 136
    Amnesty Law, 19
Brown v. Board of Education, 5
Bush, George H. W., 138
Bush, George W., 123–124
business and human rights (B&HR), 26–39
    under corporate rules and laws, 33–34
    corruption and, 33
    CSR and, 35
    due diligence process for, 30
    in EU, 35. *See also specific countries*
    in France, 35
    under Global Compact, 27–28
    government responsibility undermined by, for human rights protections, 38
    Guiding Principles for, 27–29
        critique of, 29
        institutional promotion of, 30–32
        NGO response to, 28
        responsibilities as part of, 28–29
    identification of, 35, 37
    international enforcement mechanisms for, 39
    international variations of, 32–33
        through local codes of conduct, 36–37
    in Kenya, 31
    limitations of, 35–39
        in developing countries, 35–36
        in scope of liability for, 38–39
    MDGs and, 26–27
    Norms on the Responsibilities of Transnational Corporations and Other Business Enterprises with regard to Human Rights, 28
    OBEs and, 32
    RBC, 35
    remedies for violations of, 33
    scope of, 29–30
        limitations of, 38–39
    TNCs and, 26–27
        liability of, 32, 38–39, 181
    in U. K., 35
    in US under ATCA, 33–34
    UN Human Rights Council and, 30, 32
Bybee, Jay S., 142

Cambodia, 6
    international crimes in, 20–22
    ECCC, 20–21
    Hun Sen, 7, 20–21
    under Khmer Rouge, 20
    UN Special Rapporteur on the Situation of Human Rights in Cambodia, 21
Cameroon, 6–7, 16
Carter, Jimmy, 136–139
CEDAW. *See* Convention on the Elimination of All Forms of Discrimination Against Women
CERD. *See* Convention on the Elimination of All Forms of Racial Discrimination
Chad, 6–7, 16
Charlie Hébdo attacks, 107–108
Chile, 136
China
    constitutional amendments in, 6
    technology in, 54–55
        social credit systems, 54–55
civil and political rights, 2, 21–22, 99, 110, 137, 139, 154, 167
civil society, 40–43
    in Egypt, 43
    in Libya, 43
    NGOs and, 40–42
        domestic, 42
        foreign-funded, 41–42
        international, 42
    in Middle East, 41
    OHCHR and, 42, 184
    in Syria, 43
    in Tunisia, 43
Clapham, Andrew, 39
Clinton, Bill, 120, 138–139, 145
Clinton, Hillary, 120, 123, 127, 145–147, 150–151, 197
coalition of the willing, 134
CODESA. *See* Convention for a Democratic South Africa
Cold War, 138
Colombia, 19–20
Conference on Security and Cooperation in Europe, 121–122
consensus. *See also* Washington Consensus
    on global trade, 45–46
    as human rights principle, 4, 165–167
    on women's rights, 83–84
constitutionalism of international human rights, 4–5
Convention Against Torture, 17, 140, 143
Convention for a Democratic South Africa (CODESA), 23